Healthcare Analytics Made Simple

Techniques in healthcare computing using machine learning and Python

Vikas (Vik) Kumar

BIRMINGHAM - MUMBAI

Healthcare Analytics Made Simple

Commissioning Editor: Veena Pagare
Acquisition Editor: Divya Poojari
Content Development Editor: Eisha Dsouza
Technical Editor: Sneha Hanchate
Copy Editor: Safis
Project Coordinator: Namrata Swetta
Proofreader: Safis Editing
Indexer: Rekha Nair
Graphics: Jisha Chirayil
Production Coordinator: Shantanu Zagade

First published: July 2018

Production reference: 1280718

Published by Packt Publishing Ltd.
Livery Place
35 Livery Street
Birmingham
B3 2PB, UK.

ISBN 978-1-78728-670-2

www.packtpub.com

To my parents, Viren and Sarita; my sister, Monica; and Tuly, my 2018 Person of the Year.

`mapt.io`

Mapt is an online digital library that gives you full access to over 5,000 books and videos, as well as industry leading tools to help you plan your personal development and advance your career. For more information, please visit our website.

Why subscribe?

- Spend less time learning and more time coding with practical eBooks and Videos from over 4,000 industry professionals

- Improve your learning with Skill Plans built especially for you

- Get a free eBook or video every month

- Mapt is fully searchable

- Copy and paste, print, and bookmark content

PacktPub.com

Did you know that Packt offers eBook versions of every book published, with PDF and ePub files available? You can upgrade to the eBook version at `www.PacktPub.com` and as a print book customer, you are entitled to a discount on the eBook copy. Get in touch with us at `service@packtpub.com` for more details.

At `www.PacktPub.com`, you can also read a collection of free technical articles, sign up for a range of free newsletters, and receive exclusive discounts and offers on Packt books and eBooks.

Foreword

Analytics is now an integral part of healthcare. It helps to optimize treatments, improve outcomes, and the reduce the overall cost of care. The availability of biomedical, healthcare, and operational big data enables hospitals and health systems to leverage past data to predict the future of patients and their clinical pathways. Predictive modeling and healthcare data science also help to design care pathways and operational strategies that could help in streamlining various aspects of healthcare delivery. However, healthcare analytics is an exciting field that requires skills in biomedicine, data science, and the technical stack, including databases, programming, data visualization, statistics, and machine learning. While there are several books with an in-depth account of the healthcare space and analytics tools and methods, there not many easy-to-read books that integrate these things together.

In his new and exciting book, Dr. Vikas Kumar (Vik) has now blended the critical learning points of healthcare and computer science with mathematics and machine learning. Being a physician and a data scientist, Vik has done a tremendous job in compiling complex datasets and explaining several use cases in healthcare analytics with comprehensive code in MySQL and Python.

I am sure that *Healthcare Analytics Made Simple* will be an important addition to the library of any data scientist who's interested in understanding the key concepts of biomedical and healthcare data. It will be an indispensable companion for readers from the domains of clinical informatics and health informatics to gain critical skills in the design, development, and validation of machine learning models. This book will also be useful for physicians and biomedical scientists who are interested in understanding the landscape of healthcare analytics. The book is a joy to read, and I enjoyed working through the examples. To conclude, *Healthcare Analytics Made Simple* is attempting to fill a gap in the field of healthcare analytics by providing a complete and comprehensive guide, resulting in an inter-disciplinary book that will be an easy read for computer scientists, software engineers, data scientists, and healthcare professionals alike.

Dr. Shameer Khader, PhD
Director of Healthcare Data Science and Bioinformatics
Northwell Health, New York

Contributors

About the author

Dr. Vikas (Vik) Kumar grew up in the United States in Niskayuna, New York. He earned his MD from the University of Pittsburgh, but shortly afterwards he discovered his true calling of computers and data science. He then earned his MS in the College of Computing at Georgia Institute of Technology and has subsequently worked as a data scientist for both healthcare and non-healthcare companies. He currently lives in Atlanta, Georgia.

Thank you to Mark Braunstein, James Cheng, Shameer Khader, Bryant Menn, Srijita Mukherjee, and Bob Savage for their helpful comments on the book drafts.

About the reviewer

Seungjin Kim is currently a software engineer at Arcules, transforming video data into intelligence and providing a product based on distributed machine learning architecture. Previously, he was a software engineer at a genetic startup, providing a quality frontend user experience for patients accessing genetic products. He received his M.D. from the Medical School for International Health at the Ben-Gurion University of the Negev in Israel in 2015, and he received his B.S. in computer science and Engineering from the University of California in 2008.

Packt is searching for authors like you

If you're interested in becoming an author for Packt, please visit authors.packtpub.com and apply today. We have worked with thousands of developers and tech professionals, just like you, to help them share their insight with the global tech community. You can make a general application, apply for a specific hot topic that we are recruiting an author for, or submit your own idea.

Table of Contents

Preface

The functional aim of this book is to demonstrate how Python packages are used for data analysis; how to import, collect, clean, and refine data from **Electronic Health Record (EHR)** surveys; and how to make predictive models with this data, with the help of real-world examples.

Who this book is for

Healthcare Analytics Made Simple is for you if you are a developer who has a working knowledge of Python or a related programming language, even if you are new to healthcare or predictive modeling with healthcare data. Clinicians interested in analytics and healthcare computing will also benefit from this book. This book can also serve as a textbook for students enrolled on an introductory course on machine learning for healthcare.

What this book covers

Chapter 1, *Introduction to Healthcare Analytics*, provides a definition of healthcare analytics, lists some foundational topics, provides a history of the subject, gives some examples of healthcare analytics in action, and includes download, installation, and basic usage instructions for the software in this book.

Chapter 2, *Healthcare Foundations*, consists of an overview of how healthcare is structured and delivered in the US, provides a background on legislation that's relevant to healthcare analytics, describes clinical patient data and clinical coding systems, and provides a breakdown of healthcare analytics.

Chapter 3, *Machine Learning Foundations*, describes some of the model frameworks used for medical decision making and describes the machine learning pipeline, from data import to model evaluation.

Chapter 4, *Computing Foundations – Databases*, provides an introduction to the SQL language and demonstrates the use of SQL in healthcare with a healthcare predictive analytics example.

Chapter 5, *Computing Foundations – Introduction to Python*, gives a basic overview of Python and the libraries that are important for performing analytics. We discuss variable types, data structures, functions, and modules in Python. We also give an introduction to the `pandas` and `scikit-learn` libraries.

Chapter 6, *Measuring Healthcare Quality*, describes the measures used in healthcare performance, gives an overview of value-based programs in the US, and demonstrates how to download and analyze provider-based data in Python.

Chapter 7, *Making Predictive Models in Healthcare*, describes the information contained in a publicly available clinical dataset, including downloading instructions. We then demonstrate how to make predictive models with this data, using Python, `pandas`, and scikit-learn.

Chapter 8, *Healthcare Predictive Models – A Review*, reviews some of the current progress being made in healthcare predictive analytics for select diseases and application areas by comparing machine learning results to those obtained by using traditional methods.

Chapter 9, *The Future – Healthcare and Emerging Technologies*, discusses some of the advances being made in healthcare analytics through using the internet, introduces the reader to deep learning techniques in healthcare, and states some of the challenges and limitations facing healthcare analytics.

To get the most out of this book

Helpful things to know include the following:

- High school math, such as basic probability, statistics, and algebra
- Basic familiarity with a programming language and/or basic programming concepts
- Basic familiarity with healthcare and a working knowledge of some clinical terminology

Please follow the instructions in Chapter 1, *Introduction to Healthcare Analytics* for setting up Anaconda and SQLite.

Download the example code files

You can download the example code files for this book from your account at
`www.packtpub.com`. If you purchased this book elsewhere, you can visit
`www.packtpub.com/support` and register to have the files emailed directly to you.

You can download the code files by following these steps:

1. Log in or register at `www.packtpub.com`.
2. Select the **SUPPORT** tab.
3. Click on **Code Downloads & Errata**.
4. Enter the name of the book in the **Search** box and follow the onscreen instructions.

Once the file is downloaded, please make sure that you unzip or extract the folder using the latest version of:

- WinRAR/7-Zip for Windows
- Zipeg/iZip/UnRarX for Mac
- 7-Zip/PeaZip for Linux

The code bundle for the book is also hosted on GitHub
at `https://github.com/PacktPublishing/Healthcare-Analytics-Made-Simple`. In case there's an update to the code, it will be updated on the existing GitHub repository.

We also have other code bundles from our rich catalog of books and videos available
at `https://github.com/PacktPublishing/`. Check them out!

Download the color images

We also provide a PDF file that has color images of the screenshots/diagrams used in this book. You can download it here:
`http://www.packtpub.com/sites/default/files/downloads/HealthcareAnalyticsMadeSimple_ColorImages.pdf`.

Conventions used

There are a number of text conventions used throughout this book.

`CodeInText`: Indicates code words in text, database table names, folder names, filenames, file extensions, pathnames, dummy URLs, user input, and Twitter handles. Here is an example: "Mount the downloaded `WebStorm-10*.dmg` disk image file as another disk in your system."

A block of code is set as follows:

```
string_1 = '1'
string_2 = '2'
string_sum = string_1 + string_2
print(string_sum)
```

When we wish to draw your attention to a particular part of a code block, the relevant lines or items are set in bold:

```
test_split_string = 'Jones,Bill,49,Atlanta,GA,12345'
output = test_split_string.split(',')
print(output)
```

Bold: Indicates a new term, an important word, or words that you see onscreen. For example, words in menus or dialog boxes appear in the text like this. Here is an example: "Select **System info** from the **Administration** panel."

Warnings or important notes appear like this.

Tips and tricks appear like this.

Get in touch

Feedback from our readers is always welcome.

General feedback: Email `feedback@packtpub.com` and mention the book title in the subject of your message. If you have questions about any aspect of this book, please email us at `questions@packtpub.com`.

Errata: Although we have taken every care to ensure the accuracy of our content, mistakes do happen. If you have found a mistake in this book, we would be grateful if you would report this to us. Please visit `www.packtpub.com/submit-errata`, selecting your book, clicking on the Errata Submission Form link, and entering the details.

Piracy: If you come across any illegal copies of our works in any form on the Internet, we would be grateful if you would provide us with the location address or website name. Please contact us at `copyright@packtpub.com` with a link to the material.

If you are interested in becoming an author: If there is a topic that you have expertise in and you are interested in either writing or contributing to a book, please visit `authors.packtpub.com`.

Reviews

Please leave a review. Once you have read and used this book, why not leave a review on the site that you purchased it from? Potential readers can then see and use your unbiased opinion to make purchase decisions, we at Packt can understand what you think about our products, and our authors can see your feedback on their book. Thank you!

For more information about Packt, please visit `packtpub.com`.

1
Introduction to Healthcare Analytics

This chapter is meant to introduce you to the field of healthcare analytics and is for all audiences. By the end of this chapter, you will understand the basic definition of healthcare analytics, the topics that healthcare analytics encompasses, a history of healthcare analytics, and some well-known application areas. In the second half of this chapter, we will guide you through installing the required software and provide a light introduction to Anaconda and SQLite.

In short, we will be covering the following topics in this chapter:

- Basics of healthcare analytics
- History of healthcare analytics
- Examples of healthcare analytics
- Introduction to Anaconda, Jupyter Notebook, and SQLite

What is healthcare analytics?

Unfortunately, a definition of **healthcare analytics** is not in Webster's dictionary yet. However, our own definition of healthcare analytics is *the use of advanced computing technology to improve medical care*. Let's break down this definition phrase by phrase.

Healthcare analytics uses advanced computing technology

At the time of this writing, we are approaching the year 2020, and computers and mobile phones have taken over many aspects of our lives, the healthcare industry being no exception. Most of our healthcare data is being migrated from paper charts to electronic ones, in many cases motivated by massive governmental incentives for doing so. Meanwhile, countless medical mobile applications are being written to track vital signs, including heart rates and weights, and even communicate with doctors. While this migration is not trivial, it will allow for the application of advanced computing techniques hopefully to unlock doors toward improving medical care for everyone.

What are some of these advanced computing technologies? We will discuss them in the upcoming sections.

Healthcare analytics acts on the healthcare industry (DUH!)

If you're looking for a book that demonstrates the use of machine learning to predict the year of the apocalypse, unfortunately, this is not it. Healthcare analytics is all things healthcare.

Healthcare analytics improves medical care

So far, we are using computers to do something in healthcare. What exactly are we doing? *We are trying to improve medical care.* Well that's broad, isn't it? The effectiveness of medical care is commonly measured using the so-called healthcare triple aim: improving outcomes, reducing costs, and ensuring quality (although we've seen different words used here). Let's look at each of these aims in turn.

Better outcomes

On a personal level, everyone can relate to better **healthcare outcomes**. We yearn for better outcomes in our own lives whenever we visit a doctor or a hospital. Specifically, here are some of the things about which we are concerned:

- **Accurate diagnosis**: When we see a physician, usually it is for a medical problem. The problem may be causing some amount of pain or anxiety in our lives. What we care about is that the cause of this problem will be accurately identified so that the problem may be effectively treated.
- **Effective treatment**: Treatment may be expensive, time-consuming, and may cause adverse side-effects; therefore, we want to be sure that the treatment is effective. We don't want to have to take another vacation day to see a doctor or be admitted to the hospital for the same problem two months from now–such an experience would be costly, in terms of both time and money (either through medical bills or tax dollars).
- **No complications**: We don't want to come down with a new infection or take a dangerous fall while we are seeking care for the current ailment.
- **An overall improved quality of life**: To summarize the concept of better health outcomes, while governmental bodies and physician organizations may have different ways of measuring outcomes, what we aim for is an improved quality and longevity of life that is pain- and worry-free.

Lower costs

So the goal is better health outcomes, right? Unfortunately, we can't provide 24-7 medical care to everyone all the time, because our economy would break down. We can't order whole-body x-rays to detect every cancer in advance. There is a careful balance between achieving better outcomes and decreasing costs in healthcare. The idea with healthcare analytics is that we will be able to do more with less expensive techniques. A CT scan of the chest to screen for lung cancer may cost thousands of dollars; however, doing mathematical calculations on a patient's medical history to screen for lung cancer costs much less. In this book, the plan is to show you how to make those calculations.

Ensure quality

Healthcare quality encompasses the satisfaction level of the patient after he or she receives medical care. In a capitalist system (such as the healthcare system of the United States), a tried-and-true method of improving the quality involves fair and objective measurement of how different providers are performing so that patients can make more informed decisions about their care.

Foundations of healthcare analytics

Now that we've defined and introduced healthcare analytics, it's important to give some background on the knowledge from which it draws. Healthcare analytics can be viewed as the intersection of three fields: healthcare (**Healthcare Analytics**), mathematics (**Math**), and computer science (**CS**), as seen in the following diagram. Let's explore each of these three areas in turn:

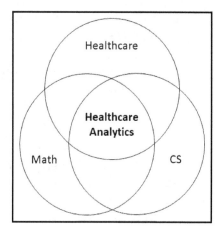

Healthcare

Healthcare is the **domain-knowledge** pillar of healthcare analytics. Here are some of the significant healthcare areas of knowledge that comprise healthcare analytics:

- **Healthcare delivery and policy**: An understanding of how the healthcare industry is structured, who the major players in healthcare are, and where the financial incentives lie can only help us in improving healthcare analytics endeavors.

- **Healthcare data**: Healthcare data is rich and complex, whether it is structured or unstructured. However, healthcare data collection often follows a specific template. Knowing the details of the typical **history and physical examination (H&P)** and how data is organized in a medical chart goes a long way in helping us turn that data into knowledge.
- **Clinical science**: A familiarity with medical terminology and diseases helps in knowing what's important in the vast ocean of medical information. Clinical science is commonly divided into two areas: **physiology**, or how the human body functions normally, and **pathology**, or how the human body functions with a disease. Some basic knowledge of both can be very helpful in doing effective healthcare analytics.

An introduction to healthcare for healthcare analytics will be provided in `Chapter 2`, *Healthcare Foundations*.

Mathematics

The second pillar of our healthcare analytics triumvirate is mathematics. We are not trying to scare you off with this list; a detailed knowledge of all of the following areas is not a prerequisite for doing effective healthcare analytics. A basic knowledge of high school math, however, may be essential. The other areas are most helpful while understanding the machine learning models that allow us to predict diseases. That being said, here are some of the significant mathematical domains that comprise healthcare analytics:

- **High school mathematics**: Subjects such as algebra, linear equations, and precalculus are essential foundations for the more advanced math topics seen in healthcare analytics.
- **Probability and statistics:** Believe it or not, every medical student takes a class in biostatistics during their training. Yes, effective medical diagnosis and treatment rely heavily on probability and statistics, including concepts such as sensitivity, specificity, and likelihood ratios.
- **Linear algebra**: Commonly, the operations done on healthcare data while making machine learning models are vector and matrix operations. You'll effectively perform plenty of these operations as you work with NumPy and scikit-learn to make machine learning models in Python.
- **Calculus and optimization**: These last two topics particularly apply to neural networks and deep learning, a specific type of machine learning that consists of layers of both linear and nonlinear transformations of data. Calculus and optimization are important for understanding for how these models are trained.

An introduction to mathematics and machine learning for healthcare analytics will be provided in `Chapter 3`, *Machine Learning Foundations*.

Computer science

Here are some of the significant computer science domains that comprise healthcare analytics:

- **Artificial intelligence**: At the center of healthcare analytics is artificial intelligence or the study of systems that interact with their environment. Machine learning is a subarea within artificial intelligence, in which predictions are made about future events using information from previous events. The models that we will study in the later parts of this book are machine learning models.
- **Databases and information management**: Healthcare data is often accessed using **relational databases**, which can often be dumped by **electronic medical record** (**EMR**) systems on demand, or which are located in the cloud. **SQL** (short for **Structured Query Language**) can be used to select the specific data in which we are interested and to make transformations on that data.
- **Programming languages**: A programming language provides an interface between the human programmer and the ones and zeros inside of a computer. A programming language allows a programmer to provide instructions to the computer to make calculations on data that humans cannot practically do. In this book, we will use Python, a popular and emerging programming language that is open source, comprehensive, and features plenty of machine learning libraries.
- **Software engineering**: Many of you are presumably learning about healthcare analytics because you are interested in deploying production-grade healthcare applications in your workplace. **Software engineering** is the study of the effective and efficient building of software systems that satisfy user and customer requirements.
- **Human-computer interaction**: The end users of healthcare analytics applications usually don't use programming to obtain their results, but instead rely on visual interfaces. Human-computer interaction is the study of how humans interact with computers and how such interfaces can be designed. A current hot topic in medicine is how EMR applications can be made more intuitive and palatable to physicians, rather than increasing the number of mouse clicks they must make per patient while writing notes.

Computer science is so pervasive in healthcare analytics that almost every chapter in this book deals with it.

History of healthcare analytics

The origin of healthcare analytics can be traced back to the 1950s, just a few years after the world's first computer (**ENIAC**) was invented in 1946. At the time, medical records were still on paper, regression analysis was done by hand, and there were no incentives given by the government for pursuing value-based care. Nevertheless, there was a burgeoning interest in developing automated applications to diagnose and treat human disease, and this is reflected in the scientific literature of the time. For example, in 1959, the journal *Science* published an article entitled *"Reasoning Foundations of Medical Diagnosis,"* by Robert S. Ledley and Lee B. Lusted that explains mathematically how physicians make a medical diagnosis (Ledley and Lusted, 1959). The paper explains many concepts that are central to modern biostatistics, although at times using terminology and symbols that we may not recognize today.

In the 1970s, as computers gained prominence and became accessible in academic research centers, there was a growing interest in developing **medical diagnostic decision support (MDDS) systems**, an umbrella term for broadly based, all-in-one computer programs that pinpoint medical diagnoses when input with patient information. The INTERNIST-1 system is the most well-known of these systems and was developed by a group of researchers at the University of Pittsburgh in the 1970s (Miller et al., 1982). Described by its inventors as "an experimental program for computer-assisted diagnosis in general internal medicine," the INTERNIST system was developed over 15 person-years of work and involved extensive consultation with physicians. Its knowledge base spanned 500 individual diseases and 3,500 clinical manifestations across all medical subspecialties. The user starts by entering positive and negative findings for a patient, after which they can check a list of differential diagnoses and see how they change as new findings are added. The program intelligently asks for specific test results until a clear diagnosis is achieved. While it showed initial promise and captured the imagination of the medical world, it ultimately failed to enter the mainstream after its recommendations were outperformed by those made by a panel of leading physicians. Other reasons for its demise (and the demise of MDDS systems in general) may include the lack of an inviting visual interface (Microsoft Windows had not been invented yet) and the fact that modern machine learning techniques were yet to be discovered.

In the 1980s, there was a rekindled interest in artificial intelligence techniques that had largely been extinguished in the late 1960s, after the limitations of perceptrons had been explicated by Marvin Minsky and Seymour Papert in their book, *Perceptrons* (Minsky and Papert, 1969). The paper *"Learning representations by back-propagating errors"* by David E. Rumelhart, Geoffrey E. Hinton, and Ronald J. Williams was published in *Nature* in 1986 and marked the birth of the back-propagation-trained, nonlinear **neural network**, which today rivals humans in its performance on a variety of artificial intelligence, such as speech and digit recognition (Rumelhart et al., 1986).

It took only a few years before such techniques were applied to the medical field. In 1990, William Baxt published a study entitled *"Use of an Artificial Neural Network for Data Analysis in Clinical Decision-Making: The Diagnosis of Acute Coronary Occlusion"* in the journal *Neural Computation* (Baxt, 1990). In the study, an artificial neural network outperformed a group of medical physicians in diagnosing heart attacks using findings from **electrocardiograms** (**EKGs**). This pioneering study helped to open the floodgates for a tsunami of biomedical machine learning research that persists even today. Indeed, searching for "machine learning" using the biomedical search engine PubMed returns only 9 results in 1990 and over 4,000 results in 2017, with the results steadily increasing in the intervening years:

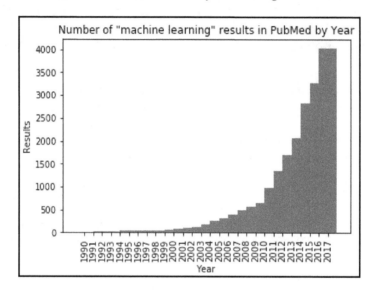

Several factors are responsible for this acceleration in biomedical machine learning research. The first is the increasing number and availability of machine learning algorithms. The neural network is just one example of this. In the 1990s, medical researchers began using a variety of alternative algorithms, including recently developed algorithms such as decision trees, random forests, and support vector machines, in addition to traditional statistical models, such as logistic and linear regression.

The second factor is the increased availability of electronic clinical data. Prior to the 2000s, almost all medical data was on paper charts and conducting computerized machine learning studies meant hours of manually entering the data into computers. The growth and eventual spread of electronic medical records made it much simpler to use this data to make machine learning models. Additionally, more data meant more accurate models.

This brings us to the present day, in which healthcare analytics is experiencing an exciting time. Today's modern neural networks (commonly referred to as *deep learning* networks) are commonly outperforming humans in tasks that are more complex than EKG interpretation, such as cancer recognition from x-ray images and predicting sequences of future medical events in patients. Deep learning often achieves this using millions of patient records, coupled together with parallel computing technology that makes it possible to train large models in shorter time spans, as well as newly developed techniques for tuning, regularizing, and optimizing machine learning models. Another exciting occurrence in present healthcare analytics is the introduction of governmental incentives to eliminate excessive spending and misdiagnosis in healthcare. Such incentives have led to an interest in healthcare analytics not just from academic researchers, but also from industrial players and companies looking to save money for healthcare organizations (and to make themselves some money as well).

While healthcare analytics and machine algorithms aren't redefining medical care just yet, the future for healthcare analytics looks bright. Personally, I like to imagine a day when hospitals, equipped with cameras, privately and securely record every aspect of patient care, including conversations between patients and physicians and patient facial expressions as they hear the results of their own medical tests. These words and images could then be passed to machine learning algorithms to predict how patients will react to future results, and what those results will be in the first place. But we are getting ahead of ourselves; before we arrive at that day, there is much work to be done!

Examples of healthcare analytics

To give you an idea of what healthcare analytics encompasses, here are some examples of healthcare analytics use cases that demonstrate the breadth and depth of modern healthcare analytics.

Using visualizations to elucidate patient care

Analytics is often divided into three subcomponents–**descriptive analytics**, **predictive analytics**, and **prescriptive analytics**. Descriptive analytics encompasses using the analytic techniques previously discussed to better describe or summarize the process under study. Understanding how care is delivered is one process that stands to benefit from descriptive analytics.

How can we use descriptive analytics to better understand healthcare delivery? The following is one example of a visualization of a toddler's **emergency department (ED)** care record when they presented complaining of an asthma exacerbation (Basole et al., 2015). It uses structured clinical data commonly found in EMR systems to summarize the temporal relationships of the care events they experienced in the ED. The visualization consists of four types of activities–administrative (yellow), diagnostic (green), medications (blue), and lab tests (red). These are encoded by color and by y-position. Along the x-axis is time. The black bar on top is divided by vertical tick marks into hour-long blocks. This patient's visit lasted a little over two hours. Information about the patient is displayed before the black time bar.

While descriptive analytical studies such as these may not directly impact costs or medical care recommendations, they serve as a starting point for exploring and understanding the patient care and often pave the way for more specific and actionable analytical methods to be launched:

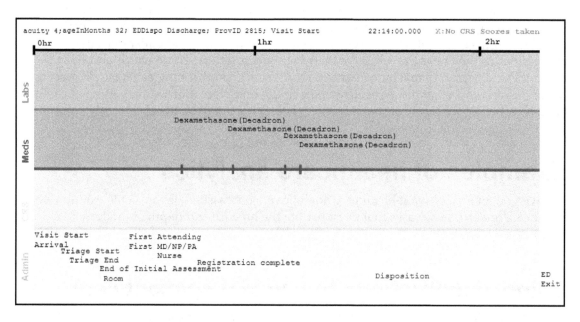

Predicting future diagnostic and treatment events

A central problem in medicine is identifying patients who are at risk of developing a certain disease. By identifying high-risk patients, steps can be taken to hinder or delay the onset of the disease or prevent it altogether. This is an example of predictive analytics at work–using information from previous events to make predictions about the future. There are certain diseases that are particularly popular for prediction research: congestive heart failure, myocardial infarction, pneumonia, and chronic obstructive pulmonary disease are just a few examples of high-mortality, high-cost diseases that benefit from early identification of high-risk patients.

Not only do we care about what diseases will occur in the future, we are also interested in identifying patients who are at risk of requiring high-cost treatments, such as hospital readmissions and doctor visits. By identifying these patients, we can take money-saving steps proactively to reduce the risk of these high-risk treatments, and we can also reward healthcare organizations that do a good job.

This is a broad example with several unknowns to consider. First: what specific event (or disease) are we interested in predicting? Second: what data will we use to make our predictions? Structured clinical data (data organized as tables) drawn from electronic medical records is currently the most popular data source; other possibilities include unstructured data (medical text), medical or x-ray images, biosignals (EEG, EKG), data recorded from devices, or even data from social media. Third: what machine learning algorithm will we use?

Measuring provider quality and performance

While making nice visualizations or predictions represent the sexier aspects of healthcare analytics, there are other types of analytics that are also important. Sometimes, it boils down to good, old number crunching. Monitoring the performance of physicians and healthcare organizations using healthcare measures is a good example of this type of analytical technique. Healthcare measures provide a mechanism by which individuals can measure and compare the compliance of participating providers on evidence-based medical recommendations. For example, it is a widely accepted recommendation that patients with diabetes receive foot exams to detect diabetic foot ulcers every three months by a physician.

A state-sponsored healthcare measure might specify guidelines for calculating the number of diabetic patients receiving care at an institution, and then determine the percentage of those patients that received appropriate foot care. Similar measures would exist for the common heart, lung, and joint diseases, among many others. This provides a way to identify the providers that provide the highest quality care, and these recommendations can be downloaded for public consumption. We will discuss specific healthcare measures in `Chapter 6`, *Measuring Healthcare Quality*.

Patient-facing treatments for disease

In rare cases, healthcare analytics comprise medical technologies that are used to actually treat diseases, not just perform research on them. An example of this is **neuroprosthetics**. Neuroprosthetics can be defined as the enhancement of nervous system function using man-made devices. Neuroprosthetics research has enabled patients with disabilities such as blindness or paraplegia to recover some of their lost function. For example, a paralyzed patient may be able to move a computer cursor on a screen not with their hand, but by using their brain signals! In this specific application, recordings of the electrical activity of specific neurons are obtained, and a machine learning model is used to determine in which direction the cursor should move given the firing of the neurons. Similar analytics can be used for visual impairments, or for visualizing what a human is seeing. A second example includes implanting devices in the body that detect seizures before they occur and proactively administer preventive medication. Certainly, the sky is the limit for analytic-driven treatments.

Exploring the software

In this section, we'll download, install, and explore Anaconda and SQLite, the distributions that we will use in this book for Python and SQL, respectively.

Anaconda

The examples in this book require the use of the Python programming language. There are many distributions of Python available. Anaconda is a free, open source Python distribution designed specifically for machine learning. It includes Python and over 1,000 data science Python libraries (for example, NumPy, scikit-learn, pandas) that can be used on top of the base Python language. It also includes **Jupyter notebook**, an interactive Python console that we will use extensively in this book. Additional tools that come with Anaconda include the Spyder IDE (short for interactive development environment) and RStudio.

Anaconda can be downloaded from `https://www.continuum.io/downloads`.

To download the Anaconda distribution of Python, complete the following steps:

1. Navigate to the preceding website.
2. Choose the appropriate Python download depending on your operating system and desired Python version. For this book, we used Anaconda 5.2.0 (the 64-bit installation for Windows, which includes Python 3.6):

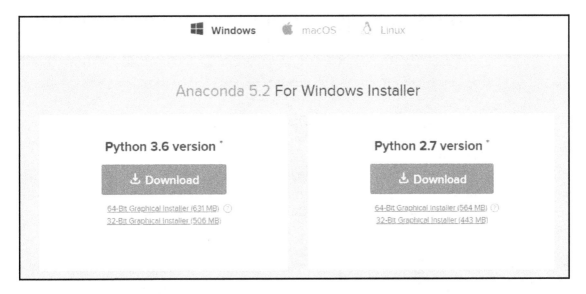

3. Click **Download**. Your browser will begin to download the file. Once it is finished, click on the file in your web browser or in your OS file manager.

4. A window will appear (shown in the following screenshot). Click on the **Next>** button:

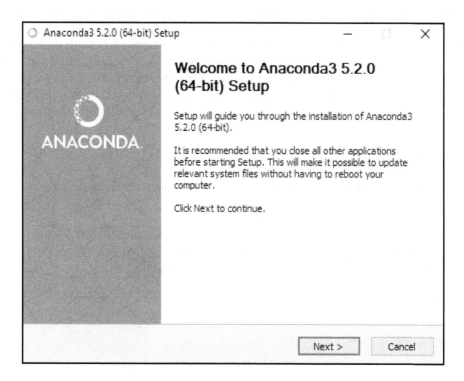

5. Continue to follow the prompts, which include accepting the license agreement, choosing the users for the installation, selecting the file destination, and choosing various options.
6. Anaconda will begin to install. Due to the number of packages included in the installation, this may take a while.
7. After the installation is complete, close the Anaconda window.

Anaconda navigator

Now that you have installed Anaconda, you can access its features by searching for Anaconda Navigator in the Windows toolbar, or by looking for Anaconda Navigator in the Applications folder of your Mac. Once you click on the icon, after a short pause, you will see a screen similar to the following:

You are currently at the **Home** tab, which lists the different applications included in Anaconda. You can access Jupyter notebook from this screen, as well as the Spyder IDE.

To see which software libraries are installed, click on the **Environments** tab on the left. You can use this tab to download and upgrade specific libraries as desired, as shown in the following screenshot:

Jupyter notebook

Now, let's explore Jupyter notebook, the Python programming tool we will use for most of this book. Go back to the **Home** tab and click the **Launch** button inside Jupyter icon. A new tab should open in your default browser that looks similar to the following screenshot:

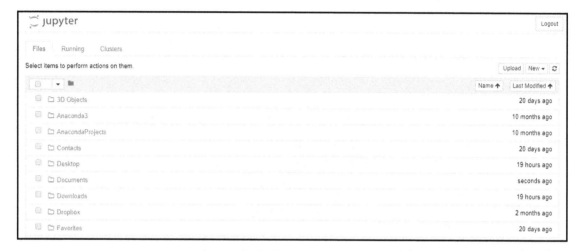

This is the **Files** tab of the Jupyter application, where you can navigate your computer's directories to launch a new Jupyter notebook, open an existing one, or manage your directories.

Let's create a new Jupyter notebook. Locate the **New** drop-down menu on the upper right of the console and click it. In the drop-down menu, click **Python 3**. Another tab will open what looks like the following screenshot:

The box labeled with `In` is called a cell. The **cell** is the functional unit of Python programming inside of Jupyter. You enter your code in a cell and then click run to execute it. After you see the result, you can create a new cell and continue with your workflow, building on the previous results if you so choose.

Let's try an example. Click in the cell body, and type the following lines:

```
message = 'Hello World!'
print(message)
```

Then, find the Play button on the top toolbar and click it. You should see the `Hello World!` message immediately following the cell. You will also see a new cell below the text. This is the way Jupyter works.

Now, in the new cell, enter the following:

```
modified_message = message + ' Also, Hello World of Healthcare Analytics!'
print(modified_message)
```

Again, click the Play button. You should see the modified message under the second cell and the appearance of a third cell. Notice that the second cell is aware of what the `message` variable contains, even though it was assigned in the first cell. Jupyter remembers every command entered into the console for each session. To clear the memory, you must shut down and restart the kernel:

Now, let's end the current session. Go back to the **Home** tab in your browser. Click on the **Running** tab in the upper left. Under the **Notebooks** menu, you should see that `Untitled.ipynb` is running. Click the **Shutdown** button to the right and the notebook will disappear.

That's enough Jupyter for now. You will get more closely acquainted with it in the coming chapters.

Spyder IDE

The Spyder IDE offers a complete environment for Python development, including a text editor, variable explorer, IPython console, and optionally, a command prompt, as seen in the following screenshot:

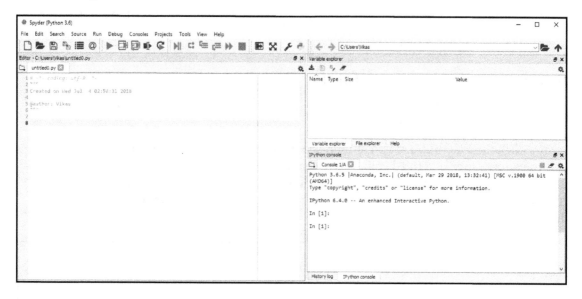

On the left half of the screen is the **Editor** window. This is where you will write your Python code. Once we are finished with the scripts, we will run them using the green Play button in the upper toolbar.

The right half of the screen is divided horizontally into two parts. The top-right window, in its most useful form, functions as a **Variable explorer** (as shown). This window lists the name, type, size, and value of every variable that is currently in your Python environment (for example, in memory). By clicking on the tabs at the bottom of the window, you can also change the window to a **File explorer** or explore Python's helper documentation.

The bottom-right window is the console. It features a Python command prompt. This is useful for running single Python commands; it can also be used to run Python scripts and for other functions. The third option for this window is a history log of previously entered commands.

We will not use Spyder extensively in this book; however, it is good to know how it works in case you would like to use it for later projects.

SQLite

Healthcare data is commonly stored in databases. To manipulate and extract the desired data from these databases, you should know SQL. SQL is a language that has many variations depending on the engine you use. We will be using **SQLite**, a free, public-domain SQL database engine.

To download SQLite, do the following:

1. Navigate to the SQLite homepage (`www.sqlite.org`). Then, click on the **Downloads** tab at the top.
2. Download the appropriate precompiled binary file for your operating system. You want the bundle file, not the DLL file (the file named with the following format: `sqlite-tools-{Your OS}-x86-{Version Number}.zip`).
3. Using a shell or command prompt, navigate to the directory containing the `sqlite3.exe` program.
4. At the prompt, type `sqlite3 test.db` and press *Enter*.

You are now in the SQLite program. Later, we will use SQLite commands to create, save, and manipulate mock patient data. SQLite commands start with a period followed by a lowercase word and then the command arguments.

To exit SQLite, type `.exit` and press *Enter*.

Command-line tools

All operating systems, whether Windows, MacOS, or Linux, come with a command-line tool for entering commands. On Mac or Linux, the shell program takes bash commands. On Windows, there are DOS commands that are different than bash. For this book, we used a Windows PC and the DOS command prompt. Where necessary, we have included the commands we used in the text along with the corresponding bash command.

Installing a text editor

Some of the data files used in this book are quite large and may not open using the standard text editor that comes with your computer. We recommend using a downloadable source code editor instead. Popular choices include Sublime (for Windows and Mac) or Notepad++ (for Windows). We used Notepad++ for this book.

Summary

Now that we have introduced the subject of healthcare analytics and set up your computer for the remainder of this book, we are ready to dive into some foundations of healthcare analytics. In `Chapter 2`, *Healthcare Foundations*, we will look at some of the healthcare foundations of healthcare analytics.

References

Basole RC, Kumar V, Braunstein ML, et al. (2015). Analyzing and Visualizing Clinical Pathway Adherence in the Emergency Department. Nashville, TN: INFORMS Healthcare Conference, July 29-31, 2015.

Baxt, WG (1990). "Use of an Artificial Neural Network for Data Analysis in Clinical Decision-Making: The Diagnosis of Acute Coronary Occlusion." *Neural Computation* 2 (4): 480-489.

Ledley RS, Lusted LB (1959). "Reasoning Foundations of Medical Diagnosis." *Science* 130 (3366): 9-21.

Miller RA, Pople Jr. HE, Myers JD (1982). "INTERNIST-1, An Experimental Computer-Based Diagnostic Consultant for General Internal Medicine." *New Engl J Med* 307: 468-476.

Minsky M, Papert SA (1969). "Perceptrons." Cambridge, MA: The MIT Press.

Rumelhart DE, Hinton GE, Williams RJ (1986). "Learning representations by back-propagating errors." *Nature* 323(9): 533-536.

Healthcare Foundations 2

This chapter is mainly aimed at developers who have limited experience of healthcare. By the end of it, you will be able to describe basic characteristics of healthcare delivery in the United States, you will be familiar with specific legislation in the US that is relevant to analytics, you will understand how data in healthcare is structured, organized, and coded, and you will be aware of frameworks for thinking about analytics in healthcare.

Healthcare delivery in the US

The healthcare industry impacts all of us, through its interactions with ourselves, our loved ones, our family, and our friends. The high costs associated with the healthcare industry are intertwined with the physical, emotional, and spiritual trauma that occurs when someone close to us becomes ill or feels pain.

In the United States, the healthcare system is in a fragile state, as healthcare expenditure exceeds 15% of the nation's total GDP; this proportion far exceeds that of other developed countries, and is expected to rise to at least 20% by the year 2040 (Braunstein, 2014; Bernaert, 2015). The rise in healthcare costs in the US, and internationally, can be attributed to several factors. One is a shift in demographics to a more elderly population. Average **life expectancy** (**LE**) rose to in excess of 80 years of age for the first time in 2011, up from 70 in 1970 (OECD, 2013). While this is a positive development, elderly patients are usually more prone to falling ill and are therefore more expensive in the eyes of the healthcare system. The second reason for rising costs is the increasing prevalence of serious chronic illnesses, such as obesity and diabetes (OECD, 2013), which increases the risk of other chronic conditions. Patients with chronic conditions account for the vast majority of healthcare expenditure (Braunstein, 2014). A third reason is misaligned incentives, which are discussed in the upcoming provider reimbursement section. A fourth reason is advancing technology, as the cost of equipment for performing expensive MRI imaging and CT scans have increased in all OECD countries (OECD, 2013).

Next, we will discuss some basic healthcare terminology and how healthcare is financed in the US.

Healthcare industry basics

Healthcare can be divided roughly into **inpatient care**, which is care that occurs in an overnight facility, such as a hospital, and **outpatient**, or **ambulatory care**, which is care that occurs on a same-day basis, usually in a physician's office. Inpatient care is usually concerned with treating conditions that have progressed to a serious state or need complex interventions, and is usually costlier than outpatient care; therefore, a central goal in healthcare is to reduce the amount of care that occurs on an inpatient basis by emphasizing adequate preventive measures.

Another way to describe healthcare is by "stages of healthcare delivery." **Primary care practitioners** (**PCPs**) usually deal with the patient's entire well-being and oversee all organ systems; in many care delivery models, they serve as "gatekeepers" to secondary and tertiary care providers. **Secondary care** denotes treatment by physicians specialized to treat certain diseases or organ systems, such as endocrinologists or cardiothoracic surgeons. **Tertiary care** is provided upon referral by a specialist and usually occurs in an inpatient setting at a facility specialized to treat very specific conditions, often via surgery.

Within healthcare, it takes a team of professionals, all having different roles, to provide optimal patient care. Physicians, physician assistants, nurse practitioners, nurses, case managers, social workers, lab technicians, and information technology professionals are just some of the other personnel you will work with directly, or indirectly, in the healthcare analytics field.

Healthcare financing

A century ago, money used to flow directly from the patient to the provider for medical services provided. Today, however, healthcare finance is more complex, with employers and governments becoming increasingly involved, and new models emerging in relation to physician reimbursement. In the US, healthcare financing is no longer completely private; in order to assist the indigent and elderly populations, state and federal governments use taxes collected from citizens to fund **Medicaid** and **Medicare**, which are government-sponsored means of paying for healthcare for the poor and elderly, respectively. Once the money reaches the various third parties (insurance companies and/or the government), or while it is still in the possession of the patient, the money must be distributed to the physicians using a variety of payment models. In the following diagram, we provide a simplified overview of how money flows within the US healthcare system.

Much of the analytics in healthcare is a response to the increased emphasis on physician performance and quality, over quantity, of care:

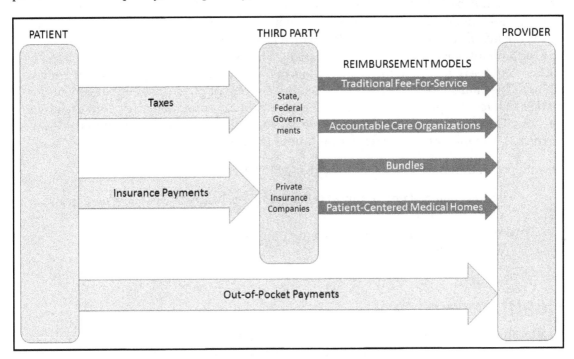

Fee-for-service reimbursement

Traditionally, physicians were reimbursed using a **fee-for-service** (FFS) payment system, in which physicians were compensated for every test or procedure that they performed, regardless of whether their patients felt better after the tests or procedures. This reimbursement method leads to conflicting incentives for physicians, who are tasked with caring for their patient efficiently while, at the same time, earning a living. Many people attribute today's exorbitant US healthcare spending to FFS. Additionally, FFS reimbursement pays each physician individually, with minimal coordination between physicians. What happens if a patient sees two doctors for the same condition? Under FFS reimbursement, the physicians could order duplicate tests and be reimbursed separately.

Value-based care

The shortcomings of FFS have led to a new vision for healthcare in the US—that of **value-based care**. Under a value-based reimbursement system, physicians are compensated based on the quality of care that they provide—which can be measured by their patient outcomes and the amount of money they save per patient. The incentive to order superfluous tests and procedures is gone, and the mutual goals of both the patient and physician become aligned. The value-based care umbrella includes a group of physician reimbursement models that reward physicians based on the quality of care provided, each with their own nuances. These models include **accountable care organizations** (**ACOs**), **bundled payments**, and **patient-centered medical homes** (**PCMHs**).

The important things to remember from this section are:

- In the United States and most other countries, healthcare expenses are growing in proportion to GDP
- Value-based care is slowly becoming the new standard for physician compensation

Healthcare policy

Healthcare reform needs support from legislators if it is to succeed, and fortunately, it has received just that. In this section, let's take a look at some legislation that has paved the way for patients' rights and privacy, the rise of EMRs, value-based care, and the advancement of big data in healthcare, all of which are relevant to healthcare analytics.

Protecting patient privacy and patient rights

Many countries around the world have enacted legislation for the protection of patient privacy. In the United States, legislation for protecting patient privacy was first signed into law in 1996 and is known as the **Health Insurance Portability and Accountability Act** (**HIPAA**). It has been revised and updated several times since then. Two of HIPAA's main components are the **Privacy Rule** and the **Security Rule**.

The Privacy Rule states the specific situations for which healthcare data can be used. In particular, any information that can be used to identify the patient (known as **protected health information** (**PHI**)) can be freely used for the purposes of medical treatment, bill payments, or other certain healthcare operations. Any other uses of the data require written authorization from the patient. A covered entity is an organization that is required to comply with HIPAA law; examples of covered entities include care providers and insurance plans. In 2013, the **Final Omnibus Rule** extended the jurisdiction of HIPAA to include business associates or independent contractors of the covered entities (which most healthcare analytics professionals can be categorized under if working with clients in the United States). Therefore, if you work with healthcare data in the United States, you must protect your patients' data or face the risk of fines and/or imprisonment.

If you are a healthcare analytics professional, how should you protect the **electronic patient health information** (**e-PHI**) in your data? The Security Rule answers this question. The Security Rule breaks down the safeguarding methods into three categories: administrative, physical, and technical. Specifically, according to the website of the US Department of Health and Human Services, healthcare data scientists should:

> *"ensure the confidentiality, integrity, and availability of all e-PHI" in their possession; protect against "reasonably anticipated threats" to the security of the information and impermissible uses or disclosures; and "ensure compliance by their workforce"*

(US Department of Health and Human Services, 2017). More specific information about safeguarding techniques can be found on the HHS website and includes the following guidelines:

- Covered entities and business associates should designate a privacy officer in charge of HIPAA enforcement and maintain training programs for employees who have access to e-PHI
- Access to hardware and software containing e-PHI should be carefully controlled, regulated, and limited to authorized individuals
- e-PHI sent over open networks (for example, via email) must be encrypted
- Covered entities and business associates are required to report any breaches of security to affected individuals and the Department of Health and Human Services

Outside of the United States, there are many countries (particularly Canada and those in Europe) that have enacted healthcare privacy laws. Regardless of the country you live in, it's considered ethical practice in healthcare analytics to protect your patients' data and privacy.

Advancing the adoption of electronic medical records

EMRs, together with healthcare analytics, are seen as a possible remedy to escalating healthcare costs. In the United States, the major piece of legislation that has promoted the use of EMRs is the **Health Information Technology for Economic and Clinical Health (HITECH) Act**, passed in 2009 as part of the American Recovery and Reinvestment Act (Braunstein, 2014). The HITECH Act provides incentive payments to healthcare organizations that do two things:

1. Adopt the use of "certified" **electronic health records (EHRs)**
2. Use the EHRs in a meaningful fashion. Starting in 2015, healthcare providers who did not use EHRs were subject to penalization from their Medicare reimbursement

In order for an EHR to be certified, it must meet several dozen criteria. Examples of such criteria include those that support clinical practice, such as allowing for computerized physician order entry and recording demographic and clinical information about patients, such as medication lists, allergy lists, and smoking statuses. Other criteria focus on maintaining the privacy and security of medical information and they call for secure access, emergency access, and access timeout after a period of inactivity. The EHR should also be able to submit clinical quality measures to the appropriate authorities. Full lists of such criteria are available at www.healthit.gov.

It is not enough for providers to have access to a certified EHR; in order to receive incentive payments, providers must use the EHR in a *meaningful* fashion, as stipulated by the meaningful use requirements. Again, dozens of requirements exist, some of which are mandatory, and some optional. These requirements are distributed across the following five domains:

- Improving care coordination
- Reducing health disparities
- Engaging patients and their families
- Improving population and public health
- Ensuring adequate privacy and security

Thanks in part to the HITECH Act, the rise of EHRs will lead to an unprecedented volume of clinical information becoming available for subsequent analysis in efforts to cut costs and improve outcomes. Later in this chapter, we will explore the creation and formatting of this clinical information in more detail.

Promoting value-based care

The **Patient Protection and Affordable Care Act (PPACA)**, also known as the **Affordable Care Act (ACA)**, was passed in 2010. It is a mammoth piece of legislation that is most well-known for its attempt to reduce the uninsured population and to provide health insurance subsidies for the majority of citizens. Some of its lesser publicized provisions, however, added new value-based reimbursement models discussed earlier in the chapter (namely, bundled payments and accountable care organizations), and created the four original value-based programs:

- **Hospital Value-Based Purchasing Program (HVBP)**
- **Hospital Readmission Reduction Program (HRRP)**
- **Hospital Acquired Conditions Reduction Program (HAC)**
- **Value Modifier Program (VM)**

These programs will be discussed in detail in `Chapter 6`, *Measuring Healthcare Quality*.

The **Medicare Access and CHIP Reauthorization Act of 2015 (MACRA)** initiated the Quality Payment Program, composed of both the **Alternative Payment Models (APM)** program and the **Merit-Based Incentive Payments System (MIPS)**. Both programs, which will be discussed in more detail in the *Measuring Provider Performance* chapter, moved the US healthcare system further away from FFS reimbursement toward value-based reimbursement.

Advancing analytics in healthcare

There are a handful of legal initiatives that are related to advancing analytics in healthcare. The most relevant of these is the **All of Us** initiative (formerly known as the **Precision Medicine Initiative**), which was enacted in 2015, and aims to collect health and genetic data from one million people by 2022 in an effort to advance precision medicine and medicine tailored to individuals.

Additionally, the following three initiatives, while not directly related to analytics, may indirectly increase funding for analytics research in healthcare. The **Brain Initiative**, passed in 2013, has the goal of radically improving our understanding of brain-related and neurological diseases such as Alzheimer's and Parkinson's disease. **Cancer Breakthroughs 2020**, passed in 2016, is focused on finding vaccines and immunotherapies against cancer. And the **21st Century Cures Act** of 2016 streamlines the **Food and Drug Administration (FDA)** drug approval process, among other provisions.

Together, the legislation of the past three decades discussed previously has set the stage for revolutionizing how healthcare analytics is performed and has created new challenges to be solved by healthcare analytics, not only in the US, but also across the globe. The new reimbursement and financing methods task us with the problem of figuring out how healthcare can be performed more efficiently, given the data that we already have.

Now let's shift gears and see what clinical data is comprised of exactly.

Patient data – the journey from patient to computer

The clinical data collection process starts when a patient starts telling a physician about his or her condition. This is known as the **patient history**, and since it is not observed directly by the physician, but instead recounted by the patient, the patient's story is known as **subjective information**. In contrast, **objective information** comes from the physician and consists of the physician's own observations about the patient, from the physical examination, lab tests, and imaging studies, to other diagnostic procedures. Together, the subjective and objective information makes up the clinical note.

There are several types of clinical notes used in healthcare. The **history and physical (H&P)** is the most thorough and comprehensive clinical note. It is usually obtained when an outpatient physician sees a patient for the first time, or when a patient is first admitted to the hospital. Collecting all the data from the patient and typing up the H&P on the hospital computer may take a total of 1-2 hours for a single patient. Usually, an H&P is only done once per physician/hospital admission. For successive outpatient visits, or an inpatient admission lasting several days, briefer clinical notes are compiled. These are termed **progress notes**, or **SOAP notes** (SOAP stands for subjective, objective, assessment, and plan). In these notes, the focus is on events that have occurred since the initial H&P or the previous progress note.

Before patient data appears in your database, it makes a long journey, starting from the patient history as interpreted by the physician team. The patient story is combined with other pieces of information from different clinical departments (for example, laboratory, imaging) to form the **electronic health record (EHR)**. When the hospital wants to make the data available to a third party for further analysis, it typically releases the data to the cloud in a database format.

Once the data is captured in a database system, the analytics professional can then use a variety of tools to visualize, pivot, analyze, and build predictive models:

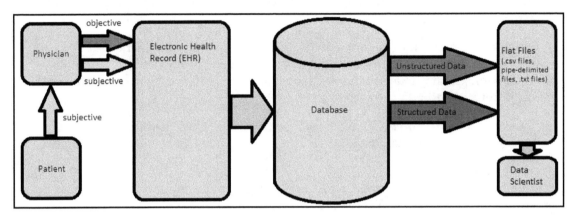

In the following subsections, we will describe the important aspects of these two types of clinical notes.

The history and physical (H&P)

As mentioned previously, the history and physical is the most comprehensive type of documentation available for patients and is usually conducted upon their admission to hospital and/or when seeing new outpatient physicians. The standard sections of the H&P clinical note are discussed in the following sections.

Metadata and chief complaint

The metadata includes basic information about the patient's visit, such as the patient's name, date of birth, date/time of admission, and the name of the admitting hospital and attending physician.

The chief complaint is the reason for the patient's visit/hospitalization, usually in the patient's own words. Example: "I'm having some chest discomfort." This chief complaint may, or may not, be translated by the history taker into the corresponding medical terminology, for example, "chest pain."

History of the present illness (HPI)

The HPI includes details surrounding the chief complaint. This section is often split into two paragraphs as follows:

The first paragraph provides the immediate details surrounding the chief complaint, usually using information obtained from the patient. The first sentence often provides important demographic details about the patient and any relevant details about the past medical history, in addition to the chief complaint. For example:

> *"Mr. Smith is a 53-year-old Caucasian male with a history of hypertension, hyperlipidemia, diabetes, and smoking, who presents to the emergency room complaining of chest pain."*

Regarding the rest of the paragraph, a first HPI paragraph usually contains the seven standard elements listed here. These seven elements tend to assume that the chief complaint is some type of pain; some chief complaints (for example, amenorrhea) require different sets of questions. The seven elements are summarized in the following table:

HPI element	Corresponding question	Example answer
Location	Where is the pain located?	The pain is left-sided and radiates to the left arm and back.
Quality	What does the pain feel like?	Patient reports a shooting, stabbing pain.
Severity	On a scale of 1-10, how bad is the pain?	Severity is 8/10.
Timing	**Onset**: When did the pain first start? **Frequency**: How often does the pain occur? **Duration**: How long are the pain episodes?	The current episode began half an hour ago. Episodes have occurred for a few months, following exercise, and for periods of up to 15-20 minutes.
Exacerbating Factors	What makes the pain worse?	Pain is exacerbated by exercise.
Alleviating Factors	What relieves the pain?	Pain is relieved by rest and weight loss.
Associated Symptoms	Do you notice any other symptoms when the pain is present?	Patient reports symptoms associated with dyspnea.

The second paragraph should contain all the previous medical care the patient has already received for their ailment. Typical questions include: Have they seen a physician already or been hospitalized previously? What labs and tests were performed? How well controlled are the patient's medical conditions relevant to the chief complaint? Which treatments were previously tried? Is there a copy of the x-ray?

Past medical history

This part of the H&P lists all current and previous medical conditions that affect the patient, including, but not limited to, hospitalizations (whether for medical, surgical, or psychiatric reasons).

Medications

Current prescription and **over-the-counter** (OTC) medications are provided in this section, usually with the following details: medication name, dose, route of administration, and frequency. Every medication listed should correspond to one of the patient's current medical conditions given in the past medical history. The route of administration and frequency are often written using abbreviations; refer to the following table for a list of common abbreviations.

Family history

The family history includes a disease history for family members up to two generations preceding the patient, with an emphasis on chronic diseases as well as diseases relevant to the chief complaint and the organ systems affected.

Social history

The social history provides details of social and risk factor information not obtained in the HPI. Included in this section are demographic factors not previously mentioned, occupation (and any occupational exposures to dangerous substances if applicable), social support (marriage, children, dependents), and substance use/abuse (tobacco, alcohol, recreational/illicit drugs).

Allergies

The allergies section commonly includes substances to which the patient is hypersensitive, including drugs, and the corresponding reaction. If the patient has no known drug allergies, it is often abbreviated using the acronym NKDA.

Review of systems

The **review of systems** (**ROS**) serves as a final screening for significant symptoms after the other parts of the history have been obtained. In this section, the patient is asked about experiencing symptoms relevant to different functional organ systems of the body (for example, gastrointestinal, cardiovascular, and pulmonary). An emphasis is placed on organ systems and symptoms relevant to the chief complaint. Symptoms for as many as 14 different organ systems may be touched upon.

Physical examination

The physician proceeds to examine the patient and records the findings in this section. The description usually starts with general patient well-being and appearance, followed by pertinent vital signs (see table for additional details), before proceeding with the **head, eyes, ears, nose, and throat** (**HEENT**), and continuing down the body with specific organs/organ systems.

Additional objective data (lab tests, imaging, and other diagnostic tests)

The physical examination marks the beginning of what is called objective data, or data about the patient that is observed, interpreted, and recorded by the physician. This is in contrast to subjective data, which is information provided to the physician by the patient first-hand, and which includes the patient history. After the physical examination, all additional objective data about the patient is provided. This includes the results of any lab tests, imaging studies if applicable, and any other tests specific to the present illness that may have been performed. Common imaging studies include **x-rays** (**XR**), **computed tomography** (**CT**) scans, and **magnetic resonance imaging** (**MRI**) scans of the body region of interest.

Assessment and plan

This is the final part of the H&P. In the assessment, the physician consolidates all of the subjective and objective data of the previous sections to make a concise summary of the chief complaint, along with significant findings from the history, physical examination, and additional tests. The physician lists the most likely causes of the patient's condition, in an itemized manner for each distinct group of complaints/findings. In the plan, the physician discusses the blueprint for treating the patient, again in an itemized fashion.

The progress (SOAP) clinical note

The SOAP note, as stated previously, is typically done on a daily basis for patients admitted to a hospital and includes one section for every letter in its acronym: **subjective, objective, assessment, and plan** (**SOAP**). The subjective section focuses on any new complaints the patient is having, or had, on the previous night. The objective section includes the daily and focused physical examination and lab, imaging, and test results from the previous day. The assessment and plan are similar to those of the H&P, updated from previous notes with all of the day's events taken into consideration.

At the end of the note documentation process, valuable information about the patient has been collected and recorded in the EMR. Before the data is tabulated, however, it is usually integrated with clinical codesets. Let's discuss clinical codesets in the next section.

Standardized clinical codesets

Being philosophical for a moment, every known object that has a significant importance attributed to it has a name. The organs you are using to read these words are known as eyes. The words are written on pieces of paper called pages. To turn the pages, you use your hands. These are all objects that we have named so that we can identify them easily.

In healthcare, important entities—diseases, procedures, lab tests, drugs, symptoms, bacteria species, for example, have names and identities too. For example, the failure of the heart valves to pump blood to the rest of the body is known as heart failure. ACE inhibitors are a class of drugs used to treat heart failure.

A problem arises, however, when healthcare industry workers associate the same entity with different identities. For example, one physician may refer to "heart failure" as "congestive heart failure", while another may refer to it as "CHF." Also, there are varying levels of specificity: a third doctor may call it "systolic heart failure" to indicate that the dysfunction is occurring during the systolic phase of the heartbeat. In medicine, accuracy and specificity are of the utmost importance. How can we ensure that all members of the healthcare team are talking and thinking about the same thing? The answer lies in clinical codes.

Clinical codes can be thought of as unique identities for medical concepts. Each code is typically comprised of a pair of objects: an alphanumeric code and a verbal description of the entity that the code represents. For example, in the ICD10-CM coding system, the code I50.9 represents "Heart failure, unspecified." There are additional, more specific codes to represent more specific heart failure diagnoses when they are known.

There are likely thousands of different coding systems that exist in the world, many of them being used only in the specific healthcare organization at which they were conceived. Fortunately, to ease confusion and promote interoperability, there are several well-known coding systems that are seen as national/international standards. Some of the more important standardized coding systems include **International Classification of Disease (ICD)** for medical diagnoses, **Current Procedural Terminology (CPT)** for medical procedures, **Logical Observation Identifiers Names and Codes (LOINC)** for laboratory tests, **National Drug Code (NDC)** for drug therapies, and **Systematized Nomenclature of Medicine (SNOMED)** for all of the preceding and more. In this section, we explore each of these coding systems in a little more detail.

International Classification of Disease (ICD)

Diseases and conditions are usually coded using the ICD coding system. ICD was started in 1899 and is revised (every 10 years) and maintained by the **World Health Organization (WHO)**. As of 2016, the tenth revision (ICD-10) is the most recent, and consists of more than 68,000 unique diagnostic codes, more than any previous revision.

ICD-10 codes may consist of up to eight alphanumeric characters. The first three characters indicate the major disease category; for example, "N18" specifies chronic kidney disease. These characters are followed by a period and then the remaining characters, which can provide an extraordinary amount of clinical detail (Braunstein, 2014). For example, code "C50.211" specifies "malignant neoplasm of upper-inner quadrant of the right female breast." With all of its precision, ICD-10 facilitates the application of analytics in healthcare.

Current Procedural Terminology (CPT)

Medical, surgical, diagnostic, and therapeutic procedures are coded using the CPT coding system. Developed by the **American Medical Association (AMA)**, CPT codes consist of four numeric characters followed by a fifth alphanumeric character. Commonly used CPT codes include those for outpatient visits, surgical procedures, radiological tests, anesthetic procedures, history and physical examination, and emerging technologies. Unlike the ICD, the CPT is not a hierarchical coding system. Some concepts, however, have multiple codes depending on factors such as the visit length (for outpatient visits) or the amount of tissue removed (for surgical procedures).

Logical Observation Identifiers Names and Codes (LOINC)

Laboratory tests and observations are coded using the LOINC coding system. Written and maintained by the Regenstrief Institute, there are over 70,000 codes, each of which is a six-digit number, the last number being separated by the other numbers with a hyphen. Like CPT codes, a specific type of laboratory test (or example, **white blood cell** (**WBC**) count) often has multiple codes that vary, depending on the timing of the sample, the measurement units, the measurement method, and so on. While each code contains a large amount of information, this may pose a problem when trying to find a code for a lab test such as a WBC count when not all of the relevant information is known.

National Drug Code (NDC)

The NDC is maintained by the US FDA. Each code is 10 digits long and has three subcomponents:

- A labeler component, which identifies the manufacturer/distributor of the drug
- A product component, which identifies the actual drug from the labeler, including strength, dosage, and formulation
- A package code, which identifies the specific package shape and size

Taken together, the three subcomponents can uniquely identify any medication that is approved by the FDA.

Systematized Nomenclature of Medicine Clinical Terms (SNOMED-CT)

SNOMED-CT is a huge coding system that uniquely identifies over 300,000 clinical concepts. These concepts may be diseases, procedures, labs, drugs, organs, infectious agents, infections, symptoms, clinical findings, and more. Additionally, SNOMED-CT defines over 1.3 million relationships between these concepts. SNOMED-CT is maintained by the **National Institutes of Health** (**NIH**) and is a subset of an even larger coding system, SNOMED, which includes concepts not relevant to clinical practice. The NIH has a software program called MetaMap (https://metamap.nlm.nih.gov/), which can be used to tag clinical concepts appearing in text, making it useful for natural language processing in healthcare.

While coding systems cannot uniquely identify every clinical concept with all of their variations and nuances, they come reasonably close, and, in so doing, make certain activities in medicine (particularly billing and analytics) much easier. In Chapter 7, *Making Healthcare Predictive Models*, we will use some coding systems to make predictive models for healthcare.

Now that we've covered healthcare fundamentals, in the next section, we will present frameworks for thinking specifically about healthcare analytics.

Breaking down healthcare analytics

So you've decided to enter the world of analytics, and you know you want to focus on the healthcare industry. However, that barely narrows down the problem space, as there are hundreds of open problems in healthcare that are being addressed with machine learning and other analytical tools. If you have ever typed the words "machine learning in healthcare" into Google or PubMed, you have probably discovered how vast the ocean of machine learning use cases in healthcare is. In academia, publications focus on problems ranging from predicting dementia onset in the elderly to predicting the occurrence of a heart attack within six months to predicting which antidepressants patients will best respond to. How do you pick the problem on which to focus? This section is all about answering that question. Choosing the appropriate problem to solve is the first essential step in healthcare analytics.

In healthcare, the problems to solve can be broken down into four categories:

- Population
- Medical task
- Data format
- Disease

We review each of these components in this section.

Population

Unfortunately, research studies cannot address every human patient on the planet, and machine learning models are no exception. In healthcare, patient **populations** are what make groups of patients, and therefore, their data and disease characteristics—homogeneous. Examples of patient populations include inpatients, outpatients, emergency room patients, children, adults, and US citizens. Geographically, populations can even be defined at the state, municipal, or local levels.

What would happen if you tried to do modeling across different populations? Data from separate populations hardly ever overlap. First of all, it may be difficult to collect the same set of features across various populations. Some of the data may simply not be collected for certain populations. If you were trying to combine inpatient and outpatient populations, for example, you wouldn't get hourly blood pressure readings or intake/output measurements for your outpatients. In addition, another contributing problem is that data for different populations will most likely come from different sources, and you probably already know that the chance of two different data sources sharing many common features is low. How can you build a model based on patients who don't have the same features? Even if there is a shared lab test, for example, variations in how the lab quantity is measured and the units in which it is expressed make it nearly impossible to produce a homogeneous, coherent dataset.

Medical task

In healthcare practice, the evaluation and treatment of patients can be broken down into different cognitive subtasks. Each of these tasks can potentially be aided by using analytics. Screening, diagnosis, prognosis measurement, outcome measurement, and response to treatment are some of these basic tasks, and we will look at each one in turn.

Screening

Screening can be defined as the identification of a disease in a patient before the onset of signs and symptoms. This is important because in many diseases, particularly chronic diseases, early detection coincides with early treatment, better outcomes, and lower costs to the healthcare provider.

Screening for some diseases has greater potential benefits than screening for others. In order for disease screening to be worthwhile, several conditions, as listed here, must be met (Martin *et al.*, 2005):

- The outcome must be alterable at the time of identifying the disease
- The screening technique should be cost-effective
- The test should have high accuracy (see `Chapter 3`, *Machine Learning Foundations* for methods for measuring test accuracy in healthcare)
- The disease should carry a large burden on the population

An example of a popular screening problem and solution is using the Pap smear to screen for cervical cancer; women are recommended to undergo this cost-effective test every 1-3 years throughout most of their lives. Lung cancer screening is an example of a problem that has yet to find an ideal solution; while using x-rays to screen for lung cancer may be accurate and may lead to earlier detection in some cases, x-rays are costly and expose patients to radiation, and there is no strong evidence that early detection influences the prognosis or outcome (Martin *et al.*, 2005). Increasingly, machine learning models are being developed in lieu of medical tests to screen for diseases including cancer, heart disease, and strokes (Esfandiari *et al.*, 2014).

Diagnosis

Diagnosis can be defined as the identification of a disease in an individual. In contrast to screening, diagnosis may happen at any time during the course of the disease. Diagnosis is important for almost every disease because it dictates how the signs or symptoms (and the underlying disease) should be treated. The exception occurs when diseases have no effective treatment, or when differentiating between diseases does not change the treatment.

A common use of machine learning in diagnosis problems is to identify potential causes of underlying disease in the face of a mysterious symptom, for example, abdominal pain. In contrast, building a machine learning model to differentiate between different types of psychiatric personality disorders may be of limited efficacy, since personality disorders are difficult to treat effectively.

Outcome/Prognosis

As discussed earlier in this chapter, healthcare is primarily concerned with producing better outcomes at a lower cost. Often, we try to determine which patients are at a high risk of a poor outcome directly, without necessarily focusing on the specific cause of their signs and symptoms. Popular outcomes for which machine learning solutions are being applied include predicting which patients will likely be readmitted to a hospital, which patients will suffer death, and which patients will be admitted to the hospital from the emergency room. As we will see in `Chapter 6`, *Measuring Healthcare Quality*, many of these outcomes are actively monitored by governments and healthcare organizations and, in some cases, governments even provide financial incentives to improve specific outcomes.

Often, instead of dividing outcomes into two classes (for example, readmission versus non-readmission), we can attempt to quantify a patient's chances of survival in terms of a specific time period, given the characteristics of the patient's disease. For example, in cancer and heart failure patients, you can attempt to predict for how many years the patient is likely to survive. This is referred to as **prognosis**, and it is also a popular machine learning problem in healthcare.

Response to treatment

In healthcare, diseases often have a variety of treatments, and predicting which treatment a patient will respond to is a problem in itself. For example, cancer patients can undergo a variety of chemotherapy regimens, and depressed patients have dozens of pharmacological treatments to choose from. Although this is a machine learning problem that is still in its infancy, it is gaining popularity and is also known as personalized medicine.

Data format

Machine learning use cases in healthcare also vary, depending on the format of the available data. The data format often dictates what methods and algorithms can be used to solve the problem, and therefore plays an important part in determining the use case.

Structured

When we think of machine learning, we usually think of the data as having a structured format. **Structured data** is data that can be organized into rows and columns having discrete values. Much of the patient data in an electronic health record may be stored in, or converted to, this format. In healthcare, individual patients or encounters often form the rows (or observations), and various features (for example, demographic variables, clinical characteristics, lab observations) of the patient/encounter form the columns. Such a format is particularly conducive to performing machine learning analyses using various algorithms.

Unstructured

Unfortunately, much of the data in an EHR (such as that in a clinical note) consists of free-form text; this is known as **unstructured data**. Provider notes generated as part of healthcare delivery provide extensive information regarding the patient and the progress of a hospital visit. Depending on the complexity of the diagnoses, radiology reports, pathology reports, and other diagnoses, notes would also include unstructured information. While unstructured data is capable of communicating far more extensive and valuable information about the patient, analysis of such data poses much more of a challenge than that of structured data.

Imaging

In certain specialties, such as radiology and pathology, data is collected using photographs and images of disease, using either photographs of lesions, pathological slides, or x-ray images. An emerging area is the automated analysis of this image data to screen, diagnose, and measure the prognosis of various diseases using these images, including benign and malignant cancers, heart disease, and strokes. We discuss examples of this in the book's final chapter.

Other data format

The **electrophysiological signal collection** is yet another data modality in healthcare; collection and analysis of such signals, be it **electroencephalographic** (EEG) signals in epilepsy patients, or **electrocardiographic** (EKG) signals in heart attack patients, can be valuable for disease diagnosis and prognosis measurement. In 2014, the popular data science competition website, Kaggle, offered a $10,000 prize for the data science team that could most effectively predict seizures in epilepsy patients using EEG data.

Disease

A fourth way in which use cases are permuted in healthcare is according to the disease. Thousands of medical diseases are actively being studied in medical research, and each one represents a potential target for machine learning models. However, in machine learning, not all diseases are created equal; some promise better potential rewards and opportunities than others.

Acute versus chronic diseases

In healthcare, diseases are often classified as being acute or chronic (Braunstein, 2014). Both types of disease are important targets for predictive modeling. **Acute diseases** are characterized by a sudden onset, are usually self-limited, and patients often experience a full recovery after the appropriate treatment. Also, risk factors for acute conditions are often not determined by patient behavior. Examples of acute diseases include influenza, kidney stones, and appendicitis.

Chronic diseases, in contrast, typically have a progressive onset and last for the lifetime of the patient. They are influenced by patient behavior, such as smoking and obesity, and also by genetic factors. Examples of chronic diseases include hypertension, atherosclerosis, diabetes, and chronic kidney disease. Chronic diseases are particularly dangerous because they tend to be linked and cause other serious chronic and acute diseases. Chronic diseases are also costly to society; billions of dollars are spent annually on preventing and treating common chronic conditions.

Acute-on-chronic diseases are particularly popular in healthcare predictive modeling. These are acute, sudden onset diseases that are caused by chronic conditions. For example, stroke and myocardial infarction are acute conditions that are by-products of the chronic conditions hypertension and diabetes. Acute-on-chronic disease modeling is popular because it allows us to filter the population to a high-risk group that has the corresponding chronic condition, increasing the yield of predictive models. For example, if you were trying to predict the onset of **congestive heart failure** (**CHF**), a useful starting place would be patients that have hypertension, which is a major risk factor. This would lead to a model with a higher percentage of true-positives than if you were to randomly sample the population. In other words, if we were trying to predict CHF onset, it wouldn't be very useful to include healthy 20-year-old males in our model.

Cancer

There are several reasons why predictive modeling for cancer has become an important use case. For one thing, cancer is the second leading cause of death among medical diseases, just behind heart attacks. It's insidious onset and course makes cancer diagnosis just that bit more surprising and devastating. No one can dispute the importance of fighting cancer with every tool in our arsenal, and that includes machine learning methods.

Second, within cancer machine learning, there are a variety of use cases that are well-suited to being solved by machine learning. For example, given a healthy patient, how likely is that patient to develop a particular type of cancer? Given a patient that has just been diagnosed with cancer, can we inexpensively predict whether the cancer is benign or malignant? How long can the patient be expected to survive? Will they likely be alive in 5 years? 10 years? To which, chemotherapy/radiotherapy regimen is the patient most likely to respond? What is the chance of cancer recurring once it is successfully treated? Questions like these benefit from mathematical answers that may be beyond the capabilities of a single doctor's reasoning or even that of a panel of doctors.

Other diseases

Certainly, there are other diseases that stand to benefit from predictive modeling. An additional point to remember is that some diseases that are particularly burdensome to society (for example, asthma and chronic kidney disease) are of particular interest to administrators and are being very actively funded and studied by both public agencies at the national, state, and local levels, as well as by private corporations.

Putting it all together – specifying a use case

Now that we've seen some of the ways in which machine learning problems can vary in healthcare, it becomes easier to specify a problem. Once you've selected a population, a medical task, an outcome measure, and disease, you can formulate a machine learning problem with a reasonable amount of specificity. We haven't included our choice of an algorithm in our discussion because, technically, it is separate from the problem being solved, and also because many problems are approached by using multiple algorithms. We will look at specific machine learning algorithms in Chapters 3 and 7, which will provide you with some background for choosing algorithms.

Here are some example use cases that can be specified using the preceding information:

"I'd like to predict which healthy elderly adults are likely to be diagnosed with Alzheimer's disease in the next five years."

"We are going to build a model that looks at images of moles and predicts whether the moles are likely to be benign or malignant."

"Can we predict whether pediatric patients presenting to the emergency room with asthma will be admitted to the hospital or discharged home?"

Summary

In Chapter 1, *Introduction to Healthcare Analytics*, we introduced the Healthcare Analytics triumvirate of healthcare, mathematics, and computer science. In this chapter, we have looked at some foundational healthcare topics. In Chapter 3, *Machine Learning Foundations*, we will look at some of the mathematical and machine learning concepts that underlie healthcare analytics.

References and further reading

Bernaert, Arnaud (2015). "Five Global Health Trends You Can't Ignore." *UPS Longitudes.* April 13, 2015. longitudes.ups.com/five-global-health-trends-you-cant-ignore/.

Braunstein, Mark (2014). *Contemporary Health Informatics.* Chicago, IL: AHIMA Press.

Esfandiari N, Babavalian MR, Moghadam A-ME, Tabar VK (2014) *Knowledge discovery in medicine: current issue and future trend. Expert Syst Appl* 41(9): 4434–4463.

Martin, GJ (2005). "Screening and Prevention of Disease." In Kasper DL, Braunwald E, Fauci AS, Hauser SL, Longo DL, Jameson JL. eds. *Harrison's Principles of Internal Medicine*, 16e. New York, NY: McGraw-Hill.

OECD (2013), Health at a Glance 2013: OECD Indicators, OECD Publishing. http://dx.doi.org/10.1787/health_glance-2013-en.

Smith, Robert C (1996). *The Patient's Story.* Boston, MA: Little, Brown.

US Department of Health and Human Services (2017). *HIPAA For Professionals.* Washington, DC: Office for Civil Rights.

Machine Learning Foundations

3

This chapter provides an introduction to the mathematical foundations behind healthcare analytics and machine learning. It is intended mainly for healthcare professionals with little background knowledge of the math required for doing healthcare analytics. By the end of the chapter, you will be familiar with the following:

- Medical decision making paradigms
- The basic machine learning pipeline

Model frameworks for medical decision making

It is a poorly publicized fact that, in addition to the basic science courses and clinical rotations that they must do during their training, physicians also take courses in biostatistics and medical decision making. In these courses, prospective physicians learn some math and statistics that will help them as they sort through different symptoms, findings, and test results to arrive at diagnoses and treatment plans for their patients. Many physicians, already bombarded with endless medical facts and knowledge, shrug these courses off. Nevertheless, whether they learned it from these courses or from their own experiences, much of the reasoning that physicians use in their daily practice resembles the math behind some common machine learning algorithms. Let's explore that assertion a bit more in this section as we look at some popular frameworks for medical decision making and compare them to machine learning methods.

Tree-like reasoning

We are all familiar with tree-like reasoning; it involves branching into various possible actions as different decision points are met. Here we look at tree-like reasoning more closely and examine its machine learning counterparts: the decision tree and the random forest.

Categorical reasoning with algorithms and trees

In one medical decision making paradigm, the clinical problem can be approached as a **tree** or an **algorithm**. Here, an algorithm does not refer to a "machine learning algorithm" in the computer science sense; it can be thought of as a structured, ordered set of rules to reach a decision. In this type of reasoning, the root of the tree represents the initiation of the patient encounter. As the physician learns more information while asking questions, they come to various branch or decision points where the physician can proceed in more than one route. These routes represent different clinical tests or alternate lines of questioning. The physician will repeatedly make decisions and pick the next branch, reaching a terminal node at which there are no more branches. The terminal node represents a definitive diagnosis or a treatment plan.

Here we have an example of a clinical management algorithm for weight and obesity management (National Heart, Lung, and Blood Institute, 2010). Each decision point (most of which are binary) is a diamond, while management plans are rectangles.

For example, suppose we have a female patient with several clinical variables that are measured: BMI = 27, waist circumference = 90 cm, and the number of cardiac risk factors = 3. Starting at node #1, we skip from Node #2 directly to Node #4, since the BMI $\geq$ 25. At Node #5, again the answer is "Yes." At Node #7, again the answer is "Yes," taking us to the management plan outlined in Node #8:

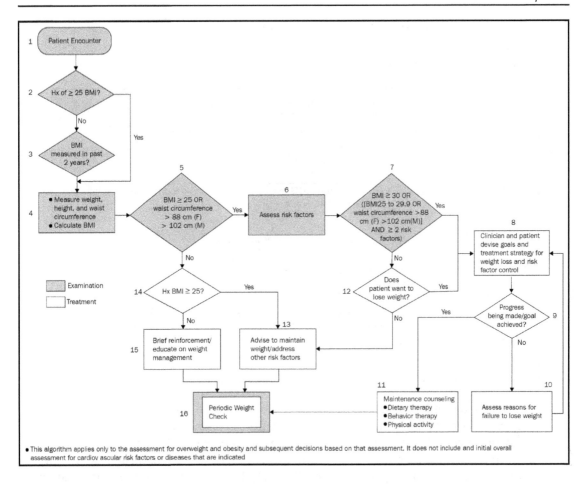

- This algorithm applies only to the assessment for overweight and obesity and subsequent decisions based on that assessment. It does not include and initial overall assessment for cardiovascular risk factors or diseases that are indicated

A second example of an algorithm that combines both diagnosis and treatment is shown as follows (Haggstrom, 2014; Kirk et al., 2014). In this algorithm for the diagnosis/treatment of pregnancy of an unknown location, a hemodynamically stable patient with no pain (a patient with stable heart and blood vessel function) is routed to have serum hCG drawn at 0 and 48 hours after presenting to the physician. Depending on the results, several possible diagnoses are given, along with corresponding management plans.

Note that in the clinical world, it is perfectly possible for these trees to be wrong; those cases are referred to as predictive errors. The goal in constructing any tree is to choose the best variables/cutpoints that minimize the error:

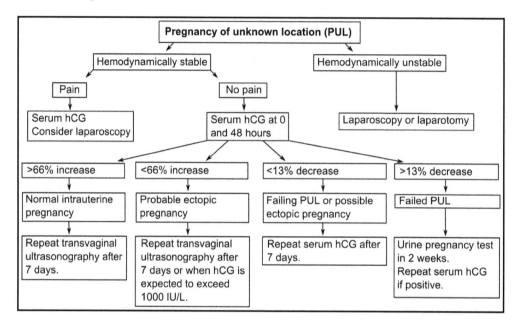

Algorithms have a number of advantages. For one, they model human diagnostic reasoning as sequences of hierarchical decisions or determinations. Also, their goal is to eliminate uncertainty by forcing the caretaker to provide a binary answer at each decision point. Algorithms have been shown to improve standardization of care in medical practice and are in widespread use for many medical conditions today not only in outpatient/inpatient practice but also prior to hospital arrival by **emergency medical technicians** (**EMTs**).

However, algorithms are often overly simplistic and don't consider the fact that medical symptoms, findings, or test results may not indicate 100% certainty. They are insufficient when multiple pieces of evidence must be weighed for arriving at a decision.

Corresponding machine learning algorithms – decision tree and random forest

In the preceding diagram, you may have noticed that the example tree most likely uses *subjectively* determined cutpoints in deciding which route to follow. For example, Diamond #5 uses a BMI cutoff of 25, and Diamond #7 uses a BMI cutoff of 30. Nice, round numbers! In the decision analysis field, trees are usually constructed based on human inference and discussion. What if we could *objectively* determine the best variables to cut (and the corresponding cutpoints at which to cut) in order to minimize the error of the algorithm?

This is just what we do when we train a formal **decision tree** using a machine learning algorithm. Decision trees evolved in the 1990s and used principles of information theory to optimize the branching variables/points of the tree to maximize the classification accuracy. The most common and simple algorithm for training a decision tree proceeds using what is known as a **greedy** approach. Starting at the first node, we take the training set of our data and **split** it based on each **variable**, using a variety of **cutpoints** for each variable. After each split, we calculate the entropy or information gain from the resulting split. Don't worry about the formulas for calculating these quantities, just know that they measure how much information is gained from the split, which correlates with how even the split is. For example, using the PUL algorithm shown previously, a split that results in eight normal intrauterine pregnancies and seven ectopic pregnancies would be favored over a split that results in 15 normal intrauterine pregnancies and zero ectopic pregnancies. Once we have the variable and cutpoint for the best split, we proceed and then repeat the method, using the remaining variables. To prevent **overfitting** the model to the training data, we stop splitting the tree when certain criteria are reached, or alternatively, we could train a big tree with many nodes and then remove (**prune**) some of the nodes.

Decision trees have some limitations. For one thing, decision trees must split the decision space linearly at each step based on a single variable. Another problem is that decision trees are prone to overfitting. Because of these issues, decision trees typically aren't competitive with most state-of-the-art machine learning algorithms in terms of minimizing errors. However, the **random forest,** which is basically an ensemble of de-correlated decision trees, is currently among the most popular and accurate machine learning methods in medicine. We will make decision trees and random forests in Chapter 7, *Making Predictive Models in Healthcare* of this book.

Probabilistic reasoning and Bayes theorem

A second, more mathematical way of approaching the patient involves initializing the baseline probability of a disease for a patient and updating the probability of the disease with every new clinical finding discovered about the patient. The probability is updated using Bayes theorem.

Using Bayes theorem for calculating clinical probabilities

Briefly, Bayes theorem allows for the calculation of the post-test probability of a disease, given a pretest probability of disease, a test result, and the 2 x 2 contingency table of the test. In this context, a "test" result does not have to be a lab test; it can be the presence or absence of any clinical finding as ascertained during the history and physical examination. For example, the presence of chest pain, whether the chest pain is substernal, the result of an exercise stress test, and the troponin result all qualify as clinical findings upon which post-test probabilities can be calculated. Although Bayes theorem can be extended to include continuously valued results, it is most convenient to binarize the test result before calculating the probabilities.

To illustrate the use of Bayes theorem, let's pretend you are a primary care physician and that a 55-year-old patient approaches you and says, "I'm having chest pain." When you hear the words "chest pain," the first life-threatening condition you are concerned about is a myocardial infarction. You can ask the question, "What is the likelihood that this patient is having a myocardial infarction?" In this case, the presence or absence of chest pain is the test (which is positive in this patient), and the presence or absence of myocardial infarction is what we're trying to calculate.

Calculating the baseline MI probability

To calculate the probability that the chest-pain patient is having a **myocardial infarction (MI)**, we must know three things:

- The pretest probability
- The 2 x 2 contingency table of the clinical finding for the disease in question (MI, in this case)
- The result of this test (in this case, the patient is positive for chest pain)

Because the presence or absence of other findings is not yet known in the patient, we can take the pretest probability to be the baseline prevalence of MI in the population. Let's pretend that in your clinic's region, the baseline prevalence of MI in any given year is 5% for a 55-year-old person. Therefore, the pretest probability of MI in this patient is 5%. We will see later that the post-test probability of disease in this patient is the pretest probability multiplied by the likelihood ratio for positive chest pain (LR+). To get LR+, we need the 2 x 2 contingency table.

2 x 2 contingency table for chest pain and myocardial infarction

Suppose the following table is the breakdown of chest pain and myocardial infarction in 400 patients who visited your clinic:

	Myocardial Infarction present (D+)	Myocardial Infarction absent (D-)	Total
Chest pain present (T+)	15 (TP)	100 (FP)	115
Chest pain absent (T-)	5 (FN)	280 (TN)	285
Total	20	380	400

Interpreting the contingency table and calculating sensitivity and specificity

In the preceding table, there are four numerical cells, labeled **TP**, **FP**, **FN**, and **TN**. These abbreviations stand for **true positives**, **false positives**, **false negatives**, and **true negatives**, respectively. The first word (true/false) indicates whether or not the test result matched the presence of disease as measured by the gold standard. The second word (positive/negative) indicates what the test result was. True positives and true negatives are desirable; this means that the test result is correct and the higher these numbers, the better the test is. On the other hand, false positives and false negatives are undesirable.

Two important quantities that can be calculated from the true/false positives/negatives include the **sensitivity** and the **specificity**. The sensitivity is a measure of how powerful the test is in detecting disease. It is expressed as the ratio of positive test results over the number of total patients who had the disease:

$$Sn = TP/(TP + FN)$$

On the other hand, the specificity is a measure of how good the test is at identifying patients who do not have the disease. It is expressed as the following:

$$Sp = TN/(TN + FP)$$

These concepts can be confusing initially, so it may take some time and iterations before you get used to them, but the sensitivity and specificity are important concepts in biostatistics and machine learning.

Calculating likelihood ratios for chest pain (+ and -)

The **likelihood ratio** is a measure of how much a test changes the likelihood of having a condition. It is often split into two quantities: the likelihood ratio of a positive test (LR+), and the likelihood ratio of a negative test (LR-).

The likelihood ratio for MI given a positive chest pain result is given by the following formulas:

$$LR+ = (TP/(TP+FN))/(FP/(FP+TN))$$

$$LR+ = Pr\,(Positive\ Test|Positive\ Disease)\,/Pr\,(Positive\ Test|Negative\ Disease)$$

$$LR+ = Sensitivity/\,(1 - Specificity)$$

The likelihood ratio for MI given a negative chest pain result would be given by the following formulas:

$$LR- = (FN/(TP+FN))/(TN/(FP+TN))$$

$$LR- = Pr\,(Negative\ Test|Positive\ Disease)\,/PR\,(Negative\ Test|Negative\ Disease)$$

$$LR- = (1 - Sensitivity)\,/Specificity$$

Since the patient is positive for the presence of chest pain, only LR+ applies in this case. To get LR+, we use the appropriate numbers:

```
LR+ = (TP/(TP + FN)) / (FP/(FP + TN))
    = (15/(15 + 5)) / (100/(100 + 280))
    = 0.750 / 0.263
    = 2.85
```

Calculating the post-test probability of MI given the presence of chest pain

Now that we have LR+, we multiply it by the pretest probability to get the post-test probability:

```
Post-Test Probability = 0.05 x 2.85 = 14.3%.
```

This approach for diagnosis and management of the patient seems very appealing; being able to calculate an exact probability of disease seemingly eliminates many issues in diagnosis! Unfortunately, Bayes theorem breaks down in clinical practice for many reasons. First, a large amount of data is required at every step to update the probability. No physician or database has access to all the contingency tables required to update the Bayes theorem with every historical element or lab test result discovered about the patient. Second, this method of probabilistic reasoning is unnatural for humans to perform. The other techniques discussed are much more conducive to a performance by the human brain. Third, while the model may work for single diseases, it doesn't work well when there are multiple diseases and comorbidities. Finally, and most importantly, the assumptions of conditional independence and exhaustiveness and exclusiveness that are fundamental to the Bayes theorem don't hold in the clinical world. The reality is that symptoms and findings are not completely independent of each other; the presence or absence of one finding can influence that of many others. Together, these facts render the probability calculated by the Bayes theorem to be inexact and even misleading in most cases, even when one succeeds in calculating it. Nevertheless, Bayes theorem is important in medicine for many subproblems when ample evidence is available (for example, using chest pain characteristics to calculate the probability of MI during the patient history).

Corresponding machine learning algorithm – the Naive Bayes Classifier

In the preceding example, we showed you how to calculate a post-test probability given a pretest probability, a likelihood, and a test result. The machine learning algorithm known as the Naive Bayes Classifier does this for every feature sequentially for a given observation. For example, in the preceding example, the post-test probability was 14.3%. Let's pretend that the patient now has a troponin drawn and it is elevated. 14.3% now becomes the pretest probability, and a new post-test probability is calculated based on the contingency table for troponin and MI, where the contingency tables are obtained from the training data. This is continued until all the features are exhausted. Again, the key assumption is that each feature is independent of all others. For the classifier, the category (outcome) having the highest post-test probability is assigned to the observation.

The Naive Bayes Classifier is popular for a select group of applications. Its advantages include high interpretability, robustness to missing data, and ease/speed for training and predicting. However, its assumptions make the model unable to compete with more state-of-the-art algorithms.

Criterion tables and the weighted sum approach

The third medical decision making paradigm we will discuss is the criterion table and its similarity to linear and logistic regression.

Criterion tables

The use of criterion tables is partially motivated by an additional shortcoming of Bayes theorem: its sequential nature of considering each finding one at a time. Sometimes, it is more convenient to consider many factors simultaneously while considering diseases. What if we imagined the diagnosis of a certain disease as an additive sum of select factors? That is, in the MI example, the patient receives a point for having positive chest pain, a point for having a history of a positive stress test, and so on. We could establish a threshold for a point total that gives a positive diagnosis of MI. Because some factors are more important than others, we could use a weighted sum, in which each factor is multiplied by an importance factor before adding. For example, the presence of chest pain may be worth three points, and a history of a positive stress test may be worth five points. This is how criterion tables work.

In the following table, we have given the modified wells criteria as an example. The modified wells criteria (derived from Clinical Prediction, 2017) are used to determine whether or not a patient may have a **pulmonary embolism** (**PE**): a blood clot in the lung that is life-threatening. Note that criterion tables not only provide point values for each relevant clinical finding but also give thresholds for interpreting the total score:

Clinical finding	Score
Clinical symptoms of deep vein thrombosis (leg swelling, pain with palpation)	3.0
Alternative diagnosis is less likely than pulmonary embolism	3.0
Heart rate > 100 beats per minute	1.5
Immobilization for > 3 days or surgery in the previous 4 weeks	1.5
Previous diagnosis of deep vein thrombosis/pulmonary embolism	1.5
Hemoptysis	1.0
Patient has cancer	1.0
Risk stratification	
Low risk for PE	< 2.0
Medium risk for PE	2.0 - 6.0
High risk for PE	> 6.0

Corresponding machine learning algorithms – linear and logistic regression

Notice that a criterion table tends to use nice, whole numbers that are easy to add. Obviously, this is so the criteria are convenient for physicians to use while seeing patients. What would happen if we could somehow determine the optimal point values for each factor, as well as the optimal threshold? Remarkably, the machine learning method called logistic regression does just this.

Logistic regression is a popular statistical machine learning algorithm that is commonly used for binary classification tasks. It is a type of model known as a generalized linear model.

To understand logistic regression, we must first understand **linear regression**. In linear regression, the ith output variable (*y-hat*) is modeled as a weighted sum of the p individual predictor variables, x_i:

$$\hat{y}_i = b_1 x_{i1} + b_2 x_{i2} + \ldots + b_p x_{ip}$$

The weights (beta) (also known as **coefficients**) of the variables can be determined by the following equation:

$$\beta = \left(X^T X\right)^{-1} X^T Y$$

Logistic regression is like linear regression, except that it applies a transformation to the output variable that limits its range to be between 0 and 1. Therefore, it is well-suited to model probabilities of a positive response in classification tasks, since probabilities must also be between 0 and 1.

Logistic regression has many practical advantages. First of all, it is an intuitively simple model that is easy to understand and explain. Understanding its mechanics does not require much advanced mathematics beyond high school statistics, and can easily be explained to both technical and nontechnical stakeholders on a project.

Second, logistic regression is not computationally intensive, in terms of time or memory. The coefficients are simply a collection of numbers that is as long as the list of predictors, and its determination only involves several matrix multiplications (see the preceding second equation for an example). One caveat to this is that the matrices may be quite large when dealing with very large datasets (for example, billions of data points), but this is true of most machine learning models.

Third, logistic regression does not require much preprocessing (for example, centering or scaling) of the variables (although transformations that move predictors toward a normal distribution can increase performance). As long as the variables are in a numeric format, that is enough to get started with logistic regression.

Finally, logistic regression, especially when coupled with regularization techniques such as lasso regularization, can have reasonably strong performance in making predictions.

However, in today's era of fast and powerful computing, logistic regression has largely been superseded by other algorithms that are more powerful, and typically more accurate. This is because logistic regression makes many major assumptions about the data and the modeling task:

- It assumes that every predictor has a linear relationship with the outcome variable. This is obviously not the case in most datasets. In other words, logistic regression is not strong at modeling nonlinearities in the data.
- It assumes that all of the predictors are independent of one another. Again, this is usually not the case, for example, two or more variables may interact to affect the prediction in a way that is more than just the linear sum of each variable. This can be partially remedied by adding products of predictors as interaction terms in the model, but choosing which interactions to model is not an easy task.
- It is highly and adversely sensitive to multiply correlated predictor variables. In the presence of such data, logistic regression may cause overfitting. To overcome this, there are variable selection methods, such as forward step-wise logistic regression, backward step-wise logistic regression, and best subset logistic regression, but these algorithms are imprecise and/or time-intensive.

Finally, logistic regression is not robust to missing data, like some classifiers are (for example, Naive Bayes).

Pattern association and neural networks

The last medical decision making framework strikes at the heart of our neurobiological understanding of how we process information and make decisions.

Complex clinical reasoning

Imagine that an elderly patient complaining of chest pain sees a highly experienced physician. Slowly, the clinician asks the appropriate questions and gets a representation of the patient as determined by the features of that patient's signs and symptoms. The patient says they have a history of high blood pressure but no other cardiac risk factors. The chest pain varies in intensity with the heartbeat (also known as pleuritic chest pain). The patient also reports they just came back to the United States from Europe. They also complain of swelling in the calf muscle. Slowly, the physician combines these lower level pieces of information (the absence of cardiac risk factors, the pleuritic chest pain, the prolonged period of immobility, a positive Homan's sign) and integrates it with memories of previous patients and the physician's own extensive knowledge to build a higher level view of this patient and realizes that the patient is having a pulmonary embolism. The physician orders a V/Q scan and proceeds to save the patient's life.

Such stories happen every day across the globe in medical clinics, hospitals, and emergency departments. Physicians use information from the patient history, exam, and test results to compose higher level understandings of their patients. How do they do it? The answer may lie in neural networks and deep learning.

Corresponding machine learning algorithm – neural networks and deep learning

How humans think and attain consciousness is certainly one of the universe's open questions. There is scarce knowledge on how human beings achieve rational thought or on how physicians make complex clinical decisions. However, perhaps the closest we have come to mimicking human brain performance in common cognitive tasks, as of this writing, is through neural networks and deep learning.

A **neural network** is modeled after the nervous system of mammals, in which predictor variables are connected to sequential layers of artificial "neurons" that aggregate and sum weighted inputs before sending their nonlinearly transformed outputs to the next layer. In this fashion, the data may pass through several layers before ultimately producing an outcome variable that indicates the likelihood of the target value is positive. The weights are usually trained by using the **backpropagation** technique, in which the negative difference between the correct output and predicted output is added to the weights at each iteration.

The neural network and the backpropagation technique was first reported in the 1980s in a famous paper published by *Nature* journal, as was discussed in `Chapter 1`, *Introduction to Healthcare Analytics* (Rumelhart et al., 1986); in the 2010s, modern computing power along with vast amounts of data led to the rebranding of neural networks as "**deep learning**." Along with the increases in computing power and data availability, there have been state-of-the-art performance gains in machine learning tasks, such as speech recognition, image and object identification, and digit recognition.

The fundamental advantage of neural networks is that they are built to handle nonlinearities and complex interactions between predictor variables in the data. This is because each layer in a neural network is essentially performing a linear regression on the output of the previous layer, not simply on the input data itself. The more layers one has in a network, the more complex functions the network can model. The presence of nonlinear transformations in the neurons also contributes to this ability.

Neural networks also easily lend themselves to **multiclass problems**, in which there are more than two possible outcomes. Recognizing digits 0 through 9 is just one example of this.

Neural networks also have disadvantages. First of all, they have low interpretability and can be difficult to explain to nontechnical stakeholders on a project. Understanding neural networks requires knowledge of college-level calculus and linear algebra.

Second of all, neural networks can be difficult to tune. There are often many parameters involved (for example, how to initialize weights, the number, and size of hidden layers, what activation functions to use, connectivity patterns, regularization, and learning rates) and tuning all of them systematically is close to impossible.

Finally, neural networks are prone to overfitting. Overfitting is when the model has "memorized" the training data and cannot generalize well to previously unseen data. This can happen if there are too many parameters/layers and/or if the data is iterated over too many times.

We will work with neural networks in `Chapter 7`, *Making Predictive Models in Healthcare*.

Machine learning pipeline

In the last section, we spent a lot of time discussing machine learning models and how they correspond to frameworks for medical decision making. But how does one actually train a machine learning model? In healthcare, machine learning usually consists of a pattern of stereotyped tasks. We can refer to the collection of these tasks as a **pipeline**. While no two pipelines are exactly the same for any two machine learning applications, pipelines allow us to describe the machine learning process. In this section, we describe a generalized pipeline that many simple machine learning projects tend to follow, particularly when dealing with **structured data**, or data that can be organized into rows and columns.

Loading the data

Before we can make computations on the data, it must be **loaded** from a storage location (usually a database or a real-time data feed) into a computing workspace. Workspaces allow the user to manipulate the data and build models using popular languages including R, Python, Hadoop, and Spark. Many commercial databases have specialized functionality in order to facilitate loading into workspaces. The machine learning languages themselves also have functions that read from text files and connect to and read from databases. Sometimes the user may also prefer to perform data quality control and cleansing directly in the database. This typically includes steps such as building a patient index, data normalization, and data cleaning. In `Chapter 4`, *Computing Foundations – Databases*, we discuss the manipulation of databases using the **Structured Query Language** (**SQL**) and in `Chapter 5`, *Computing Foundations – Introduction to Python*, we discuss methods for loading the data into a Python workspace.

Cleaning and preprocessing the data

There is a popular saying in data science that goes along the lines of, "For every 10 hours of a data scientist's time, 7 hours are spent cleaning the data." There are several subtasks that can be classified under **data cleansing**, and we will look at them now.

Aggregating data

Data is usually organized in a database as separate tables that may be bound together by common patient or encounter identifiers. Machine learning algorithms usually work on a single data structure at a time. Therefore, combining and merging the data from several tables into one final table is an important task. Along the way, you'll have to make some decisions as to which data to preserve (demographic data is usually indispensable) along with which data you can safely forget (the exact timestamps of anti-asthmatic medication administrations may not be important if you are trying to predict cancer onset, for example).

Parsing data

There are cases in which some or all of the data we need is in a condensed form. An example includes flat files of healthcare survey data in which each survey is encoded as an *N*-character string, with the characters at each position corresponding to specific survey responses. In these cases, the data we want must be broken down into its various components and converted into a useful format before we can use it. We refer to this activity as **parsing**. Even data that is expressed using particular medical coding systems may require some parsing.

Converting types

If you are familiar at all with programming, you know that data can be stored as different **variable types**, ranging from simple integers to complex decimals to string (character) types. These types differ in terms of the operations that can be performed on them. For example, if the numbers 3 and 5 are stored as integer types, we can easily calculate 3+5= 8 using code. However, if they are stored as string types, adding "3" to "5" may yield an error, or it may yield "35," and this would cause all sorts of problems with our data, as you can imagine. Part of cleaning and inspecting the data is making sure every variable is stored as its proper type. Numerical data should correspond to numerical types, and most other data should correspond to string or categorical types.

In addition to the variable type, in many modeling languages, decisions must be made as to how to store data using more complex **data containers**, such as lists, vectors, and dataframes in R and lists, dictionaries, tuples, and dataframes in Python. Various importing and modeling functions may assume different choices of data structures, so once again, interconversion between data structures is usually necessary in order to achieve the desired result, and this is a crucial part of data cleansing. We will cover Python-related data structures in Chapter 5, *Computing Foundations – Introduction to Python*.

Dealing with missing data

Part of the reason why machine learning is so uniquely difficult in healthcare is its propensity for **missing data**. Inpatient hospital-data collection is often dependent on the nurses and other clinical staff to be completed thoroughly, and given how busy nurses and other clinical staff are, it's no wonder that many inpatient datasets have certain features, such as urinary intake and output or timestamps of medication administrations, inconsistently reported. Another example is diagnosis codes: a patient may be eligible for a dozen medical diagnoses but in the interest of time, only five are entered into the chart by the outpatient physician. When details such as these are left out of our data, our models will be that much less accurate when applied to real patients.

Even more problematic than the lack of detail is the effect of the missing data on our algorithms. Even one missing value in a dataframe that consists of thousands of patients and hundreds of features can prevent a model from running successfully. A quick fix might be simply to type in or impute a zero where the missing value is. But if the variable is a hemoglobin lab value, surely a hemoglobin of 0.0 is impossible. Should we impute the missing data with the mean hemoglobin lab value instead? Do we use the overall mean or the gender-specific mean? Questions such as these are the reasons why dealing with missing data is practically a data science field in itself. The importance of having the basic awareness of missing data in your dataset cannot be overemphasized. In particular, it is important to know the difference between zero-valued data and missing data. Also, gaining some familiarity with concepts such as **zero**, **NaN** ("not a number"), **NULL** ("missing"), or **NA** ("not applicable") and how they are expressed in your languages of choice, whether SQL, Python, R, or some other language, is important.

The final goal of the data-cleansing stage is usually a single **data frame**, which is a single data structure that organizes the data into a matrix-like object of rows and columns, where rows comprise the individual events or observations and columns reflect different features of the observations using various data types. In an ideal world, all of the variables will have been inspected and converted to the appropriate type, and there would be no missing data. It should be noted that there may be some back-and-forth iterations between data cleansing, exploring, visualizing, and feature selection before reaching this final milestone. Data exploration/visualization and feature selection are the two pipeline steps that we'll discuss next.

Exploring and visualizing the data

To be done in close conjunction with parsing and cleaning the data, data exploration and visualization is an important part of the model-building process. This part of the pipeline is hard to define concretely–what exactly is one looking for when exploring the data? The underlying theory is that humans can do certain things much better than computers can–things such as making connections and identifying patterns. The more one looks at and analyzes the data, the more one will discover about how the variables are related and how they can be used to predict the target variable.

A popular exploratory activity in this step is to take a stock of all of the predictor variables; that is, their formats (for example, whether they are binary, categorical, or continuous) and how many missing values there are in each. For **binary variables**, it is helpful to count how many responses are positive and how many are negative; for **categorical variables**, it is helpful to count how many possible values each variable can take and the frequency histograms for each; and for **continuous variables**, calculating some measures of central tendency (for example, mean, median, mode) and dispersion (for example, standard deviation, percentiles) is a good idea.

Additional exploratory and visualization activities can be done to elucidate the relationships between selected predictor variables and the target variable. Specific plots vary depending on the formats (binary, categorical, continuous). For example, when both the predictor variable and target variable are continuous, a **scatterplot** is a popular visualization; to make a scatterplot the values of each variable are plotted on separate axes. If the predictor variable is continuous and the target variable is binary or categorical, a **dual overlapping frequency histogram** is a good tool, as is a **box-and-whisker plot**.

In many cases, there are so many predictor variables that it becomes impossible to inspect manually and visualize each relationship. In these cases, automatic analyses, and calculating measures and statistics, such as correlation coefficients, become important.

Selecting features

When building models, more features are not always better. From an implementation perspective, a predictive pipeline modeling real-time clinical settings that interacts with multiple devices, health informatics systems, and source databases is more likely to fail than a simplified version with a minimal number of features. Specifically, while cleaning and exploring your data, you will find that not all of the features will be significantly related to the outcome variable.

Furthermore, many of the variables may be highly correlated with other variables and will offer little new information for making accurate predictions. Leaving these variables in your model could, in fact, reduce the accuracy of your model because they add random noise to the data. Therefore, a usual step in the machine learning pipeline is to perform **feature selection** and remove unwanted features from your data. The number and which variables to remove depends on many factors, including the choice of your machine learning algorithm and how interpretable you want the model to be.

There are many approaches to removing extraneous features from the final model. Iterative approaches, in which features are removed and the resulting model is built, evaluated, and compared to previous models, are popular because they allow one to measure how adjustments affect the performance of the model. Several algorithms for selecting features include **best subset selection** and forward and backward **step-wise regression**. There are also a variety of measures for feature importance, and these include the relative risk ratio, odds ratio, *p*-value significance, lasso regularization, correlation coefficient, and random forest out-of-bag error, and we will explore some of these measures in Chapter 7, *Making Predictive Models in Healthcare*.

Training the model parameters

Once we have our final data frame, we can think of the machine learning problem as minimizing an error function. All we are trying to do is make the best predictions on unseen patients/encounters; we are trying to minimize the difference between the predicted value and the observed value. For example, if we are trying to predict cancer onset, we want the predicted likelihood of cancer occurrence to be high in patients that developed cancer and low in patients that have not developed cancer. In machine learning, the difference between the predicted values and the observed values is known as an **error function** or **cost function**. Cost functions can take various forms, and machine learning practitioners often tinker with them while performing modeling. When minimizing the cost function, we need to know what weights we assign to certain features. In most cases, features that are more highly correlated to the outcome variable should be given more mathematical importance than features that are less highly correlated to the outcome variable. In a simplistic sense, we can refer to these "importance variables" as weights, or parameters. One of the major goals of supervised machine learning is all about finding that unique set of parameters or weights that minimizes our cost function. Almost every machine learning algorithm has its own way of assigning weights to different features. We will study this part of the pipeline in greater detail for the logistic regression, random forest, and neural network algorithms in Chapter 7, *Making Predictive Models in Healthcare*.

Evaluating model performance

Finally, after building the model, it is important to evaluate its performance against the ground truth, so that we can adjust it if needed, compare different models, and report the results of our model to others. Methods for evaluating model performance depend on the structure of the target variable being predicted.

Often, the first step in evaluating a model is making a 2 x 2 contingency table, an example of which is shown as follows (Preventive Medicine, 2016). In a 2 x 2 contingency table, all of the observations are split into four categories, which are further discussed in the following chart:

		CONDITION determined by "Gold Standard"	
	TOTAL POPULATION	CONDITION POS	CONDITION NEG
TEST OUT-COME	TEST POS	True Pos TP	*Type I Error* False Pos FP
	TEST NEG	*Type II Error* False Neg FN	True Neg TN

For binary-valued target variables (for example, classification problems), there will be four types of observations:

- Those that had a positive outcome for which we predicted a positive outcome
- Those that had a positive outcome for which we predicted a negative outcome
- Those that had a negative outcome for which we predicted a positive outcome
- Those that had a negative outcome for which we predicted a negative outcome

These four classes of observations are referred to respectively as:

- **True positives (TP)**
- **False negatives (FN)**
- **False positives (FP)**
- **True negatives (TN)**

Various performance measures can then be calculated from these four quantities. We will cover the popular ones in the following sections.

Sensitivity (Sn)

The **sensitivity**, also known as the **recall**, answers the question, "How effective is my model at incorrectly detecting observations that are positive for disease?"

Its formula is given as the following:

$$Sn = True\ Positives/All\ Positives = TP/(TP + FN)$$

Specificity (Sp)

The **specificity** answers the question: "How effective is my model at incorrectly detecting observations that are negative for disease?"

Its formula is given as the following:

$$Sp = True\ Negatives/All\ Negatives = TN/(TN + FP)$$

The sensitivity and specificity are complementary performance measures and are often reported together to measure the performance of a model.

Positive predictive value (PPV)

The **positive predictive value** (**PPV**), also known as the **precision**, answers the question: "Given a positive prediction of my model, how likely is it to be correct?"

Its formula is given as the following:

$$PPV = True\ Positives/All\ Positive\ Predictions = TP/(TP + FP)$$

Negative predictive value (NPV)

The **negative predictive value** (**NPV**) answers the question: "Given a negative prediction of my model, how likely is it to be correct?"

Its formula is given as the following:

$$NPV = True\ Negatives/All\ Negative\ Predictions = TN/(TN+FN)$$

False-positive rate (FPR)

The **false-positive rate** (**FPR**) answers the question: "Given a negative observation, what is the likelihood that my model will classify it as positive?"

Its formula is given as the following:

$$FPR = False\ Positives/All\ Negatives = FP/(FP+TN)$$

It is also equal to one minus the *specificity (1 - Sp)*.

Accuracy (Acc)

The **accuracy** (**Acc**) answers the question, "Given any observation, what is the likelihood that my model will classify it correctly?" It can be used as a standalone measure of model performance.

Its formula is the following:

$$Acc = Correct\ Predictions/All\ Observations = (TP+TN)/(TP+FP+FN+TN)$$

Receiver operating characteristic (ROC) curves

When the target variable is binary, many machine learning algorithms will return the prediction for the observation in the form of a score that ranges from 0 to 1. Therefore, the positive or negative value of the prediction depends on where we set the threshold in that range. For example, if we build a model to predict cancer malignancy and determine that a particular patient's malignancy likelihood is 0.65, choosing a positive threshold of 0.60 makes a positive prediction for that patient, while choosing a threshold of 0.70 makes a negative prediction for that patient. All of the performance scores vary according to where we set the threshold. Certain thresholds will lead to better performance than others, depending on our goal for detection. For example, if we are interested in cancer detection, setting a threshold to a low value such as 0.05 will increase the sensitivity of our model, at the expense of the specificity, but this may be desired because we may not mind the false positives as long as we can identify every patient who is possibly at risk for cancer.

Perhaps the most common performance measurement paradigm for binary-valued outcome variables is to construct a **receiver operating characteristic (ROC) curve**. In this curve, we plot the values of two measures, the false-positive rate, and the sensitivity, as we vary the threshold from 0 to 1. The sensitivity is usually inversely related to the false-positive rate, yielding a lowercase-r-shaped curve in most cases. The stronger the model, the higher the sensitivity and the lower the false positive rate will generally be, and the **area under the curve (AUC)** will tend to approach 1. The AUC can, therefore, be used to compare models (for the same use case) while removing the dependency on the threshold's value.

The example ROC plot (Example ROC Curves, 2016) shown as follows has two ROC curves, a dark one and a light one. Because the red (dark) curve has a greater area under the curve than the lighter curve, the model measured by the dark curve can be seen as being better performing than that reflected by the lighter curve:

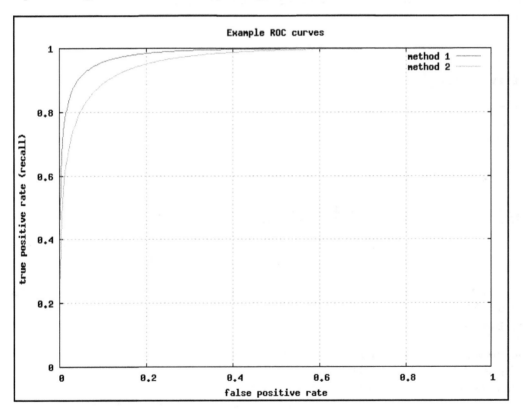

Precision-recall curves

The **precision-recall curve** is an alternative to the ROC curve when the target variable is imbalanced (for example, when the positive-negative ratio is very low or very high). In healthcare, many use cases have a low positive-negative ratio, so you may see this curve often. It plots the positive predictive value of the sensitivity as the threshold varies from 0 to 1. In most cases, this yields an uppercase-L-shaped curve.

Continuously valued target variables

For continuously valued target variables (for example, regression problems), there is no concept of true positives or false positives, so the previously discussed measures and curves cannot be calculated. Instead, the **residual sum of squares (RSS) error** is usually calculated: it is the sum of the squared distances between the actual values and the predicted values.

Summary

In this chapter, we have toured some of the machine learning and mathematical foundations for performing healthcare analytics. In the next chapter, we'll continue exploring the foundational triumvirate of healthcare analytics by moving on to the computing leg.

References and further reading

Clinical Prediction (2017). "Wells Clinical Prediction Rule for Pulmonary Embolism." http://www.clinicalprediction.com/wells-score-for-pe/. Accessed June 6, 2018.

"File: Example ROC curves.png." Wikimedia Commons, the free media repository. 26 Nov 2016, 05:26 UTC. 11 Jul 2018, 01:53 https://commons.wikimedia.org/w/index.php?title=File:Example_ROC_curves.pngoldid=219960771.

"File: Preventive Medicine Statistics Sensitivity TPR, Specificity TNR, PPV, NPV, FDR, FOR, ACCuracy, Likelihood Ratio, Diagnostic Odds Ratio 2 Final.png." Wikimedia Commons, the free media repository. 26 Nov 2016, 04:26 UTC. 11 Jul 2018, 01:42 https://commons.wikimedia.org/w/index.php?title=File:Preventive_Medicine_Statistics_Sensitivity_TPR,_Specificity_TNR,_PPV,_NPV,_FDR,_FOR,_ACCuracy,_Likelihood_Ratio,_Diagnostic_Odds_Ratio_2_Final.pngoldid=219913391.

Häggström, Mikael (2014). "Medical gallery of Mikael Häggström 2014". WikiJournal of Medicine 1 (2). DOI:10.15347/wjm/2014.008. ISSN 2002-4436. Public Domain.

James G, Witten D, Hastie T, Tibshirani R (2014). *An Introduction to Statistical Learning.* New York: Springer.

Kirk E, Bottomley C, Bourne T (2014). "Diagnosing ectopic pregnancy and current concepts in the management of pregnancy of unknown location". Hum. Reprod. Update 20 (2): 250–61. DOI:10.1093/humupd/dmt047. PMID24101604.

Mark, DB (2005). "Decision-Making in Clinical Medicine." In Kasper DL, Braunwald E, Fauci AS, Hauser SL, Longo DL, Jameson JL. eds. *Harrison's Principles of Internal Medicine,* 16e. New York, NY: McGraw-Hill.

National Heart, Lung, and Blood Institute (2010). "Treatment Algorithm." *Guidelines on Overweight and Obesity: Electronic Textbook.* https://www.nhlbi.nih.gov/health-pro/guidelines/current/obesity-guidelines/e_textbook/txgd/algorthm/algorthm.htm. Accessed June 3, 2018.

Rumelhart DE, Hinton GE, Williams RJ (1986). "Learning representations by backpropagating errors." *Nature* 323(9): 533-536.

4
Computing Foundations – Databases

This chapter will introduce you to databases and the **Structured Query Language** (**SQL**). It is mainly for healthcare professionals and beginner data scientists and programmers who are interested in working with healthcare databases. By the end of the chapter, you will know what a database is and how to use basic SQL to extract and manipulate information in clinical databases. We will present an example task and SQL statements useful for manipulating data in a sample mini-database of five patients.

Introduction to databases

A **database** can be defined as a collection of related data (Elmasri and Navathe, 2010). Databases are often subcategorized as **SQL databases** or **NoSQL databases**. In SQL databases, data is recorded in tables and consists of rows and columns. The related data may be distributed across several tables in a trade-off between efficient storage and convenience. The **database management system** (**DBMS**) is a piece of software that enables the database to serve several functions. For one thing, it allows for the *retrieval* of data using the SQL language (for SQL databases). Another function is to update the data when needed, also using SQL. Additional functions of a DBMS include protecting and securing the data.

Database management is a complex field of its own. In this book, we will place an emphasis on *using SQL to retrieve and update clinical data that is usually distributed across multiple related tables*. For additional comprehensive resources on databases, see the *References* section at the end of this chapter.

Data engineering with SQL – an example case

For this chapter, let's pretend you secured a predictive analytics assignment with a cardiology practice located in the United States. The practice wants you to predict which patients are at risk of dying within 6 months of their visit to the clinic. They make their data available to you in the form of a database that includes six tables. For simplicity, we truncate the database to include the information for five patients only. Our task is to manipulate the data using the SQL language to consolidate it into a single table so that it can be used for machine learning. We will first go over the patients in the database and the database structure. Then, we will introduce basic SQL concepts for engineering and manipulate the data into a form amenable to machine learning.

Case details – predicting mortality for a cardiology practice

The cardiology practice you are working with has two physicians on staff: Dr. Johnson and Dr. Wu. While the practice has many patients, they are interested in identifying which patients who visit are at high risk of all-cause mortality within the next 6 months. Having an outpatient visit sometime in 2016 makes up the inclusion criteria for the analytics. The target variable is whether the patient passed away within 6 months of their visit.

Now that we've reviewed the details of the modeling assignment, let's take a look at the five patients in the database. The preliminary data sent to you by the cardiology practice includes information on five patients, distributed across six tables. The following are case vignettes for each of the patients. Note that this section is heavy on clinical terminology related to cardiovascular diseases. We encourage you to use available online resources to answer your questions about this terminology. A comprehensive clinical reference is *Harrison's Principles of Internal Medicine* (Kasper et al., 2005), the information for which is given at the end of the chapter.

The following is the information about the patients:

- **Patient ID-1**: Patient #1 in the database is a 65-year-old male who has **congestive heart failure (CHF)**, a chronic condition in which the heart is unable to pump blood properly to the rest of the body. He also has hypertension (high blood pressure), which is a risk factor for CHF. He visited his cardiologist, Dr. Johnson, on 9/1/2016 and 17/1/2016. On his January 9th visit, he was found to have an elevated BP (154/94) and an elevated B-natriuretic peptide (BNP) lab value of 350. BNP is a marker of CHF severity. He was subsequently placed on lisinopril and furosemide, which are first-line treatments for CHF and hypertension. Unfortunately, he passed away on May 15th, 2016.

- **Patient ID-2**: Patient #2 is a 39-year-old female with a history of angina pectoris (cardiovascular-related chest pain upon exercising) and diabetes mellitus. Diabetes mellitus is a risk factor for myocardial infarction (heart attack; a late, often fatal manifestation of atherosclerotic heart disease), and angina pectoris can be seen as an early manifestation of atherosclerotic heart disease. She visited her cardiologist, Dr. Wu, on January 15th, 2016, at which time she was found to have an elevated blood glucose level of 225, a sign of uncontrolled diabetes. She was started on metformin for her diabetes, as well as nitroglycerin, aspirin, and metoprolol for her angina.

- **Patient ID-3**: Patient #3 is a 32-year-old female who sees Dr. Johnson for management of her hypertension. During her visit on February 1st, 2016 her blood pressure was elevated at 161/100. She was started on valsartan/hydrochlorothiazide, an anti-hypertensive combination.

- **Patient ID: 4**: Patient #4 is a 51-year-old male who has severe CHF with pulmonary hypertension. He saw Dr. Wu on February 27th, 2016. During that visit, his weight was 211 lbs and his blood pressure was slightly elevated at 143/84. His BNP level was highly elevated at 1,000. He was given lisinopril and furosemide for his CHF as well as diltiazem for his pulmonary hypertension. Unfortunately, he passed away on June 8th, 2016.

- **Patient ID-5**: The last patient in our database, patient #5, is a 58-year-old male who presented to Dr. Wu on March 1st, 2016 with a history of CHF and diabetes mellitus Type 2. During the visit, his glucose was elevated at 318 and BNP was moderately elevated at 400. He was started on lisinopril and furosemide for his CHF and metformin for his diabetes.

The clinical database

Now that we've gotten to know the five patients whose information is contained in our database, we can describe the table structure and fields contained in the database, for six mock tables: PATIENT, VISIT, MEDICATIONS, LABS, VITALS, and MORT. Although every clinical database is different, I've tried to use a structure that is commonly seen in healthcare. Typically, tables are presented by clinical domains (for an example of a research study that received tables in such a distributed format, see Basole et al., 2015). For example, there is often one table that contains demographic and personal information, one table for lab results, one for medications, and so on, so that is how we constructed the database in this example. They tend to be tied together by a common identifier, which in our case is the Pid field.

As we describe the tables, we must keep our end-goal of the data engineering phase in mind–to combine the relevant information from the six tables into a single table, whose columns include the target variable (mortality in this case) in addition to predictor variables, which should be useful for predicting the target variable. This will enable us to make a machine learning model with popular packages such as Python's scikit-learn. With this in mind, we will highlight selected fields that will be useful for our assignment.

The PATIENT table

In our example, the PATIENT table, which we can see in the following screenshot, contains the demographic and identifying information of our patients–their names, contact information, birthdays, and biological sex. In this example, there are only five observations and 11 columns; in real practice, this table would contain all of the patients affiliated with the healthcare organization. The number of rows in this table might range from hundreds to hundreds of thousands, while the table could potentially include dozens of columns containing detailed demographic information:

```
sqlite> select * from PATIENT;
Pid    Fname      Minit      Lname      Bdate       Street           City        State      Zip        Phone       Sex
-----  ---------- ---------- ---------- ----------  ---------------- ----------  ---------- ---------- ----------  ------
1      John       A          Smith      01/01/1952  1206 Fox Hollow Rd.  Pittsburgh  PA         15213      6789871234  M
2      Candice    P          Jones      02/03/1978  1429 Orlyn Dr.   Los Angele  CA         90024      3107381419  F
3      Regina     H          Wilson     04/23/1985  765 Chestnut Ln. Albany      NY         12065      5184590206  F
4      Harold                Lee        11/15/1966  2928 Policy St.  Providence  RI         02912      6593482691  M
5      Stan       P          Davis      12/30/1958  4271 12th St.    Atlanta     GA         30339      4049814933  M
```

In the database, every unique patient is assigned to an identifier (the field labeled as Pid), which in our case is simply numbered 1 - 5. The Pid column allows us to keep track of the patients across different tables. Also, notice that there is one and only one entry for each distinct patient ID.

After identifying the indispensable identifer column, the focus should be on which variables to keep and which to discard. Certainly, age and sex are important demographic predictors of mortality. If race were in this table, that would be another important demographic variable.

Another notable variable in this table is the zip code. Increasingly, socioeconomic data is being used in machine learning analyses. The zip code can potentially be tied to publicly available census data; that data can then be joined to the data in this table on the zip code and could potentially provide information on the average education level, income, and healthcare coverage for each patient's zip code. There are even organizations who sell household-level information; however, with that data comes a great responsibility for privacy protection and data security. For this example, we will omit the zip code to keep our final table simple.

Information we'll leave out from our final table includes names, street addresses, and phone numbers. As long as we have the patient ID, these fields shouldn't have much of a predictive impact on our target variable.

The VISIT table

While the PATIENT table contains basic administrative information about each patient, our assignment is to predict the mortality risk on the basis of each *visit*. The VISIT table contains one observation for each patient visit, along with some clinical information about each visit:

```
sqlite> SELECT * FROM VISIT;
Pid       Visit_id   Visit_date  Attending_md  Pri_dx_icd  Pri_dx_name               Sec_dx_icd  Sec_dx_name
--------  ---------  ----------  ------------  ----------  ------------------------  ----------  --------------------------------
1         10001      01/09/2016  JOHNSON       I50.9       Heart failure, unspecified  I10       Essential (primary) hypertension
1         10002      01/17/2016  JOHNSON       I50.9       Heart failure, unspecified  I10       Essential (primary) hypertension
2         10003      01/15/2016  WU            I20.9       Angina pectoris, unspecifi  E11.9     Type 2 diabetes mellitus without
3         10004      02/01/2016  JOHNSON       I10         Essential (primary) hypert
4         10005      02/27/2016  WU            I27.0       Primary pulmonary hyperten  I50.9     Heart failure, unspecified
5         10006      03/01/2016  WU            I50.9       Heart failure, unspecified  E11.9     Type 2 diabetes mellitus without
```

Notice that the patient ID is no longer the primary identifier of this table, since Patient #1 had two visits; instead, there is a Visit_id field that is numbered from 10001 to 10006 in this example, with one distinct ID per visit.

This table also contains Visit_date. Since the cardiology practice indicated they want to know the mortality risk within 6 months of the patient visit, we will have to use this field later when we compute the target variable.

Two of the fields in this table contain ICD (diagnosis) codes. Actual tables may contain dozens of codes for each visit. For each coded field, there is a corresponding name field that contains the name of the condition that the code represents. A popular approach in healthcare is to make, in the final table, a column for every clinical code we are interested in tracking (Futoma et al., 2015; Rajkomar et al., 2018). We will adopt this approach later in the chapter.

Finally, we note that the name of the attending physician is included, which can be used to measure physician performance.

The MEDICATIONS table

The MEDICATIONS table contains one entry for every medication being taken by our five patients. In this example, there is no single column that serves as a primary key for this table. As we can see in the following screenshot, this table includes information about the medication name, dose, frequency, route, prescribing physician, and prescription date. The NDC code of each medication is also included; we covered NDC codes in Chapter 2, *Healthcare Foundations*:

```
sqlite> SELECT * FROM MEDICATIONS;
Pid          Rx_name      Rx_dose      Rx_freq      Rx_route     Prescribing_md   Rx_date      Rx_ndc
----------   ----------   ----------   ----------   ----------   --------------   ----------   ------------
1            LISINOPRIL   5 mg         bid          po           JOHNSON          01/09/2016   68180-513-01
1            FUROSEMIDE   20 mg        bid          po           JOHNSON          01/09/2016   50742-104-01
2            NITROGLYCE   0.4 mg       tid          sl           WU               01/15/2016   59762-3304-1
2            METFORMIN    500 mg       bid          po           WU               01/15/2016   65162-175-10
2            ASPIRIN      81 mg        qdaily       po           WU               01/15/2016   63981-563-51
2            METOPROLOL   25 mg        bid          po           WU               01/15/2016   62332-112-31
3            VALSARTAN    160/12.5 m   qdaily       po           JOHNSON          02/01/2016   51655-950-52
4            DILTIAZEM    300 mg       qdaily       po           WU               02/27/2016   52544-693-19
4            LISINOPRIL   10 mg        bid          po           WU               02/27/2016   68180-514-01
4            FUROSEMIDE   40 mg        bid          po           WU               02/27/2016   68788-1966-1
5            LISINOPRIL   5 mg         bid          po           WU               03/01/2016   68180-513-01
5            FUROSEMIDE   20 mg        bid          po           WU               03/01/2016   50742-104-01
5            METFORMIN    500 mg       bid          po           WU               03/01/2016   65162-175-10
```

Including medications in our final table will not be straightforward. For example, the information in the tables does not indicate the class of each medication. The NDC code is present, but the NDC code is even more granular than the medication name since it includes the route of administration and dosage in making each unique code; therefore, multiple forms of lisinopril could have different NDC codes. In order to make a column for each medication, we could potentially separately make a table for each medication, which contains all of the medications that compose it, and then merge that information into our table.

If we choose to include dosage information, that field will require some cleaning. Notice that Patient #3 is receiving an anti-hypertensive combination drug–the valsartan component has a dosage of 160 mg, while the hydrochlorothiazide component has a dosage of 12.5 mg. This could possibly be coded as two separate drugs, but creating a script that splits combination drugs into two rows is not trivial.

The LABS table

Laboratory information is an important part of clinical diagnostics, and many laboratory test results make for good predictor variables (Donze et al., 2013; Sahni et al., 2018). The LABS table includes fields that describe the laboratory test name, abbreviation, LOINC code, and result:

```
sqlite> SELECT * FROM LABS;
Pid          Lab_name              Lab_abbrev  Lab_loinc  Lab_value  Ordering_md  Lab_date
----------   --------------------  ----------  ---------  ---------  -----------  ----------
1            Natriuretic peptide B BNP         42637-9    350        JOHNSON      01/09/2016
2            Natriuretic peptide B BNP         42637-9    100        WU           01/15/2016
2            Glucose               GLU         2345-7     225        WU           01/15/2016
2            Troponin I            TROP        10839-9    <0.004     WU           01/15/2016
4            Natriuretic peptide B BNP         42637-9    1000       WU           02/27/2016
5            Natriuretic peptide B BNP         42637-9    400        WU           03/01/2016
5            Glucose               GLU         2345-7     318        WU           03/01/2016
```

There are some different approaches to including lab information in the final table. One way would be to include the raw lab result as a continuous variable. However, this leads to a problem because the result would be NULL for most labs. We could potentially navigate around this issue by imputing a value in the normal range when it is missing. Another approach would be to have a binary variable for a lab test result that is in the abnormal range. This solves the missing data problem, since if the result is missing it would be zero. However, a BNP value of 1,000 (which indicates severe CHF) would be no different than a BNP value of 350 (which indicates mild CHF) with this method. We will demonstrate both approaches in this chapter.

Also note that the Lab_value field sometimes contains special characters, for example in the troponin result. These will need to be removed and the lab values interpreted accordingly. Culture results (not included in this example) are completely textual, often naming specific bacterial strains instead of numbers.

Again, we repeat that this is a simplified example and that many of the common labs that would be drawn for these patients (for example, WBC count, hemoglobin, sodium, potassium, and so on) are excluded here.

The VITALS table

Vital signs are important indicators of a patient's health status and can be good predictors in healthcare machine learning models (Sahni et al., 2018). Vital signs are typically taken at every patient visit, so they can easily be included in their raw (numerical) form to preserve granularity.

In the following screenshot of the table, we notice that while height and weight are present, the **body mass index** (**BMI**) is missing. We will demonstrate the calculation of the BMI in Chapter 5, *Computing Foundations – Introduction to Python*. Second, Visit #10004 is missing a temperature reading. This is common in healthcare and may be caused by an oversight in care:

```
sqlite> SELECT * FROM VITALS;
Pid        Visit_id   Height_in   Weight_lb   Temp_f     Pulse      Resp_rate   Bp_syst    Bp_diast    SpO2
---------  ---------  ----------  ----------  ---------  ---------  ----------  ---------  ----------  -----
1          10001      70          188.4       98.6       95         18          154        94          97
1          10002      70          188.4       99.1       85         17          157        96          100
2          10003      63          130.2       98.7       82         16          120        81          100
3          10004      65          120.0                  100        19          161        100         98
4          10005      66          211.4       98.2       95         19          143        84          93
5          10006      69          150.0       97.6       77         18          130        86          99
```

The VITALS table

Later in the chapter, we will impute the normal temperature for this visit.

The MORT table

Finally, we come to the table that contains the target variable. The MORT table contains just two fields, the patient identifier, and the date the patient passed away. Patients not listed in this table can be assumed to be living:

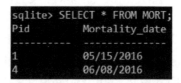

```
sqlite> SELECT * FROM MORT;
Pid        Mortality_date
---------  --------------
1          05/15/2016
4          06/08/2016
```

Later, we will learn how to transfer the information from this table into a binary target variable.

Starting an SQLite session

The database engine we will use to transform our database is **SQLite**. In Chapter 1, *Introduction to Healthcare Analytics*, we went over installation instructions as well as basic SQLite commands. It should be mentioned that SQL comes in many variants, and the SQL specific to SQLite has minor differences to that specific to MySQL or SQL Server databases. However, the underlying principles remain constant across all SQL dialects.

At this time, do the following:

1. Navigate to the directory containing the sqlite3.exe program in your shell or command prompt (using the cd command).
2. Type sqlite3 mortality.db and press *Enter*. You should see a prompt that looks like the following: sqlite>. This prompt indicates that you are in the SQLite program.
3. Throughout the remainder of this chapter, we are going to create some tables and execute some SQLite commands on them in the SQLite program.
4. To exit the session at any time, type .exit and press *Enter*.

Data engineering, one table at a time with SQL

Let's now look at how to perform data engineering with SQLite. First, we have to create our tables in the database. Then, we will manipulate them, one by one, to get the desired final table.

Query Set #0 – creating the six tables

In this mock assignment, let's pretend that the portal at which the data can be downloaded from the cardiology practice is not working. Instead, one of the technicians sends you SQLite commands that you can use to create the six tables. You can follow along with the book and type each command manually. Alternatively, you can go to the book's official code repository and download the commands from there.

Query Set #0a – creating the PATIENT table

One way to create a table in our database is to specify its schema manually. Let's do that here with our first table, the PATIENT table:

```
sqlite> CREATE TABLE PATIENT(
  Pid VARCHAR(30) NOT NULL,
  Fname VARCHAR(30) NOT NULL,
  Minit CHAR,
  Lname VARCHAR(30) NOT NULL,
  Bdate TEXT NOT NULL,
  Street VARCHAR(50),
  City VARCHAR(30),
  State VARCHAR(2),
  Zip VARCHAR(5),
  Phone VARCHAR(10) NOT NULL,
  Sex CHAR,
  PRIMARY KEY (Pid)
);
```

In the preceding example, notice that the name of the table appears after the CREATE TABLE phrase. Following that, there is an open parenthesis, and on each line a new column is named (for example, Pid and Fname). On each line, following the column names, are the types of each column. We use VARCHAR(n) for most columns in this example, where n is the maximum number of characters that the column contains. A CHAR column contains just one character. Finally, some of the important fields (such as names and identifiers) we will not allow to be blank, and we specify that for those columns by using the NOT NULL phrase.

Now that we created the schema of our table, the next step is to populate the table with data. As we said, in the database we just have five patients, therefore the PATIENT table will have five rows. We use an INSERT command to insert each row into the table as shown here:

```
sqlite> INSERT INTO PATIENT (Pid, Fname, Minit, Lname, Bdate, Street, City,
State, Zip, Phone, Sex)
VALUES ('1','John','A','Smith','1952-01-01','1206 Fox Hollow
Rd.','Pittsburgh','PA','15213','6789871234','M');

sqlite> INSERT INTO PATIENT (Pid, Fname, Minit, Lname, Bdate, Street, City,
State, Zip, Phone, Sex)
VALUES ('2','Candice','P','Jones','1978-02-03','1429 Orlyn Dr.','Los
Angeles','CA','90024','3107381419','F');

sqlite> INSERT INTO PATIENT (Pid, Fname, Minit, Lname, Bdate, Street, City,
State, Zip, Phone, Sex)
VALUES ('3','Regina','H','Wilson','1985-04-23','765 Chestnut
```

```
    Ln.','Albany','NY','12065','5184590206','F');

sqlite> INSERT INTO PATIENT (Pid, Fname, Minit, Lname, Bdate, Street, City,
State, Zip, Phone, Sex)
VALUES ('4','Harold','','Lee','1966-11-15','2928 Policy
St.','Providence','RI','02912','6593482691','M');

sqlite> INSERT INTO PATIENT (Pid, Fname, Minit, Lname, Bdate, Street, City,
State, Zip, Phone, Sex)
VALUES ('5','Stan','P','Davis','1958-12-30','4271 12th
St.','Atlanta','GA','30339','4049814933','M');
```

Notice that the INSERT statements first specify that fields that will be inserted, before using the VALUES keyword, after which the actual data elements are listed. If VARCHAR or CHAR is used, the data elements should be surrounded by single quotes.

Query Set #0b – creating the VISIT table

Let's now make the VISIT table. Again, first we use a CREATE TABLE statement, followed by six INSERT statements:

```
sqlite> CREATE TABLE VISIT(
  Pid VARCHAR(30) NOT NULL,
  Visit_id VARCHAR(30) NOT NULL,
  Visit_date DATE NOT NULL,
  Attending_md VARCHAR(30) NOT NULL,
  Pri_dx_icd VARCHAR(20) NOT NULL,
  Pri_dx_name VARCHAR(100) NOT NULL,
  Sec_dx_icd VARCHAR(20),
  Sec_dx_name VARCHAR(100),
  PRIMARY KEY (Visit_id)
);

sqlite> INSERT INTO VISIT (Pid, Visit_id, Visit_date, Attending_md,
Pri_dx_icd, Pri_dx_name, Sec_dx_icd, Sec_dx_name)
VALUES ('1','10001','2016-01-09','JOHNSON','I50.9','Heart failure,
unspecified','I10','Essential (primary) hypertension');

sqlite> INSERT INTO VISIT (Pid, Visit_id, Visit_date, Attending_md,
Pri_dx_icd, Pri_dx_name, Sec_dx_icd, Sec_dx_name)
VALUES ('1','10002','2016-01-17','JOHNSON','I50.9','Heart failure,
unspecified','I10','Essential (primary) hypertension');

sqlite> INSERT INTO VISIT (Pid, Visit_id, Visit_date, Attending_md,
Pri_dx_icd, Pri_dx_name, Sec_dx_icd, Sec_dx_name)
VALUES ('2','10003','2016-01-15','WU','I20.9','Angina pectoris,
```

```
    unspecified','E11.9','Type 2 diabetes mellitus without complications');

sqlite> INSERT INTO VISIT (Pid, Visit_id, Visit_date, Attending_md,
Pri_dx_icd, Pri_dx_name, Sec_dx_icd, Sec_dx_name)
VALUES ('3','10004','2016-02-01','JOHNSON','I10','Essential (primary)
hypertension','','');

sqlite> INSERT INTO VISIT (Pid, Visit_id, Visit_date, Attending_md,
Pri_dx_icd, Pri_dx_name, Sec_dx_icd, Sec_dx_name)
VALUES ('4','10005','2016-02-27','WU','I27.0','Primary pulmonary
hypertension','I50.9','Heart failure, unspecified');

sqlite> INSERT INTO VISIT (Pid, Visit_id, Visit_date, Attending_md,
Pri_dx_icd, Pri_dx_name, Sec_dx_icd, Sec_dx_name)
VALUES ('5','10006','2016-03-01','WU','I50.9','Heart failure,
unspecified','E11.9','Type 2 diabetes mellitus without complications');
```

Query Set #0c – creating the MEDICATIONS table

To create the MEDICATIONS table, use the following code:

```
sqlite> CREATE TABLE MEDICATIONS(
    Pid VARCHAR(30) NOT NULL,
    Rx_name VARCHAR(50) NOT NULL,
    Rx_dose VARCHAR(20),
    Rx_freq VARCHAR(10),
    Rx_route VARCHAR(10),
    Prescribing_md VARCHAR(30) NOT NULL,
    Rx_date DATE NOT NULL,
    Rx_ndc VARCHAR(30)
);

sqlite> INSERT INTO MEDICATIONS (Pid, Rx_name, Rx_dose, Rx_freq, Rx_route,
Prescribing_md, Rx_date, Rx_ndc)
VALUES ('1', 'LISINOPRIL','5
mg','bid','po','JOHNSON','01/09/2016','68180-513-01');

sqlite> INSERT INTO MEDICATIONS (Pid, Rx_name, Rx_dose, Rx_freq, Rx_route,
Prescribing_md, Rx_date, Rx_ndc)
VALUES ('1', 'FUROSEMIDE','20
mg','bid','po','JOHNSON','01/09/2016','50742-104-01');

sqlite> INSERT INTO MEDICATIONS (Pid, Rx_name, Rx_dose, Rx_freq, Rx_route,
Prescribing_md, Rx_date, Rx_ndc)
VALUES ('2', 'NITROGLYCERIN','0.4
mg','tid','sl','WU','01/15/2016','59762-3304-1');
```

```
sqlite> INSERT INTO MEDICATIONS (Pid, Rx_name, Rx_dose, Rx_freq, Rx_route,
Prescribing_md, Rx_date, Rx_ndc)
VALUES ('2', 'METFORMIN','500
mg','bid','po','WU','01/15/2016','65162-175-10');

sqlite> INSERT INTO MEDICATIONS (Pid, Rx_name, Rx_dose, Rx_freq, Rx_route,
Prescribing_md, Rx_date, Rx_ndc)
VALUES ('2', 'ASPIRIN','81
mg','qdaily','po','WU','01/15/2016','63981-563-51');

sqlite> INSERT INTO MEDICATIONS (Pid, Rx_name, Rx_dose, Rx_freq, Rx_route,
Prescribing_md, Rx_date, Rx_ndc)
VALUES ('2', 'METOPROLOL TARTRATE','25
mg','bid','po','WU','01/15/2016','62332-112-31');

sqlite> INSERT INTO MEDICATIONS (Pid, Rx_name, Rx_dose, Rx_freq, Rx_route,
Prescribing_md, Rx_date, Rx_ndc)
VALUES ('3', 'VALSARTAN HCTZ','160/12.5
mg','qdaily','po','JOHNSON','02/01/2016','51655-950-52');

sqlite> INSERT INTO MEDICATIONS (Pid, Rx_name, Rx_dose, Rx_freq, Rx_route,
Prescribing_md, Rx_date, Rx_ndc)
VALUES ('4', 'DILTIAZEM HYDROCHOLORIDE','300
mg','qdaily','po','WU','02/27/2016','52544-693-19');

sqlite> INSERT INTO MEDICATIONS (Pid, Rx_name, Rx_dose, Rx_freq, Rx_route,
Prescribing_md, Rx_date, Rx_ndc)
VALUES ('4', 'LISINOPRIL','10
mg','bid','po','WU','02/27/2016','68180-514-01');

sqlite> INSERT INTO MEDICATIONS (Pid, Rx_name, Rx_dose, Rx_freq, Rx_route,
Prescribing_md, Rx_date, Rx_ndc)
VALUES ('4', 'FUROSEMIDE','40
mg','bid','po','WU','02/27/2016','68788-1966-1');

sqlite> INSERT INTO MEDICATIONS (Pid, Rx_name, Rx_dose, Rx_freq, Rx_route,
Prescribing_md, Rx_date, Rx_ndc)
VALUES ('5', 'LISINOPRIL','5
mg','bid','po','WU','03/01/2016','68180-513-01');

sqlite> INSERT INTO MEDICATIONS (Pid, Rx_name, Rx_dose, Rx_freq, Rx_route,
Prescribing_md, Rx_date, Rx_ndc)
VALUES ('5', 'FUROSEMIDE','20
mg','bid','po','WU','03/01/2016','50742-104-01');
```

```
sqlite> INSERT INTO MEDICATIONS (Pid, Rx_name, Rx_dose, Rx_freq, Rx_route,
Prescribing_md, Rx_date, Rx_ndc)
VALUES ('5', 'METFORMIN','500
mg','bid','po','WU','03/01/2016','65162-175-10');
```

Query Set #0d – creating the LABS table

To create the LABS table, use the following code:

```
sqlite> CREATE TABLE LABS(
  Pid VARCHAR(30) NOT NULL,
  Lab_name VARCHAR(50),
  Lab_abbrev VARCHAR(20),
  Lab_loinc VARCHAR(10) NOT NULL,
  Lab_value VARCHAR(20) NOT NULL,
  Ordering_md VARCHAR(30),
  Lab_date DATE NOT NULL
);

sqlite> INSERT INTO LABS (Pid, Lab_name, Lab_abbrev, Lab_loinc, Lab_value,
Ordering_md, Lab_date)
VALUES ('1','Natriuretic peptide
B','BNP','42637-9','350','JOHNSON','2016-01-09');

sqlite> INSERT INTO LABS (Pid, Lab_name, Lab_abbrev, Lab_loinc, Lab_value,
Ordering_md, Lab_date)
VALUES ('2','Natriuretic peptide
B','BNP','42637-9','100','WU','2016-01-15');

sqlite> INSERT INTO LABS (Pid, Lab_name, Lab_abbrev, Lab_loinc, Lab_value,
Ordering_md, Lab_date)
VALUES ('2','Glucose','GLU','2345-7','225','WU','2016-01-15');

sqlite> INSERT INTO LABS (Pid, Lab_name, Lab_abbrev, Lab_loinc, Lab_value,
Ordering_md, Lab_date)
VALUES ('2','Troponin I','TROP','10839-9','<0.004','WU','2016-01-15');

sqlite> INSERT INTO LABS (Pid, Lab_name, Lab_abbrev, Lab_loinc, Lab_value,
Ordering_md, Lab_date)
VALUES ('4','Natriuretic peptide
B','BNP','42637-9','1000','WU','2016-02-27');

sqlite> INSERT INTO LABS (Pid, Lab_name, Lab_abbrev, Lab_loinc, Lab_value,
Ordering_md, Lab_date)
VALUES ('5','Natriuretic peptide
B','BNP','42637-9','400','WU','2016-03-01');
```

```
sqlite> INSERT INTO LABS (Pid, Lab_name, Lab_abbrev, Lab_loinc, Lab_value,
Ordering_md, Lab_date)
VALUES ('5','Glucose','GLU','2345-7','318','WU','2016-03-01');
```

Query Set #0e – creating the VITALS table

Notice that the VITALS table uses numeric types such as FLOAT and INT. To create the
VITALS table, use the following code:

```
sqlite> CREATE TABLE VITALS(
  Pid VARCHAR(30) NOT NULL,
  Visit_id VARCHAR(30) NOT NULL,
  Height_in INT,
  Weight_lb FLOAT,
  Temp_f FLOAT,
  Pulse INT,
  Resp_rate INT,
  Bp_syst INT,
  Bp_diast INT,
  SpO2 INT
);

sqlite> INSERT INTO VITALS (Pid, Visit_id, Height_in, Weight_lb, Temp_f,
Pulse, Resp_rate, Bp_syst, Bp_diast, SpO2)
VALUES ('1','10001',70,188.4,98.6,95,18,154,94,97);

sqlite> INSERT INTO VITALS (Pid, Visit_id, Height_in, Weight_lb, Temp_f,
Pulse, Resp_rate, Bp_syst, Bp_diast, SpO2)
VALUES ('1','10002',70,188.4,99.1,85,17,157,96,100);

sqlite> INSERT INTO VITALS (Pid, Visit_id, Height_in, Weight_lb, Temp_f,
Pulse, Resp_rate, Bp_syst, Bp_diast, SpO2)
VALUES ('2','10003',63,130.2,98.7,82,16,120,81,100);

sqlite> INSERT INTO VITALS (Pid, Visit_id, Height_in, Weight_lb, Temp_f,
Pulse, Resp_rate, Bp_syst, Bp_diast, SpO2)
VALUES ('3','10004',65,120.0,NULL,100,19,161,100,98);

sqlite> INSERT INTO VITALS (Pid, Visit_id, Height_in, Weight_lb, Temp_f,
Pulse, Resp_rate, Bp_syst, Bp_diast, SpO2)
VALUES ('4','10005',66,211.4,98.2,95,19,143,84,93);

sqlite> INSERT INTO VITALS (Pid, Visit_id, Height_in, Weight_lb, Temp_f,
Pulse, Resp_rate, Bp_syst, Bp_diast, SpO2)
VALUES ('5','10006',69,150.0,97.6,77,18,130,86,99);
```

Query Set #0f – creating the MORT table

To create the MORT table, use the following code:

```
sqlite> CREATE TABLE MORT(
  Pid VARCHAR(30) NOT NULL,
  Mortality_date DATE NOT NULL,
  PRIMARY KEY (Pid)
);

sqlite> INSERT INTO MORT (Pid, Mortality_date)
VALUES ('1', '2016-05-15');

sqlite> INSERT INTO MORT (Pid, Mortality_date)
VALUES ('4', '2016-06-08');
```

Query Set #0g – displaying our tables

To confirm that a table (for example, PATIENT) was made correctly, we can use the SELECT * FROM PATIENT; query (we will explain this syntax further in Query Set #2):

```
sqlite> SELECT * FROM PATIENT;
1 John A Smith 1952-01-01 1206 Fox Hollow Rd. Pittsburgh PA 15213
6789871234 M
2 Candice P Jones 1978-02-03 1429 Orlyn Dr. Los Angele CA 90024 3107381419
F
3 Regina H Wilson 1985-04-23 765 Chestnut Ln. Albany NY 12065 5184590206 F
4 Harold Lee 1966-11-15 2928 Policy St. Providence RI 02912 6593482691 M
5 Stan P Davis 1958-12-30 4271 12th St. Atlanta GA 30339 4049814933 M
```

Query Set #1 – creating the MORT_FINAL table

The first query we write will create the table using a CREATE TABLE statement. In one version of a CREATE TABLE statement, each variable is spelled out with its corresponding datatype. We used this version to create our six tables from scratch in the previous examples. Alternatively, one can create a table by copying from an existing table. We will opt for the second option here.

Now that we've answered that question, a second one remains–which table should we copy from? It might be tempting to copy the patient information from the PATIENT table to our final table, since it contains one row for each patient, and it contains basic demographic information. However, we must remember that the use case is based on each *visit*, not patient. Therefore, if a patient has two visits (such as Patient #1), technically that patient will receive two risk scores: one for each visit. Therefore, we should start by copying information from the VISIT table. This will create a table with six rows, one for each visit.

So we start our query using a CREATE TABLE clause, with MORT_FINAL being the name of our new table. Then we use the AS keyword. The next two lines of the query specify which information to copy using a SELECT-FROM-WHERE construct:

```
sqlite> CREATE TABLE MORT_FINAL AS
SELECT Visit_id, Pid, Attending_md, Visit_date, Pri_dx_icd, Sec_dx_icd
FROM VISIT;
```

A SELECT-FROM-WHERE statement is a systematic way of selecting the information we want from a table. The SELECT part acts as a *column* selector–following the SELECT keyword are the columns that we want to copy into the new table. Note that we left out the names of the diagnoses (Pri_dx_name, Sec_dx_name) since those technically aren't predictor variables, as long we have each code and we can refer to their meanings. The FROM keyword specifies the table name from which we wish to copy (VISIT, in this case). The WHERE keyword is an optional clause that allows us to select only those *rows* that meet certain conditions. For example, if we were interested in restricting our model to those visits in which the patient had heart failure, we could say WHERE Pri_dx_code == 'I50.9'. Because we are interested in including all visits in this example, we do not need a WHERE clause for this query. We will see the WHERE clause in action in the next query set.

Query Set #2 – adding columns to MORT_FINAL

In this section, we will demonstrate two ways to add additional columns. One method uses an ALTER TABLE statement, while the second method uses a JOIN operation.

Query Set #2a – adding columns using ALTER TABLE

Now that we've populated information from the VISIT table into the MORT_FINAL table, it's time to start integrating the other tables as well. We'll start with the PATIENT table; specifically, we would like to add in the birthdate and sex from this table. We start with the birthdate.

In Query Set #2, we demonstrate the basic query pattern for adding a new column (the birthdate) to our table. We start with an ALTER TABLE statement, followed by the name of the table, the operation (ADD COLUMN, in this case), the name of our new column, and the variable type. Although standard SQL supports a DATE variable type for dates, in SQLite, we use the TEXT type. Dates are always specified in YYYY-MM-DD format.

After we've initialized the new column with our ALTER TABLE statement, the next step is to populate the actual birthdates from the PATIENT table. For this, we use an UPDATE statement. We specify the table we are updating, followed by a SET statement and the name of the column we are modifying, with an equals sign.

The SELECT-FROM-WHERE block is the basic *retrieval* query of the SQL language. We are trying to *retrieve* information from the PATIENT table and populate into our new Bdate column, so we use a SELECT-FROM-WHERE statement, enclosed in parentheses, after the equals sign. Think of the SQL statement as issuing the following order to the database with its SELECT statement: "For every row in the MORT_FINAL table, find me the birthdate from the PATIENT table where the Pid in the PATIENT table equals the Pid in the MORT_FINAL table."

Following the UPDATE statement for the Bdate column, we use the same sequence of queries (ALTER TABLE and UPDATE) to retrieve the Sex column from the PATIENT table:

```
sqlite> ALTER TABLE MORT_FINAL ADD COLUMN Bdate TEXT;

sqlite> UPDATE MORT_FINAL SET Bdate =
(SELECT P.Bdate
FROM PATIENT AS P
WHERE P.Pid = MORT_FINAL.Pid);

sqlite> ALTER TABLE MORT_FINAL ADD COLUMN Sex CHAR;

sqlite> UPDATE MORT_FINAL SET Sex =
(SELECT P.Sex
FROM PATIENT AS P
WHERE P.Pid = MORT_FINAL.Pid);
```

Query Set #2b – adding columns using JOIN

While the ALTER TABLE and UPDATE sequence is a good way to add columns to a table one at a time, it can be tedious when you want to copy many columns from the same table. A JOIN operation gives us a second option for copying many columns from the same table.

In a JOIN operation, two tables are combined to produce a single table. In the following example query, the selected columns of the VITALS table are appended on the end of the MORT_FINAL table.

However, the MORT_FINAL table and VITALS table both contain several rows. How does the query know which rows of each table correspond to each other? This is specified using an ON clause (at the end of the query). The ON clause says, "When joining the tables, combine those rows where the visit IDs are equal." So for each row of the MORT_FINAL table, there will be one and only one row of the VISITS table to which it corresponds: the row that has the same visit ID. This makes sense because we are interested in collecting the information from individual visits in their own separate rows.

Another thing to know about JOINs is that there are four different JOIN types in standard SQL: LEFT JOINs, RIGHT JOINs, INNER JOINs, and OUTER JOINs. A LEFT JOIN (referred to as a LEFT OUTER JOIN in SQLite) is the type we use here; it says, "For every row of the first table (MORT_FINAL, in this case), add the corresponding VISIT columns where the visit IDs are equal, and add NULL values if there is no corresponding visit ID in the VISIT table." In other words, all of the rows of the first table are preserved, whether or not there is a corresponding row in the right table. Visits that have a row in the second table but are missing from the first table are discarded.

In a RIGHT JOIN, the opposite is true: unique visit IDs of the second table are preserved, and they are aligned to the corresponding visit IDs of the first table. Visit IDs present in the first table but missing in the second table are discarded. INNER JOINs include in the final result: only visit IDs that are present in both tables. OUTER JOINs include all rows of both tables and replace all missing entries with NULL values. As a note, we should add that RIGHT JOINs and OUTER JOINs are not supported in SQLite.

So why did we choose a LEFT JOIN? Fundamentally, our job is to specify a prediction for every single visit, whether or not vital signs were recorded at that visit. Therefore, every visit ID present in the MORT_FINAL table should be in the final result, and the LEFT JOIN ensures that will be true.

In the following code, we see that by using a JOIN, only one total query is needed to add eight columns of the VITALS table. What are the downsides of this method? For one thing, notice that a new table is created: MORT_FINAL_2. We cannot append to the old MORT_FINAL table; a new table must be created. Also, notice that we have to type out each column that we wish to preserve in the final result. In SQL, the asterisk (*) indicates to add *all* columns from both tables; we could have written SELECT * FROM MORT_FINAL .... However, if we used an asterisk, there would be duplicate columns (for example, the Visit_id column would be present twice, since it is in both tables).

Then we would have to exclude the duplicate columns with a SELECT statement. Nevertheless, JOINs are useful when there are many columns in a second table that you would like to merge into a first table:

```
sqlite> CREATE TABLE MORT_FINAL_2 AS
SELECT M.Visit_id, M.Pid, M.Attending_md, M.Visit_date, M.Pri_dx_icd,
M.Sec_dx_icd, M.Bdate, M.Sex, V.Height_in, V.Weight_lb, V.Temp_f, V.Pulse,
V.Resp_rate, V.Bp_syst, V.Bp_Diast, V.SpO2
FROM MORT_FINAL AS M LEFT OUTER JOIN VITALS AS V ON M.Visit_id =
V.Visit_id;
```

Query Set #3 – date manipulation – calculating age

So far, our MORT_FINAL_2 table contains 16 columns: 6 from the VISIT table, 2 from the PATIENT table, and 8 from the VITALS table (you can verify this by using the SELECT * FROM MORT_FINAL_2; command). In this query set, we transform one of these variables, the birthdate variable, into a usable form using date manipulation: we calculate the patients' age.

As we said earlier in Query Set #2a, dates are stored in SQLite as TEXT variable types and are in the YYYY-MM-DD format. Calculating the age takes two calls to the julianday() function. In SQLite, the julianday() function takes a date in YYYY-MM-DD as input and returns the number of days since November 24th, 4714 BC 12:00 PM as a float. By itself, it may not seem very useful, but when used in combination with another julianday() call and a subtraction sign, it allows you to find the number of days that have elapsed between two dates. Following that, we calculate the Julian day difference between the visit date and the birthdate and divide the result by 365.25 to give us the patient ages in years. We also apply the ROUND() function to this result and round to two places after the decimal point (which is what the 2 indicates before the final parentheses are closed):

```
sqlite> ALTER TABLE MORT_FINAL_2 ADD COLUMN Age_years REAL;

sqlite> UPDATE MORT_FINAL_2 SET Age_years =
ROUND((julianday(Visit_date) - julianday(Bdate)) / 365.25,2);
```

Query Set #4 – binning and aggregating diagnoses

In our example database, the VISIT table contains the diagnostic codes for the visit. Although they didn't get their own table in our example, the diagnostic codes are among the most important pieces of information for many analytics problems. For one thing, they allow us to select the observations that are relevant to our model. For example, if we were building a model to predict malignant cancers, we would need the diagnosis codes to tell us which patients have cancer and to filter out the other patients. Second, they often serve as good predictor variables (Futoma et al., 2015). For example, as we will see in Chapter 7, *Making Predictive Models in Healthcare*, many chronic diseases increase the likelihood of poor healthcare outcomes by a large amount. Clearly, we must leverage the information given to us in the diagnostic codes to optimize our predictive models.

We will introduce two transformations for coded variables here. The first transformation, **binning**, converts the categorical variable to a series of binary variables for specific diagnoses. The second transformation, **aggregating**, groups many of the binary binned variables into a single binary or numerical variable. These transformations apply not only to diagnostic codes, but to the procedure, medication, and laboratory codes as well. The following are examples of both of these transformations.

Query Set #4a – binning diagnoses for CHF

Here, we see the binning transformation for congestive heart failure diagnoses. First, we initialize the new column, Chf_dx, as an integer using an ALTER TABLE statement. The DEFAULT 0 statement means that all rows are initialized to be zero. Next, we set the column equal to 1 if and only if there is a code corresponding to CHF in the Pri_dx_icd column or the Sec_dx_icd column:

```
sqlite> ALTER TABLE MORT_FINAL_2 ADD COLUMN Chf_dx INTEGER DEFAULT 0;

sqlite> UPDATE MORT_FINAL_2 SET Chf_dx = 1
WHERE Pri_dx_icd = 'I50.9' OR Sec_dx_icd = 'I50.9';
```

Query Set #4b – binning diagnoses for other diseases

Here, we see the same type of transformation for every single diagnosis code in our five-patient dataset. The queries for binning hypertension, angina, diabetes, and pulmonary hypertension are as follows:

```
sqlite> ALTER TABLE MORT_FINAL_2 ADD COLUMN Htn_dx INTEGER DEFAULT 0;

sqlite> UPDATE MORT_FINAL_2 SET Htn_dx = 1
WHERE Pri_dx_icd = 'I10' OR Sec_dx_icd = 'I10';

sqlite> ALTER TABLE MORT_FINAL_2 ADD COLUMN Angina_dx INTEGER DEFAULT 0;

sqlite> UPDATE MORT_FINAL_2 SET Angina_dx = 1
WHERE Pri_dx_icd = 'I20.9' OR Sec_dx_icd = 'I20.9';

sqlite> ALTER TABLE MORT_FINAL_2 ADD COLUMN Diab_dx INTEGER DEFAULT 0;

sqlite> UPDATE MORT_FINAL_2 SET Diab_dx = 1
WHERE Pri_dx_icd = 'E11.9' OR Sec_dx_icd = 'E11.9';

sqlite> ALTER TABLE MORT_FINAL_2 ADD COLUMN Pulm_htn_dx INTEGER DEFAULT 0;

sqlite> UPDATE MORT_FINAL_2 SET Pulm_htn_dx = 1
WHERE Pri_dx_icd = 'I27.0' OR Sec_dx_icd = 'I27.0';
```

Query Set #4c – aggregating cardiac diagnoses using SUM

While binning is important for separating out individual diagnoses, in practice, we often want to group similar or near-identical diagnostic codes together as a single variable. Aggregating combines two or more binary variables into a single binary/numeric variable. Here, we aggregate all cardiac diagnostic codes in our dataset (CHF, hypertension, and angina are cardiac diseases) using the + operator. The result is a count of the number of total cardiac diagnoses for each of the five patients:

```
sqlite> ALTER TABLE MORT_FINAL_2 ADD COLUMN Num_cardiac_dx INTEGER;

sqlite> UPDATE MORT_FINAL_2 SET Num_cardiac_dx = Chf_dx + Htn_dx +
Angina_dx;
```

Query Set #4d – aggregating cardiac diagnoses using COUNT

In Query Sets #4b and #4c, we binned and then aggregated three diagnostic codes using the + operator on the column names individually. However, we may be interested in binning and aggregating dozens, hundreds, or even thousands of diagnostic codes. The method of Query Sets #4b and #4c quickly becomes impractical for large aggregations.

Here, we use the COUNT function and a supplemental table to aggregate the diagnostic codes listed in the table. We first use a CREATE TABLE statement to create a CARDIAC_DX table. The format of this CREATE TABLE statement is a bit different than that of Query Set #1. In that example, we simply created a table by copying columns from an existing table. Here, we create the table from scratch by including parentheses and the column name, variable type, and NOT NULL statement enclosed in parentheses. If there were more than one column, they would be separated by commas within the parentheses.

After creating the table, we insert our three diagnostic codes into it using an INSERT statement: I50.9, I10, and I20.9. Then we add a column to our MORT_FINAL_2 table called Num_cardiac_dx_v2.

The final query updates the Num_cardiac_dx_v2 column by adding the number of codes from the table that are present in the Pri_dx_icd or Sec_dx_icd column. It accomplishes that by using a SELECT-FROM-WHERE block for each column, inside the original UPDATE statement. Therefore, this type of query is called a *nested* query. Within each SELECT block, the COUNT(*) statement simply returns the number of rows of the resulting query as an integer. So for example, in Visit #10001, there is a cardiac code in the Pri_dx_icd column and there is also one match in the Sec_dx_icd column. The first SELECT block would return a value of 1, since the query without COUNT would have returned a table with 1 row. By wrapping COUNT around *, 1 is returned as an integer. The second SELECT block also detects a match and returns a value of 1. The + operator makes 2 the final result. By comparing the Num_cardiac_dx and Num_cardiac_dx_2 columns, we see the result is exactly the same. So, which method is better? For small, simple aggregations, the first method is easier, because one simply has to make a column for each code and then aggregate them in a single statement with the + operator. However, in practice, you may wish to edit which codes are aggregated together to create features quite frequently. In this case, the second method is easier:

```
sqlite> CREATE TABLE CARDIAC_DX(
 Dx_icd TEXT NOT NULL);

sqlite> INSERT INTO CARDIAC_DX (Dx_icd)
VALUES ('I50.9'),('I10'),('I20.9');
```

```
sqlite> ALTER TABLE MORT_FINAL_2 ADD COLUMN Num_cardiac_dx_v2 INTEGER;

sqlite> UPDATE MORT_FINAL_2 SET Num_cardiac_dx_v2 =
(SELECT COUNT(*)
FROM CARDIAC_DX AS C
WHERE MORT_FINAL_2.Pri_dx_icd = C.Dx_icd) +
(SELECT COUNT(*)
FROM CARDIAC_DX AS C
WHERE MORT_FINAL_2.Sec_dx_icd = C.Dx_icd);
```

Query Set #5 – counting medications

Now we'll move on to the medications. Let's add a feature that simply tallies the number of medications each patient is taking. In Query Set #5 (as follows) we first add the Num_meds column using an ALTER TABLE statement. Then, we use a SELECT-FROM-WHERE block inside of an UPDATE statement to find the number of medications for each patient. The query works by tallying, for each patient ID in the MORT_FINAL_2 table, the number of rows in the MEDICATIONS table where the corresponding patient ID is equal. Again, we use the COUNT function to get the number of rows. We introduce a new function in this query, DISTINCT. DISTINCT removes any rows containing duplicate values for the column in parentheses. So for example, if LISINOPRIL was listed twice for a patient, the DISTINCT(Rx_name) function call would ensure it is only counted once:

```
sqlite> ALTER TABLE MORT_FINAL_2 ADD COLUMN Num_meds INTEGER;

sqlite> UPDATE MORT_FINAL_2 SET Num_meds =
(SELECT COUNT(DISTINCT(Rx_name))
FROM MEDICATIONS AS M
WHERE MORT_FINAL_2.Pid = M.Pid);
```

Query Set #6 – binning abnormal lab results

Several research articles have found lab values to be important predictors for clinical outcomes such as readmission (Donze et al., 2013). Lab results are problematic, however, because they are missing in most patients. No lab result type will be present for every patient; for example, in our example, not every patient got blood drawn for lab tests during their visit. Indeed, of the three different types of lab tests present in our data, the most common test was the BNP, drawn in four out of six patients. What do we do with the other two patients?

One way around this is to set up a "flag" for the presence of an abnormal result. This is accomplished in Query Set #6 for the glucose lab test. After the first query adds the `Abnml_glucose` column with an `ALTER TABLE` statement, the next query sets the result equal to the number of times that specific lab test exceeds a value of 200 for each patient visit. Notice the multiple `AND` clauses; they are necessary for selecting the right patient, date, and lab test of interest. So, only visits with an excessive result will have a value greater than zero for this feature. Notice we use the `CAST()` function to convert the values from `TEXT` to `FLOAT` before testing the value:

```
sqlite> ALTER TABLE MORT_FINAL_2 ADD COLUMN Abnml_glucose INTEGER;

sqlite> UPDATE MORT_FINAL_2 SET Abnml_glucose =
(SELECT COUNT(*) FROM LABS AS L
WHERE MORT_FINAL_2.Pid = L.Pid
AND MORT_FINAL_2.Visit_date = L.Lab_date
AND L.Lab_name = 'Glucose'
AND CAST(L.Lab_value AS FLOAT) >= 200);
```

While this solves the missing lab data problem, a limitation of this method is that it treats missing results and normal results as being the same. In Query Set #7, we will study basic methods for filling in missing values.

Query Set #7 – imputing missing variables

While the method presented in Query Set #6 solves the missing data problems for labs, all of the information contained in the actual lab values is discarded. For BNP, for example, only two of the patients don't have a value, and for the temperature vital sign, only one patient is missing.

Some previous studies have experimented with this principle and have obtained good results with predictive models while using it. In (Donze et al., 2013), some of the patient discharges (around 1%) had missing data. This data was filled in by assuming it was in the normal range.

In SQL, **single imputation** can easily be done. We demonstrate this here.

Query Set #7a – imputing missing temperature values using normal-range imputation

Here, we use an UPDATE statement to set the temperature variable to 98.6 where it is missing:

```
sqlite> UPDATE MORT_FINAL_2 SET Temp_f = 98.6
WHERE Temp_f IS NULL;
```

Query Set #7b – imputing missing temperature values using mean imputation

Here, we use **mean imputation** instead of normal-value imputation to fill in the missing temperature value. As such, the 98.6 value from Query Set #7a is replaced with a SELECT-FROM-WHERE block that finds the mean of the temperature variable (98.4, in this case) where it is not missing. The AVG() function returns the mean of a collection of values. The AVG() function and similar functions (MIN(), MAX(), COUNT(), SUM(), and so on) are termed **aggregate functions** because they describe an aggregation of values using a single value:

```
sqlite> UPDATE MORT_FINAL_2 SET Temp_f =
(SELECT AVG(Temp_f)
FROM MORT_FINAL_2
WHERE Temp_f IS NOT NULL)
WHERE Temp_f IS NULL;
```

Query Set #7c – imputing missing BNP values using a uniform distribution

While imputing the single missing temperature value was not difficult in our example, imputing the two missing BNP values is more problematic for a number of reasons:

- There is a higher proportion of visits that have a missing BNP value.
- While the normal temperature range is simply 98.6, BNP has a huge normal range of 100 - 400 pg/mL. How do we select which value to impute when doing normal-value imputation?

- The mean of the BNP values in our dataset is 462.5, which is, in fact, abnormal. This means that if we tried mean imputation with this variable, we would be imputing an abnormal value for all patients who didn't have blood drawn, a highly unlikely scenario.

While there is no perfect answer for this problem, if we do try to salvage the raw BNP values (which means imputing the missing values), in this query set, we impute from a uniform distribution of values in the normal range:

```
sqlite> ALTER TABLE MORT_FINAL_2 ADD COLUMN Raw_BNP INTEGER;

sqlite> UPDATE MORT_FINAL_2 SET Raw_BNP =
(SELECT CAST(Lab_value as INTEGER)
FROM LABS AS L
WHERE MORT_FINAL_2.Pid = L.Pid
AND MORT_FINAL_2.Visit_date = L.Lab_date
AND L.Lab_name = 'Natriuretic peptide B');

sqlite> UPDATE MORT_FINAL_2 SET Raw_BNP =
ROUND(ABS(RANDOM()) % (300 - 250) + 250)
WHERE Raw_BNP IS NULL;
```

Query Set #8 – adding the target variable

We are almost done with our table. We've gone through all of the data. The only thing left to add is the target variable. See the following:

```
sqlite> ALTER TABLE MORT_FINAL_2 ADD COLUMN Mortality INTEGER DEFAULT 0;

sqlite> UPDATE MORT_FINAL_2 SET Mortality =
(SELECT COUNT(*)
FROM MORT AS M
WHERE M.Pid = MORT_FINAL_2.Pid
AND julianday(M.Mortality_date) -
julianday(MORT_FINAL_2.Visit_date) < 180);
```

Query Set #9 – visualizing the MORT_FINAL_2 table

To visualize our end result, we can do the following:

```
sqlite> .headers on
sqlite> SELECT * FROM MORT_FINAL_2;
Visit_id|Pid|Attending_md|Visit_date|Pri_dx_icd|Sec_dx_icd|Bdate|Sex|Height
_in|Weight_lb|Temp_f|Pulse|Resp_rate|Bp_syst|Bp_diast|SpO2|Age_years|Chf_dx
|Htn_dx|Angina_dx|Diab_dx|Pulm_htn_dx|Num_cardiac_dx|Num_cardiac_dx_v2|Num_
meds|Abnml_glucose|Raw_BNP|Mortality
10001|1|JOHNSON|2016-01-09|I50.9|I10|1952-01-01|M|70|188.4|98.6|95|18|154|9
4|97|64.02|1|1|0|0|0|2|2|2|0|350|1
10002|1|JOHNSON|2016-01-17|I50.9|I10|1952-01-01|M|70|188.4|99.1|85|17|157|9
6|100|64.04|1|1|0|0|0|2|2|2|0|266|1
10003|2|WU|2016-01-15|I20.9|E11.9|1978-02-03|F|63|130.2|98.7|82|16|120|81|1
00|37.95|0|0|1|1|0|1|1|4|1|100|0
10004|3|JOHNSON|2016-02-01|I10||1985-04-23|F|65|120.0|98.44|100|19|161|100|
98|30.78|0|1|0|0|0|1|1|1|0|291|0
10005|4|WU|2016-02-27|I27.0|I50.9|1966-11-15|M|66|211.4|98.2|95|19|143|84|9
3|49.28|1|0|0|0|1|1|1|3|0|1000|1
10006|5|WU|2016-03-01|I50.9|E11.9|1958-12-30|M|69|150.0|97.6|77|18|130|86|9
9|57.17|1|0|0|1|0|1|1|3|1|400|0
```

Summary

In this chapter, we learned how to engineer healthcare data in a database format using SQL. We downloaded and installed SQLite, and wrote some SQL queries to get the data in a format that we want for modeling.

Next, in `Chapter 5`, *Computing Foundations – Introduction to Python*, we will continue our discussion of computing foundations with an exploration of the Python programming language.

References and further reading

Basole RC, Braunstein ML, Kumar V, Park H, Kahng M, Chau DH, Tamersoy A, Hirsh DA, Serban N, BostJ, Lesnick B, Schissel BL, Thompson M (2015). Understanding variations in pediatric asthma care processes in the emergency department using visual analytics. *Journal of the American Medical Informatics Association* 22(2): 318–323, https://doi.org/10.1093/jamia/ocu016.

Donze J, Aujesky D, Williams D, Schnipper JL (2013). Potentially avoidable 30-day hospital readmissions in medical patients: derivation and validation of a prediction model. *JAMA Intern Med* 173(8): 632-638.

Elmasri R, Navathe S (2010). Fundamentals of Database Systems, 6th Edition. Boston, MA: Addison Wesley.

Futoma J, Morris J, Lucas J (2015). A comparison of models for predicting early hospital readmissions. *Journal of Biomedical Informatics* 56: 229-238.

Kasper DL, Braunwald E, Fauci AS, Hauser SL, Longo DL, Jameson JL (2005), eds. *Harrison's Principles of Internal Medicine,* 16e. New York, NY: McGraw-Hill.

Rajkomar A, Oren E, Chen K, Dai AM, Hajaj N, Hardt M, et al. (2018). Scalable and accurate deep learning with electronic health records. *npj Digital Medicine* 1:18; doi:10.1038/s41746-018-0029-1.

Sahni N, Simon G, Arora R (2018). *J Gen Intern Med* 33: 921. https://doi.org/10.1007/s11606-018-4316-y

SQLite Home Page. http://www.sqlite.org/. Accessed 04/03/2017.

5
Computing Foundations – Introduction to Python

This chapter will provide an introduction to Python for analytics. It is meant mainly for novice programmers or developers who are not familiar with Python. By the end of the chapter, you will have a basic familiarity with the features of the Python base language, which is integral for healthcare analytics and machine learning. You will also understand how to get started using `pandas` and `scikit-learn`, two important Python libraries for analytics.

If you would like to follow along using the Jupyter Notebook, we encourage you to refer to the directions in `Chapter 1`, *Introduction to Healthcare Analytics*, to start a new Jupyter session. The notebook for this chapter is also available online at the book's official code repository.

Variables and types

Basic variable types in Python consist of strings and numeric types. Let's look at both of these types in this section.

Strings

In Python, a **string** is a variable type that stores text characters such as letters, numbers, special characters, and punctuation. In Python, we use single or double quotation marks to indicate that the variable is a string rather than a number:

```
var = 'Hello, World!'
print(var)
```

Strings cannot be used for mathematical operations on numbers. But they can be used for other useful operations, as we see in the following example:

```
string_1 = '1'
string_2 = '2'
string_sum = string_1 + string_2
print(string_sum)
```

The result of the preceding code is to print string `'12'`, not `'3'`. Instead of adding the two numbers, the + operator performs concatenation (appending the second string to the end of the first string) in Python when operating on two strings.

Other operators that act on strings include the ∗ operator (for repeating strings n number of times, for example, `string_1 * 3`) and the < and > operators (to compare the ASCII values of the strings).

To convert data from a numeric type to a string, we can use the `str()` method.

Because strings are sequences (of characters), we can index them and slice them (like we can do with other data containers, as you will see later). A slice is a contiguous section of a string. To index/slice them, we use integers enclosed in square brackets to indicate the character's position:

```
test_string = 'Healthcare'
print(test_string[0])
```

The output is shown as follows:

```
H
```

To slice strings, we include the beginning and end positions, separated by a colon, in the square brackets. Note that the end position will include all the characters *up to but not including* the end position, as we see in the following example:

```
print(test_string[0:6])
```

The output is as follows:

```
Health
```

Earlier, we mentioned the `str()` method. There are dozens of other methods for strings. A full list of them is available in the online Python documentation at `www.python.org`. Methods include those for case conversion, finding specific substrings, and stripping whitespace. We'll discuss one more method here–the `split()` method. The `split()` method acts on a string and takes a `separator` argument.

The output is a list of strings; each item in the list is a component of the original string, split by `separator`. This is very useful for parsing strings that are delimited by punctuation characters such as `,` or `;`. We will discuss lists in the next section. Here is an example of the `split()` method:

```
test_split_string = 'Jones,Bill,49,Atlanta,GA,12345'
output = test_split_string.split(',')
print(output)
```

The output is as follows:

```
['Jones', 'Bill', '49', 'Atlanta', 'GA', '12345']
```

Numeric types

The two numeric types in Python that are most useful for analytics are **integers** and **floating-point** numbers. To convert to these types, you can use the `int()` and `float()` functions, respectively. The most common operations on numbers are supported with the usual operators: +, −, *, /, <, and >. Modules containing special methods for numeric types that are particularly useful for analytics include `math` and `random`. More information on numeric types is available in the online Python documentation (see the link in the previous section).

Note that with some Python versions, dividing two integers using the / operator performs **floor division** (with the numbers after the decimal place omitted); for example, 10/4 would equal 2, not 2.5. This is a stealthy yet egregious error that can throw off numerical calculations. However, with the version of Python we are using in this book, we don't need to worry about this error.

The **Boolean type** is a special integer type that can be used to represent the True and False values. To convert an integer to a Boolean type, you can use the `bool()` function. A zero gets converted to False; any other integer would get converted to True. Boolean variables behave like 1 (True) and 0 (False), except that they return True and False, respectively, when converted to strings.

Data structures and containers

In the last section, we talked about variable types that store single values. Now we will move on to data structures that can hold multiple values. These data structures are lists, tuples, dictionaries, and sets. Lists and tuples are commonly referred to as sequences in Python. In this book, we will use the terms data structures and data containers interchangeably.

Lists

Lists are a widely used data structure that can hold multiple values. Let's look at some features of lists:

- To make a list, we use square brackets, `[]`.
  Example: `my_list = [1, 2, 3]`.
- Lists can hold any combination of numeric types, strings, Boolean types, tuples, dictionaries, or even other lists.
  Example: `my_diverse_list = [51, 'Health', True, [1, 2, 3]]`.
- Lists, like strings, are sequences and support indexing and slicing.
  For example, in the preceding example, `my_diverse_list[0]` would equal 51. `my_diverse_list[0:2]` would equal `[51, 'Health']`. To access the 3 of the nested list, we can use `my_diverse_list[3][2]`.
- Lists are **mutable** (unlike strings and tuples), meaning that we can change individual components using indices.
  For example, if we entered the `my_diverse_list[2] = False` command, our new `my_diverse_list` would be equal to `[51, 'Health', False, [1, 2, 3]]`.

Notable advantages of lists for analytics include their vast array of helper methods, such as `append()`, `extend()`, and `join()`, and their interchangeability with the `pandas` and `numpy` data structures.

Tuples

Tuples are similar to lists. To make a tuple, we use parentheses, `()`. Example: `my_tuple = (1, 2, 3)`. The main difference between tuples and lists is that tuples are **immutable**, so we cannot change any components of a tuple. If we tried `my_tuple[0] = 4`, an error would be thrown. Because their values are immutable, tuples are useful for setting constant variables.

Dictionaries

A **dictionary** is a common data structure in Python. It is used to store unidirectional mappings from keys to values. For example, if we wanted to create a dictionary that stored a list of patient names and their corresponding room numbers, we could use the following code:

```
rooms = {
    'Smith': '141-A',
    'Davis': '142',
    'Williams': '144',
    'Johnson': '145-B'
}
```

Let's talk about the preceding code snippet in more detail:

- The names in the `rooms` dictionary are referred to as **keys**. The keys in a dictionary must be unique. To access them, we can use the `keys()` function, `rooms.keys()`.
- The room numbers in the `rooms` dictionary are referred to as **values**. To access all of the values, we can use the `values()` function, `rooms.values()`. To access an individual value, we just supply the name of its key in square brackets. For example, `rooms['Smith']` will return `'141-A'`. For this reason, we say that a dictionary maps keys to their values.
- To access a nested list of tuples that contains each key along with its corresponding value, we can use the `items()` function, `rooms.items()`.
- Dictionaries don't have to just be strings; in fact, the values can be any data type/structure. The keys can be particular variables such as integers or strings. While the values are mutable, the keys are immutable.
- Dictionaries have no intrinsic order, so indexing and slicing by number is not supported.

Sets

Although in Python the set doesn't receive as much attention as its popular cousin the list, sets play an important role in analytics, so we include them here. To make a set, we use the built-in set() function. There are three things you need to know about sets:

- They are immutable
- They are unordered
- The elements of a set are unique

Therefore, sets in Python are very similar to their mathematical counterparts if you are familiar with the basic set theory. The set methods also duplicate typical set operations and include union(), intersection(), add(), and remove(). These functions come in handy when wanting to perform typical set-like operations on data structures, such as lists or tuples, following conversions to sets.

Programming in Python – an illustrative example

In the previous sections, we discussed variable types and data containers. There are many more aspects of Python programming, such as control flow with if/else statements, loops, and comprehensions; functions; and classes and object-oriented programming. Commonly, Python programs are packaged into **modules**, which are self-standing scripts that can be run from the command line to perform computing tasks.

Let's introduce some of these concepts in Python with a "module" of our own (you can use the Jupyter Notebook for this):

```python
from math import pow


LB_TO_KG = 0.453592
IN_TO_M = 0.0254


class Patient:
    def __init__(self, name, weight_lbs, height_in):
        self.name = name
        self.weight_lbs = weight_lbs
        self.weight_kg = weight_lbs * LB_TO_KG
        self.height_in = height_in
        self.height_m = height_in * IN_TO_M
```

```
        def calculate_bmi(self):
            return self.weight_kg / pow(self.height_m, 2)
        def get_height_m(self):
            return self.height_m

if __name__ == '__main__':
    test_patients = [
        Patient('John Smith', 160, 68),
        Patient('Patty Johnson', 180, 73)
    ]
    heights = [patient.get_height_m() for patient in test_patients]
    print(
        "John's height: ", heights[0], '\n',
        "Patty's height: ", heights[1], '\n',
        "John's BMI: ", test_patients[0].calculate_bmi(), '\n',
        "Patty's BMI: ", test_patients[1].calculate_bmi()
    )
```

When you run this code, you should see the following output:

```
John's height:  1.7271999999999998
 Patty's height:  1.8541999999999998
 John's BMI:  24.327647271211504
 Patty's BMI:  23.74787410486812
```

The preceding code is a Python module that prints the height and **body mass indices** (**BMIs**) for two mock patients. Let's take a more detailed look at each element of this code:

- The first line of the code block is an **import statement**. This allows us to import functions and classes that have been written in other modules that are either distributed with Python, written as open source software, or written by ourselves. A **module** can simply be thought of as a file that contains Python functions, constants, and/or classes. It has a `.py` extension. To import a module in its entirety, we can simply use the `import` word followed by the module name, for example, `import math`. Notice we used the `from` keyword as well because we only want to import a specific function, the `pow()` function. This also saves us from the inconvenience of having to type `math.pow()` every time we want to raise something to a power.
- The next two lines contain **constants** that we will use to perform unit conversions. Constants are usually indicated by capital letters.

- Next, we define a `Patient` class that has a **constructor** and two **methods**. The constructor takes three arguments–the name, height, and weight–and sets three attributes of the specific `Patient` instance to equal those three values. It also converts the weight from pounds to kilograms and the height from inches to meters, and stores those values in two extra attributes.

- The two methods are coded as **functions**, using the `def` keyword. `calculate_bmi()` returns the BMI of the patient, while `get_height()` simply returns the height in meters.

- Next, we have a mini `if` statement. All that this `if` statement is saying is to run the subsequent code only if it is the main module invoked at the command line. Other `if` statements may have multiple `elif` clauses and can also include a final `else` clause.

- Next, we create a list of two patients, John Smith and Patty Johnson, with their heights and weights as listed in the code.

- The following line uses a list **comprehension** to create a list of heights of the two patients. Comprehensions are very popular in Python programming and can also be performed with dictionaries.

- Finally, our `print` statement prints the four numbers as the output (the two heights and the two BMI values).

 Further references for the base Python programming language are given at the end of this chapter. You can also check out the online documentation at `www.python.org`.

Introduction to pandas

Almost all of the features we've discussed so far are features of *base* Python; that is, no external packages or libraries were required. The truth of the matter is that the majority of the code we write in this book will pertain to one of several *external* Python packages commonly used for analytics. The **pandas** library (`http://pandas.pydata.org`) is an integral part of the later programming chapters. The functions of pandas for machine learning are threefold:

- Import data from flat files into your Python session
- Wrangle, manipulate, format, and cleanse data using the pandas DataFrame and its library of functions
- Export data from your Python session to flat files

Let's review each of these functions in turn.

Flat files are popular methods of storing healthcare-related data (along with HL7 formats, which are not covered in this book). A **flat file** is a text file representation of data. Using flat files, data can be represented as rows and columns, similar to databases, except that punctuation or whitespace are used as column delimiters, while carriage returns are used as row delimiters. We will see an example flat file in Chapter 7, *Making Predictive Models in Healthcare*.

pandas allows us to import data into a tabular Python data structure, called a **DataFrame**, from a variety of other Python structures and flat files, including Python dictionaries, pickle objects, **comma-separated values** (**csv**) files, **fixed-width format** (**fwf**) files, Microsoft Excel files, JSON files, HTML files, and even SQL database tables.

Once the data is in Python, there are additional functions that you can use to explore and transform the data. Need to perform a mathematical function on a column, such as finding its sum? Need to perform SQL-like operations, such as JOINs or adding columns (see Chapter 3, *Machine Learning Foundations*)? Need to filter rows by a condition? All of the functionality is there in pandas' API. We will make good use of some of pandas' functionality in Chapter 6, *Measuring Healthcare Quality* and in Chapter 7, *Making Predictive Models in Healthcare*.

Finally, when we are done exploring, cleansing, and wrangling our data, if we can choose to export it out as most of the formats listed. Or we can convert it to a NumPy array and train machine learning models, as we will do later in this book.

What is a pandas DataFrame?

A **pandas DataFrame** can be thought of as a two-dimensional, matrix-like data structure that consists of rows and columns. A pandas DataFrame is analogous to a dataframe in R or a table in SQL. Advantages over traditional matrices and other Python data structures include the ability to have columns of different types in the same DataFrame, a wide array of predefined functions for easy data manipulation, and one-line interfaces that allow quick conversion to other file formats including databases, flat file formats, and NumPy arrays (for integration with scikit-learn's machine learning functionality). Therefore, pandas is indeed the glue that holds together many machine learning pipelines, from data importation to algorithm application.

The limitations of pandas include slower performance and lack of built-in parallel processing for pandas functionality. Therefore, if you are working with millions or billions of data points, **Apache Spark** (https://spark.apache.org/) may be a better option, since it has parallel processing built into its language.

Importing data

In this section, we demonstrate how to load data into Python via dictionaries, flat files, and databases.

Importing data into pandas from Python data structures

The first step in working with pandas DataFrames is to create one using the pandas constructor function, DataFrame(). The constructor takes many Python data structures as input. It also takes as input NumPy arrays and pandas **Series**, another type of one-dimensional pandas data structure that is similar to a list. Here we demonstrate how to convert a dictionary of lists into a DataFrame:

```
import pandas as pd
data = {
    'col1': [1, 2, 3],
    'col2': [4, 5, 6],
    'col3': ['x', 'y', 'z']
}

df = pd.DataFrame(data)
print(df)
```

The output is as follows:

```
   col1  col2 col3
0     1     4    x
1     2     5    y
2     3     6    z
```

Importing data into pandas from a flat file

Because healthcare data can often be in flat file format, such as `.csv` or `.fwf`, it is important to know of the `read_csv()` and `read_fwf()` functions that import data into `pandas` from these two formats, respectively. Both of the functions take as mandatory arguments the full path of the flat file, along with over a dozen additional optional arguments that specify options including the data types of the columns, the header rows, the columns to include in the DataFrame, and so on (a full listing of the function arguments is available online). It is often easiest to import all the columns as string types and convert the columns to other data types later on. In the following example, a DataFrame called `data` is created by using the `read_csv()` function to read in a flat `.csv` file that contains one header row (`row #0`):

```
pt_data = pd.read_csv(data_full_path, header=0, dtype='str')
```

Because fixed-width files have no explicit character separator, the `read_fwf()` function needs an additional argument, `widths`, which is a list of integers specifying the column widths for each column. The length of `widths` should match the number of columns in the file. As an alternative, the `colspecs` argument takes in a list of tuples specifying the starting points and endpoints of each column:

```
pt_data = pd.read_fwf(source, widths=data_widths, header=None, dtype='str')
```

Importing data into pandas from a database

The `pandas` library also has functions to support the import of tables directly from SQL databases. Functions that can accomplish this include `read_sql_query()` and `read_sql_table()`. Before using these functions, the connection to the database must be established so that it can be passed to the function. In the following example, a table from a SQLite database is read into a DataFrame using the `read_sql_query()` function:

```
import sqlite3

conn = sqlite3.connect(pt_db_full_path)
table_name = 'TABLE1'
pt_data = pd.read_sql_query('SELECT * from ' + table_name + ';', conn)
```

If you wish to connect to a standard database, such as a MySQL database, the code would be similar, except for the connection statement, which would use the corresponding function for a MySQL database.

Common operations on DataFrames

In this section, we'll go over DataFrame operations useful for performing analytics. For descriptions of additional operations, please refer to the official pandas documentation at `https://pandas.pydata.org/`.

Adding columns

Adding columns is a common operation in analytics, whether adding new columns from scratch or transforming existing columns. Let's go over both types of operations here.

Adding blank or user-initialized columns

To add a new column of a DataFrame, you can follow the name of the DataFrame with the name of the new column (enclosed in single quotes and square brackets) and set it equal to whatever value you like. To add a column of empty strings or integers, you can set the column equal to `""` or `numpy.nan`, respectively (the latter requires importing `numpy` beforehand). To add a column of zeros, set the column equal to `0`. The following examples illustrate these points:

```
df['new_col1'] = ""
df['new_col2'] = 0
print(df)
```

The output is as follows:

```
   col1  col2 col3 new_col1  new_col2
0     1     4    x                  0
1     2     5    y                  0
2     3     6    z                  0
```

Adding new columns by transforming existing columns

In some cases, you might wish to add a new column that is a function of existing columns. In the following example, the new column, titled example_new_column_3, is added as a sum of the existing columns, old_column_1 and old_column_2. The axis=1 argument indicates that you wish to take the horizontal sum across the columns instead of the vertical sum of columns:

```
df['new_col3'] = df[[
    'col1','col2'
]].sum(axis=1)

print(df)
```

The output is as follows:

	col1	col2	col3	new_col1	new_col2	new_col3
0	1	4	x		0	5
1	2	5	y		0	7
2	3	6	z		0	9

The following second example accomplishes a similar task using the pandas apply() function. apply() is a special function because it allows you to apply any function to columns in a DataFrame (including your own custom functions):

```
old_column_list = ['col1','col2']
df['new_col4'] = df[old_column_list].apply(sum, axis=1)
print(df)
```

The output is as follows:

	col1	col2	col3	new_col1	new_col2	new_col3	new_col4
0	1	4	x		0	5	5
1	2	5	y		0	7	7
2	3	6	z		0	9	9

Dropping columns

To drop columns, you can use pandas' drop() function. It takes a single column as well as a list of columns, and in this example, additional optional arguments indicate which is the axis along which to drop and whether or not to drop columns in place:

```
df.drop(['col1','col2'], axis=1, inplace=True)
print(df)
```

The output is as follows:

```
   col3 new_col1  new_col2  new_col3  new_col4
0    x                  0         5         5
1    y                  0         7         7
2    z                  0         9         9
```

Applying functions to multiple columns

To apply a function over multiple columns in a DataFrame, the list of columns can be iterated over using a `for` loop. In the following example, a predefined list of columns is converted from the string type to the numeric type:

```
df['new_col5'] = ['7', '8', '9']
df['new_col6'] = ['10', '11', '12']

for str_col in ['new_col5','new_col6']:
    df[[str_col]] = df[[str_col]].apply(pd.to_numeric)
print(df)
```

Here is the output:

```
   col3 new_col1  new_col2  new_col3  new_col4  new_col5  new_col6
0    x                  0         5         5         7        10
1    y                  0         7         7         8        11
2    z                  0         9         9         9        12
```

Combining DataFrames

DataFrames can also be combined with each other, as long as they have the same number of entries along the combining axis. In this example, two DataFrames are concatenated vertically (for example, they contain the same number of columns, and their rows are stacked upon each other). DataFrames can also be concatenated horizontally (if they contain the same number of rows) by specifying the `axis` parameter. Note that the column names and row names should correspond to each other across the DataFrames; if they do not, new columns will be formed and NaN values will be inserted for any missing values.

First, we create a new DataFrame name, `df2`:

```
df2 = pd.DataFrame({
    'col3': ['a', 'b', 'c', 'd'],
    'new_col1': '',
    'new_col2': 0,
    'new_col3': [11, 13, 15, 17],
```

```
        'new_col4': [17, 19, 21, 23],
        'new_col5': [7.5, 8.5, 9.5, 10.5],
        'new_col6': [13, 14, 15, 16]
});
print(df2)
```

The output is as follows:

```
  col3 new_col1  new_col2  new_col3  new_col4  new_col5  new_col6
0   a            0        11        17       7.5        13
1   b            0        13        19       8.5        14
2   c            0        15        21       9.5        15
3   d            0        17        23      10.5        16
```

Next, we perform the concatenation. We set the optional `ignore_index` argument equal to `True` to avoid duplicate row indices:

```
df3 = pd.concat([df, df2] ignore_index = True)
print(df3)
```

The output is as follows:

```
  col3 new_col1  new_col2  new_col3  new_col4  new_col5  new_col6
0   x            0         5         5       7.0        10
1   y            0         7         7       8.0        11
2   z            0         9         9       9.0        12
3   a            0        11        17       7.5        13
4   b            0        13        19       8.5        14
5   c            0        15        21       9.5        15
6   d            0        17        23      10.5        16
```

Converting DataFrame columns to lists

To extract the contents of a column into a list, you can use the `tolist()` function. After being converted to a list, the data can then be iterated over using `for` loops and comprehensions:

```
my_list = df3['new_col3'].tolist()
print(my_list)
```

The output is as follows:

```
[5, 7, 9, 11, 13, 15, 17]
```

Getting and setting DataFrame values

The `pandas` library offers two main methods for selectively getting and setting values in DataFrames: `loc` and `iloc`. The `loc` method is mainly for **label-based indexing** (for example, identifying rows/columns using their indices/column names, respectively), while the `iloc` method is primarily for **integer-based indexing** (for example, identifying rows/columns using their integer positions in the DataFrame). The specific labels/indices of the rows and columns you wish to access are provided following the name of the DataFrame using square brackets, with row labels/indices preceding column labels/indices and separated from them by a comma. Let's look at some examples.

Getting/setting values using label-based indexing with loc

The `.loc` attribute of a DataFrame is used to select values using the labels of the entries. It can be used to retrieve single scalar values from a DataFrame (using singular string labels for both row and column), or multiple values from a DataFrame (using lists of row/column labels). Single and multiple indexing can also be used in combination to get multiple values from a single row or column. The following lines of code illustrate the retrieval of a single scalar value from the `df` DataFrame:

```
value = df3.loc[0,'new_col5']
print(value)
```

The output will be `7.0`.

Single/multiple values can also be set using the `.loc` attribute and an equals sign:

```
df3.loc[[2,3,4],['new_col4','new_col5']] = 1
print(df3)
```

The output is as follows:

	col3	new_col1	new_col2	new_col3	new_col4	new_col5	new_col6
0	x		0	5	5	7.0	10
1	y		0	7	7	8.0	11
2	z		0	9	1	1.0	12
3	a		0	11	1	1.0	13
4	b		0	13	1	1.0	14
5	c		0	15	21	9.5	15
6	d		0	17	23	10.5	16

Getting/setting values using integer-based labeling with iloc

The `.iloc` attribute works very similarly to the `.loc` attribute, except that it uses the integer positions of the rows and columns being accessed, not their labels. In the following example, the value in the 101st row (not the 100th row, since indexing starts at 0) and the 100th column is transferred to `scalar_value`:

```
value2 = df3.iloc[0,5]
print(value2)
```

The output is `7.0`.

Note that, similarly to `.loc`, lists containing multiple values can be passed to the `.iloc` attribute to change multiple entries of a DataFrame at once.

Getting/setting multiple contiguous values using slicing

Sometimes, the multiple values that we wish to get or set are coincidentally in neighboring (contiguous) columns. When this is the case, we can use **slicing** within the square brackets to select multiple values. With slicing, we specify the starting point and endpoint of the data that we wish to access. We can use slicing with both `.loc` and `.iloc`, although slicing using integers and `.iloc` is more common. The following lines of code illustrate slicing to retrieve part of a DataFrame (we can also assign elements using an equals sign). Note that slicing can also be used to access values in lists and tuples (as covered previously in the current chapter):

```
partial_df3 = df3.loc[1:3,'new_col2':'new_col4']
print(partial_df3)
```

The output is as follows:

```
   new_col2   new_col3   new_col4
1         0          7          7
2         0          9          1
3         0         11          1
```

Fast getting/setting of scalar values using at and iat

If we are certain that we only wish to get/set single values in a DataFrame, we can use the `.at` and `.iat` attributes, along with singular labels/integers, respectively. Just remember, the `i` in `.iloc` and `.iat` stands for "integer":

```
value3 = df3.iat[3,3]
print(value3)
```

The output is 11.

Other operations

Two other common operations are filtering rows using a Boolean condition and sorting rows. Here we will review each of these operations.

Filtering rows using Boolean indexing

So far, we've discussed using labels, integers, and slicing to select values in DataFrames. Sometimes, it is convenient to select certain rows that meet a certain condition in one of their statements. For example, if we wanted to restrict an analysis on people whose age is greater than or equal to 50 years.

pandas DataFrames support **Boolean indexing**, that is, indexing using a vector of Boolean values to indicate which values we wish to include, provided that the length of the Boolean vector is equal to the number of rows in the DataFrame. Because a conditional statement involving a DataFrame column yields exactly that, we can index DataFrames using such conditional statements. In the following example, the df DataFrame is filtered to include only rows in which the value of the age column is equal to or exceeds 50:

```
df3_filt = df3[df3['new_col3'] > 10]
print(df3_filt)
```

The output is as follows:

```
  col3 new_col1  new_col2  new_col3  new_col4  new_col5  new_col6
3    a                  0        11         1       1.0        13
4    b                  0        13         1       1.0        14
5    c                  0        15        21       9.5        15
6    d                  0        17        23      10.5        16
```

Conditional statements can be chained together using logical operators such as | or &.

Sorting rows

If you wish to sort a DataFrame by the value of one of its columns, that can be done using the sort_values() function; simply specify the column name as the first parameter. ascending is an optional parameter that lets you specify the sorting direction:

```
df3 = df3.sort_values('new_col4', ascending=True)
print(df3)
```

The output is as follows:

```
   col3 new_col1  new_col2  new_col3  new_col4  new_col5  new_col6
2    z               0         9         1       1.0        12
3    a               0        11         1       1.0        13
4    b               0        13         1       1.0        14
0    x               0         5         5       7.0        10
1    y               0         7         7       8.0        11
5    c               0        15        21       9.5        15
6    d               0        17        23      10.5        16
```

SQL-like operations

For people who are used to working with heterogeneously typed tables in SQL, switching to similar analyses in Python may seem like a daunting task. Fortunately, there are a number of pandas functions that can be combined to yield results similar to those yielded by common SQL queries, using operations such as grouping and joining. There is even a subsection in the pandas documentation (https://pandas.pydata.org/pandas-docs/stable/comparison_with_sql.html) that describes how to perform SQL-like operations with pandas DataFrames. We provide two such examples in this section.

Getting aggregate row COUNTs

Sometimes, you may wish to get a count or tally of the occurrences of particular values in a column. For example, you might have a healthcare dataset and you want to know how many times particular payment methods were used during patient visits. In SQL, you could write a query that uses a GROUP BY clause in conjunction with an aggregate function (in this case, COUNT(*)) to get a tally of the payment methods:

```
SELECT payment, COUNT(*)
FROM data
GROUP BY payment;
```

In pandas, the same result is accomplished by chaining together the groupby() and size() functions:

```
tallies = df3.groupby('new_col4').size()
print(tallies)
```

The output is as follows:

```
new_col4
1     3
5     1
7     1
21    1
23    1
dtype: int64
```

Joining DataFrames

In Chapter 4, *Computing Foundations – Databases*, we discussed merging data from two database tables using the JOIN operation. To use a JOIN operation, you need to specify the names of the two tables, along with the type of JOIN (left, right, outer, or inner) and the columns on which to join:

```
SELECT *
FROM left_table OUTER JOIN right_table
ON left_table.index = right_table.index;
```

In pandas, you can accomplish table joins using the merge() or join() functions. By default, the join() function joins data on the index of the tables; however, other columns can be used by specifying the on parameter. If column names are overlapping in the two tables being joined, you will need to specify a rsuffix or lsuffix argument that renames the columns so they no longer have identical names:

```
df_join_df2 = df.join(df2, how='outer', rsuffix='r')
print(df_join_df2)
```

The output is as follows (note the NaN values in Row 3, a row that was not present in df):

	col3	new_col1	new_col2	new_col3	new_col4	new_col5	new_col6	col3r	\
0	x		0.0	5.0	5.0	7.0	10.0	a	
1	y		0.0	7.0	7.0	8.0	11.0	b	
2	z		0.0	9.0	9.0	9.0	12.0	c	
3	NaN	NaN	NaN	NaN	NaN	NaN	NaN	d	

	new_col1r	new_col2r	new_col3r	new_col4r	new_col5r	new_col6r
0		0	11	17	7.5	13
1		0	13	19	8.5	14
2		0	15	21	9.5	15
3		0	17	23	10.5	16

Introduction to scikit-learn

Entire books have been written on **scikit-learn** (`http://scikit-learn.org/stable/`). The scikit-learn library has numerous submodules. Only a few of these submodules will be used in this book (in `Chapter 7`, *Making Predictive Models in Healthcare*). These include the `sklearn.linear_model` and `sklearn.ensemble` submodules, for example. Here we will give an overview of some of the more commonly used submodules. For convenience, we have grouped the relevant modules into various segments of the data science pipeline discussed in `Chapter 1`, *Introduction to Healthcare Analytics*.

Sample data

scikit-learn includes several sample datasets in the `sklearn.datasets` submodule. At least two of these datasets, `sklearn.datasets.load_breast_cancer` and `sklearn.datasets.load_diabetes`, are healthcare-related. These datasets have been already preprocessed and are small in size, spanning only dozens of features and hundreds of patients. The data we will use in `Chapter 7`, *Making Predictive Models in Healthcare* is much bigger and resembles the data you are likely to receive from modern healthcare organizations. These sample sklearn datasets, however, are useful for experimenting with scikit-learn functions.

Data preprocessing

Data preprocessing functionality is present in the `sklearn.preprocessing` submodule, among others. Some of the relevant functions of this module are discussed in the following sections.

One-hot encoding of categorical variables

Almost every dataset has some categorical data contained in it. **Categorical data** is discrete data in which the value can take on a finite number of possible values (usually encoded as a "string"). Because Python's scikit-learn can handle only numeric data, before performing machine learning with scikit-learn, we must find alternative ways of encoding categorical variables.

With **one-hot encoding**, also known as a **1-of-K encoding scheme**, a single categorical variable having *k* possible values is converted into *k* different binary variables, each one is positive if and only if the column's value for that observation equaled the value it represents. In Chapter 7, *Making Predictive Models in Healthcare*, we provide a detailed example of what one-hot encoding is and use a pandas function called get_dummies() to perform one-hot encoding on a real clinical dataset. scikit-learn also has a class used to perform one-hot encoding, however, it is the OneHotEncoder class in the sklearn.preprocessing module.

For instructions on how OneHotEncoder is used, you can visit the scikit-learn documentation: http://scikit-learn.org/stable/modules/preprocessing.html#encoding-categorical-features.

Scaling and centering

For some machine learning algorithms, it is preferable to transform not only the categorical variables (using one-hot encoding, discussed previously) but also the continuous variables. Recall from Chapter 1, *Introduction to Healthcare Analytics* that a continuous variable is numerical and can take on any rational value (although in many cases they are restricted to integers). A particularly common practice is to **standardize** each continuous variable so that the *mean of the variable is zero and the standard deviation is one*. For example, take the AGE variable: it typically ranges from 0 to about 100, with a mean of perhaps 40. Let's pretend that for a particular population, the mean of our AGE variable is 40 with a standard deviation of 20. If we were to center and rescale our AGE variable, a person whose age was 40 would be represented as zero in the transformed variable. A person who was 20 years old would be represented as -1, a person who was 60 years old would be represented as 1, a person who was 80 years old would be represented as 2, and a person who was 50 years old would be 0.5. This transformation prevents variables with larger ranges from being overrepresented in the machine learning algorithm.

scikit-learn has many built-in classes and functions for centering and scaling data, including sklearn.preprocessing.StandardScaler(), sklearn.preprocessing.MinMaxScaler(), and sklearn.preprocessing.RobustScaler(). These various tools are specialized for centering and scaling different types of continuous data, such as normally distributed variables, or variables that have many outliers.

For instructions on how the scaling classes are used, you can check out the scikit-learn documentation: http://scikit-learn.org/stable/modules/preprocessing.html#standardization-or-mean-removal-and-variance-scaling.

Binarization

Binarization is yet another type of transformation in which continuous variables are transformed into binary variables. For example, if we had a continuous variable named AGE, we could binarize the variable around 50 years by thresholding ages 50 and above to have a value of one, and ages with values below 50 to have a value of zero. Binarizing is good to save time and memory when you have many variables; however, in practice, the raw continuous values usually perform better since they are more informative.

While binarization can also be performed in pandas using the code demonstrated earlier, scikit-learn comes with a Binarizer class that can also be used to binarize features. For instructions on using the Binarizer class, you can visit http://scikit-learn.org/stable/modules/preprocessing.html#binarization.

Imputation

In Chapter 1, *Introduction to Healthcare Analytics*, we mentioned the importance of handling missing data. **Imputation** is one strategy for dealing with missing values in which missing values are filled in with estimates that are derived based on the data that is present. In healthcare, two common types of imputation are **zero imputation**, in which missing data is taken to be zero (for example, if a particular diagnosis has a value of NULL, most likely that is because it is not present in the patient chart) and **mean imputation**, in which the missing data is taken to be the mean of the distribution of the present data (for example, if a patient has a missing age, we can impute it as 40). We demonstrated various imputation methods in Chapter 4, *Computing Foundations – Databases*, and we will write our own custom functions for performing imputation in Chapter 7, *Making Predictive Models in Healthcare*.

Scikit-learn comes with an Imputer class for performing different types of imputation. You can see details on how it is used at http://scikit-learn.org/stable/modules/preprocessing.html#imputation-of-missing-values.

Feature-selection

In machine learning, there is often a misconception that the more data you have, the better off you are. This is usually true with observations (for example, the number of rows in the dataset). However, with features, more isn't always better. In some cases, the performance may be paradoxically better with fewer features, because multiple features with high correlation are biasing the predictions, or because there are more features present than the number of observations.

In other cases, the performance may be the same or infinitesimally worse with, say, half the features, but the smaller number of features may be desirable for a number of reasons, including time considerations, memory availability, or ease of explanation and interpretation to other non-technical stakeholders. In any case, it is almost always a good idea to perform some feature selection on the data. Even if you don't wish to remove any features, performing feature selection and ranking the feature importance can give you great insight into your model and understanding its predictive behavior and performance.

There are a number of classes and functions in the `sklearn.feature_selection` module that are built for feature selection, and different sets of classes correspond to different methods of performing feature selection. For example, univariate feature selection involves measuring the statistical dependency between each predictor variable and the target variable, and this can be done using the `SelectKBest` or `SelectPercentile` classes, among others. The `VarianceThreshold` class removes features that have a low variance across observations, for example, those features that are almost always zero. And the `SelectFromModel` class prunes features that don't meet a certain strength requirement (in terms of either coefficient or feature importance) after the model has been fit.

For a full list of the feature selection classes in scikit-learn, you can visit `http://scikit-learn.org/stable/modules/feature_selection.html#univariate-feature-selection`.

Machine learning algorithms

Machine learning algorithms provide a mathematical framework for making predictions for new observations. scikit-learn supports dozens of different ML algorithms that have different strengths and weaknesses. We will discuss some of these algorithms and their corresponding scikit-learn API functionality briefly here. We will use some of these algorithms in `Chapter 7`, *Making Predictive Models in Healthcare*.

Generalized linear models

As we discussed in `Chapter 3`, *Machine Learning Foundations*, a **linear model** can be thought of casually as a weighted combination of features (for example, a weighted sum) to predict a target value. The features are determined by the observations; the weights of each feature are determined by the model. Linear regression predicts a continuous variable, while logistic regression can be thought of as an extended form of linear regression in which the predicted target undergoes a **logit transformation** to be converted to a variable that has a range between zero and one. Such a transformation is useful for performing binary classification tasks such as when there are two possible outcomes.

In scikit-learn, these two algorithms are represented by the `sklearn.linear_model.LogisticRegression` and `sklearn.linear_model.LinearRegression` classes. We will demonstrate logistic regression in `Chapter 7`, *Making Predictive Models in Healthcare*.

Ensemble methods

Ensemble methods involve making predictions using combinations of different ML models. For example, a **random forest** is a collection of decision tree classifiers that have been decorrelated from each other by choosing and using specific feature sets for each tree. Additionally, **AdaBoost** is an algorithm that fits many weak learners on the data to make effective predictions. These algorithms are supported by the `sklearn.ensemble` module.

Additional machine learning algorithms

Some other popular machine learning algorithms include the Naive Bayes algorithm, k-nearest neighbors, neural networks, decision trees, and support vector machines. These are supported in scikit-learn by the `sklearn.naive_bayes`, `sklearn.neighbors`, `sklearn.neural_network`, `sklearn.tree`, and `sklearn.svm` modules, respectively. In `Chapter 7`, *Making Predictive Models in Healthcare*, we will make neural network models on a clinical dataset.

Performance assessment

Lastly, once we make our model using our desired algorithm, it is important to measure its performance. The `sklearn.metrics` module is useful for this. As discussed in `Chapter 3`, *Machine Learning Foundations*, the confusion matrix is particularly important for classification tasks, and it is supported by the `sklearn.metrics.confusion_matrix()` function. Determining the receiver operating characteristic (ROC) curve and calculating the **area under the curve** (**AUC**) can be accomplished using the `sklearn.metrics.roc_curve()` and `sklearn.metrics.roc_auc_score()` functions, respectively. Precision-recall curves are an alternative to the ROC curve that are important for imbalanced datasets, and they are supported by the `sklearn.metrics.precision_recall_curve()` function.

Additional analytics libraries

Here we mention three important packages that are frequently used for analytics: NumPy, SciPy, and matplotlib.

NumPy and SciPy

NumPy (`www.numpy.org`) is Python's matrix library. Using `numpy.array()` and similar constructs, large matrices can be created and various mathematical operations (including matrix addition and multiplication) can be performed on them. NumPy also has many functions for manipulating the shapes of matrices. Another feature of NumPy is the presence of familiar mathematical functions such as `sin()`, `cos()`, and `exp()`.

SciPy (`www.scipy.org`) is a toolbox that contains many advanced mathematical modules. Its machine-learning-related subpackages include `cluster`, `stats`, `sparse`, and `optimize`. SciPy is an important package that enables scientific computing in Python.

matplotlib

matplotlib (`https://matplotlib.org`) is a popular Python 2-D plotting library. According to its website, one "can generate plots, histograms, power spectra, bar charts, error charts, scatterplots, and so on, with just a few lines of code." Its plotting library comes with a myriad of options and features to enable a high degree of customization.

Summary

In this chapter, we took a whirlwind tour of the base Python language, along with two Python libraries that are important for performing analytics: pandas, and scikit-learn. We have now completed the foundational chapters of this book.

In `Chapter  6`, *Measuring Healthcare Quality*, we will dive into some real-world healthcare provider performance data and analyze it using pandas.

6
Measuring Healthcare Quality

This chapter is intended for all audiences and will show you how healthcare providers are evaluated and rewarded/penalized under current value-based programs in the US. We will look at examples of actual provider data that's been downloaded from the web and wrangle it all using Python to extract the information we need. By the end of this chapter, you will be able to locate provider-based data on a given program of interest and manipulate it in `pandas` to identify those providers who are high-performing and those who could benefit from an analytic solution.

Introduction to healthcare measures

A **healthcare measure** is a calculation made on the care activities of a provider that indicates the level of quality provided by the caregiver. As providers are increasingly being rewarded based on the quality rather than the quantity of services they provide, healthcare measures are playing a more important role in determining which care providers are rewarded or penalized. The **Centers for Medicare and Medicaid Services (CMS)** is just one of the federal-level agencies in the United States that publishes standardized measures; in addition, states publish measures as well. Providers calculate the measures using the data of their own patients and then submit their calculations to be audited by the issuing agency. The results partially determine how the providers are reimbursed by the agency.

A typical measure in healthcare is usually a ratio or percentage that correlates with care quality. There are typically two parts that make up a measure: a **numerator** and a **denominator**. The denominator is some quantification of the eligible population or number of encounters that were seen by the provider during a specific time range. Determining the denominator usually involves applying **inclusion criteria** and/or **exclusion criteria** to the overall provider population to reach the desired measurement population or encounter pool. Once the denominator is determined, the numerator is calculated based on the number of items in the denominator that received a certain positive or negative outcome or event.

This outcome or event is usually suggested by basic and/or clinical research as being a recommended part of patient care (or a marker for adverse care). Finally, dividing the numerator by the denominator yields the final percentage. This percentage may be used on a standalone basis or may be integrated into more complex formulas and weighting schemes with other measures to determine an overall quality score.

For example, an agency that wishes to measure the quality of diabetes care provided by outpatient facilities in a state could start composing a measure by surveying the literature for diabetes care recommendations. Among other things, diabetes patients are supposed to receive multiple foot examinations (to check for ulcers and nerve damage) and hemoglobin-A1c tests (to check for elevated blood glucose) during each year. To calculate the denominator, the inclusion criteria are that the patient has received an ICD code diagnosis of diabetes mellitus at least once in the past year. The agency only wants to consider the standard adult population; therefore, children less than 18 years of age and elderly adults greater than 65 years of age will be excluded. One clinic may have 4,000 patients overall, of which 500 meet these criteria; 500 is then the denominator for this measure. There are then two numerators to calculate:

- The number of these patients who received at least three foot exams in the past year
- The number of these patients who received at least two HgbA1c tests during the past year

For example, let's say that the numbers for our clinic are 350 and 400, respectively. The final measures are 350/500 = 0.70 for diabetic foot exam performance and 400/500 = 0.80 for diabetic blood work measurement. These can then be averaged together to give an overall rating of 0.75 for diabetes care at this clinic.

Measures have their share of problems; no measure is above loopholes that allow providers to manipulate their measurement scores without really improving care. Also, many measures may unfairly penalize providers who may have had patients act against medical advice or refuse proper treatment. However, if care quality is to be rewarded, then there must be a way to quantify care quality, and measures in healthcare are an important means of achieving that.

US Medicare value-based programs

In Chapter 2, *Healthcare Foundations*, we discussed that a **fee-for-service** (**FFS**) reimbursement model has been used in medicine, in which physicians are reimbursed by the volume of care they provided rather than the value of that care. More recently, there has been a push toward rewarding providers based on the quality of care rather than the quantity of care given.

In order to facilitate the movement from FFS reimbursement to value-based reimbursement, the CMS has implemented value-based programs. These programs reward or penalize providers for the quality of care that they provide to Medicare patients. In 2018, there are a total of eight such programs. They are the following:

- **The Hospital Value-Based Purchasing (HVBP) program**
- **The Hospital Readmission Reduction (HRR) program**
- **The Hospital Acquired Conditions (HAC) program**
- **The End-Stage Renal Disease (ESRD) quality initiative program**
- **The Skilled Nursing Facility Value-Based Program (SNFVBP)**
- **The Home Health Value-Based Program (HHVBP)**
- **Alternative Payment Models (APMs)**
- **The Merit-Based Incentive Payment System (MIPS)**

In the following sections, we will take a detailed look at these programs.

The Hospital Value-Based Purchasing (HVBP) program

The HVBP program rewards hospitals with incentive payments for the quality of care they give to Medicare patients. The HVBP program was enacted through the Affordable Care Act in 2010 and began in 2012.

Domains and measures

In 2018, there are approximately 20 measures in the HVBP program that span four different domains of hospital care quality. The list is ever expanding and will include approximately 25 measures by 2023. Let's take a look at each domain and measure here.

The clinical care domain

The clinical care domain measures clinical care quality predominantly by using mortality measures. The **mortality rate** refers to the patient death rate for a specific disease. There are five mortality measures used in this domain (listed here). The sixth measure is the complications rate for the total hip/knee arthroplasty (a.k.a. replacement) procedure:

- **MORT-30-AMI**: 30-day mortality for patients that have an acute myocardial infarction
- **MORT-30-HF**: 30-day mortality for patients that have heart failure
- **MORT-30-PN**: 30-day mortality for patients that have pneumonia
- **THA/TKA**: The number of THA/TKA procedures with complications
- **MORT-30-COPD**: 30-day mortality for patients that have COPD
- **MORT-30-CABG**: 30-day mortality for patients that undergo coronary artery bypass grafting

The patient- and caregiver-centered experience of care domain

The measures in the patient- and caregiver-centered experience of care domain are determined using information from the **Hospital Consumer Assessment of Healthcare Providers and Systems (HCAHPS)** survey. The HCAHPS survey is administered to a random sample of Medicare patients shortly after they are discharged from the hospital. More than a dozen questions focus on the eight measures listed here:

- Communication with nurses
- Communication with doctors
- Responsiveness of hospital staff
- Communication about medicines
- Cleanliness and quietness of the hospital environment
- Discharge information
- Overall rating of hospital
- Three-item care transition

Safety domain

The measures in this domain evaluate the safeness of hospitals for incidents such as adverse events and nosocomial infections. All of the measures in this domain are described in the later section on the HAC program (except for the PC-01 measure, which is described as follows):

- **AHRQ Composite (PSI-90)**: Please see the section on the HAC program for a detailed description.
- **Catheter-associated urinary tract infection (CAUTI)**: Please see the section on the HAC program for a detailed description.
- **Central line-associated bloodstream infection (CLABSI)**: Please see the section on the HAC program for a detailed description.
- **Clostridium difficile infection (CDI)**: Please see the section on the HAC program for a detailed description.
- **Methicillin-resistant Staphylococcus aureus infection (MRSA)**: Please see the section on the HAC program for a detailed description.
- **Surgical site infection (SSI)**: Please see the section on the HAC program for a detailed description.
- **PC-01 – Elective delivery prior to 39 weeks completed gestation**: Guidelines recommend that pregnancies are delivered as close as possible to 40 weeks.

Efficiency and cost reduction domain

The four measures in this domain examine the cost of care associated with each hospital. One measure (MSPB) relates to overall spending per patient; the three remaining measures pertain to spending for three specific conditions:

- **Medicare spending per beneficiary (MSPB)**
- **Acute myocardial infarction (AMI)** payment
- **Heart failure (HF)** payment
- **Pneumonia (PN)** payment

The Hospital Readmission Reduction (HRR) program

An alternative way to measure inpatient care quality is by using the readmission rate of hospitals for patients diagnosed with specific conditions during their initial (index) visits. It is expected that if patients are receiving proper care at the facility for those specific conditions, the readmission rate will be at or below an acceptable rate. Rates higher than a baseline rate are subject to lower reimbursements. Accordingly, the HRR program started in 2012. It is a program that provides incentive payments (up to 3% of their prospective inpatient payments from Medicare) to hospitals that reduce their inpatient 30-day readmission rates for the following conditions:

- **Acute myocardial infarction (AMI)**
- **Heart failure (HF)**
- **Pneumonia (PN)**
- **Chronic obstructive pulmonary disease (COPD)**
- **Total hip/knee arthoplasty** (replacement) **(THA/TKA)**
- **Coronary artery bypass graft surgery (CABG)**

The Hospital-Acquired Conditions (HAC) program

Yet another method for measuring inpatient care quality is to consider the number of nosocomial or iatrogenic illnesses at that facility. An **iatrogenic** condition is one that is caused by medical examination or treatment, while a **nosocomial** illness refers to an illness (usually an infection) originating at a hospital. Often, nosocomial infections are resistant to multiple antibiotics and are quite difficult to treat.

Under the HACRP, which started in 2014, hospitals are penalized 1% of their total Medicare payments if their patients are at a high risk of getting hospital-acquired infections. More specifically, hospitals that meet a certain score threshold based on how often their patients get five common healthcare-acquired infections and their AHRQ **Patient Safety Indicator (PSI)** 90 composite measure performance are eligible for a 1% reduction in Medicare reimbursement.

There are six measures comprising the HAC program that span two domains of care. Five of the six measures relate to infection rates for patients at hospitals. The sixth measure is a composite measure that looks at a variety of adverse patient safety events.

We will now take a more detailed look at the domains and measures.

The healthcare-acquired infections domain

The five healthcare-acquired infections are the following:

- **Catheter-associated urinary tract infection (CAUTI)**: A CAUTI occurs when a urinary catheter is inserted into the urethra using the improper (aseptic) technique, causing germs to colonize the urinary tract.
- **Central line-associated bloodstream infection (CLABSI)**: Similarly, a CLABSI occurs when a central line is improperly inserted into the body, causing germs to colonize the blood (**sepsis**).
- **Clostridium difficile infection (CDI)**: Sick patients who are being treated at hospitals for infections are highly susceptible to the clostridium difficile bacterium, which colonizes the GI tract after antibiotic therapy wipes out the native GI flora. Poor sanitary conditions and improper washing of hands among medical personnel are additional risk factors for C. difficile infection.
- **Methicillin-resistant *Staphylococcus aureus* (MRSA) infection**: MRSA is a common, particularly virulent strain of the S. aureus bacterium that commonly infects the skin and blood and is resistant to multiple antibiotics. It is commonly contracted in hospitals and can be avoided by rapid treatment and care to avoid transmission.
- **Surgical site infection (SSI)**: This results from improper sterilization techniques during or after surgeries, resulting in infection of the wound or surgical site.

The patient safety domain

The PSI 90 is a patient safety/complication measure produced by the **Agency for Healthcare Research and Quality (AHRQ)**. In 2017, it measured the patient safety and complication rates at hospitals using 10 measures:

- **PSI 03: Pressure Ulcer Rate**: Pressure ulcers are skin lesions that form when the patient has been in a bed in the same position for too long. It is commonly used as a measure of hospital care quality/neglect.

- **PSI 06: Iatrogenic Pneumothorax Rate**: A pneumothorax is a tear in the lung wall that causes air to fill up in the cavity surrounding the lung, preventing the patient from breathing properly. Some pneumothoraces are caused by hospital procedures and these are known as iatrogenic pneumothoraces.
- **PSI 08: In-Hospital Fall with Hip Fracture Rate**: Falls are common in elderly patients in hospitals, especially following an operation or procedure. There are certain precautions that can be taken to prevent falls in such patients, and hospitals that fail to do so are often labeled as providing poor quality of care.
- **PSI 09: Perioperative Hemorrhage or Hematoma Rate**: This measure gauges the amount of excessive bleeding that occurs when patients undergo procedures at the hospital.
- **PSI 10: Postoperative Acute Kidney Injury Rate**: Following procedures or operations, patients are at risk for injury to their kidneys due to decreased blood flow or harmful contrast agents for x-rays.
- **PSI 11: Postoperative Respiratory Failure Rate**: Following an operation, complications also include respiratory failure, which is a life-threatening condition that requires placing the patient on a ventilator under anesthesia and constant supervision in an **intensive care unit** (ICU). Respiratory failure incidents can be reduced by coaching patients to perform proper breathing exercises.
- **PSI 12: Perioperative Pulmonary Embolism (PE) or Deep Vein Thrombosis (DVT) Rate**: DVT is a blood clot that forms in the veins of the lower leg muscles. Pulmonary embolism is when the clot travels via the bloodstream to the lung and is a life-threatening complication. Many DVTs can be prevented by administering heparin and other treatments during the hospital stay and encouraging the patient to be active.
- **PSI 13: Postoperative Sepsis Rate**: This measure gauges how often patients that undergo operations at the hospital get infected after the operation. Sepsis is a life-threatening condition in which bacteria have colonized the bloodstream and are affecting organ function.
- **PSI 14: Postoperative Wound Dehiscence Rate**: Wound dehiscence is the failure of the operative site to close or heal correctly following the surgery. It is a sign of poor surgical procedure and/or poor nutrition following the surgery.
- **PSI 15: Unrecognized Abdominopelvic Accidental Puncture/Laceration Rate**: This measure gauges the frequency with which accidental punctures/lacerations occur during abdominal or pelvic surgery.

More information can be found at `https://www.qualityindicators.ahrq.gov/News/PSI90_Factsheet_FAQ.pdf`.

The End-Stage Renal Disease (ESRD) quality incentive program

The ESRD quality incentive program measures the quality of care received at dialysis centers by Medicare ESRD patients. There are a total of 16 measures: 11 clinical and 5 reporting, and they are detailed here:

- **NHSN bloodstream infection in hemodialysis outpatients**: Infections may occur from hemodialysis when the improper sterilization technique is used. This measure examines the number of infections that occur (the numerator) and compares it to the expected amount (the denominator).
- **ICH CAHPS**: This measure examines the quality of care received at the dialysis center through assessment of patient survey responses.
- **Standardized readmission ratio**: The standardized readmission ratio is the number of actual unplanned 30-day readmissions divided by the expected unplanned 30-day readmissions.
- **Kt/V dialysis adequacy measure – hemodialysis**: Kt/V is a formula that quantifies the dialysis treatment adequacy. The four Kt/V measures examine how many treatment sessions met a certain Kt/V threshold for different dialysis patient populations:
    - **Kt/V dialysis adequacy measure – Peritoneal dialysis**
    - **Kt/V dialysis adequacy measure – Pediatric hemodialysis**
    - **Kt/V dialysis adequacy measure – Pediatric peritoneal dialysis**
- **Standardized transfusion ratio**: This measure compares the number of actual versus expected red blood cell transfusions in dialysis patients (blood transfusions are undesirable consequences of dialysis).
- **Vascular access – Fistula**: The vascular access measures quantify whether or not proper access was provided to the patient's bloodstream. The Fistula measure evaluates how many arteriovenous fistula sites used two needles for access.

- **Vascular access – Catheter** - The Catheter measure determines how many of the catheters have been present in the patient for more than 90 days, which is an infection risk.
- **Hypercalcemia**: This measure looks at how many months for which patients experienced hypercalcemia, an adverse effect of dialysis.
- **Mineral metabolism reporting**: The five reporting measures examine how well various aspects of the dialysis patient's care were reported by each facility. The measures examine mineral metabolism reporting, anemia management reporting, pain assessment, depression screening, and flu vaccine for personnel reporting:
    - Anemia management reporting
    - Pain assessment and follow-up reporting
    - Clinical depression screening and follow-up reporting
    - Flu vaccine for personnel reporting

The Skilled Nursing Facility Value-Based Program (SNFVBP)

The SNFVBP is scheduled to start in 2019. It will base Medicare reimbursement from the government to SNFs partially on two outcome-related measures:

- The 30-day all-cause readmission rate
- The 30-day potentially preventable readmission rate

The rates apply to residents of SNFs who are admitted to other hospitals. When this program begins SNFs could benefit from collaborating with machine learning practitioners who predict which patients are at risk for readmission.

More information about the SNFVBP can be found at the following link: https://www.cms.gov/Medicare/Quality-Initiatives-Patient-Assessment-Instruments/Value-Based-Programs/Other-VBPs/SNF-VBP.html.

The Home Health Value-Based Program (HHVBP)

The HHVBP was started in January 2016 in nine of the 50 US states. It provides payment adjustments to Medicare-certified **Home Health Agencies** (**HHAs**) based on the quality of their care. The program will use 22 measures to gauge the quality of care provided by the HHAs. These measures include survey, process, and outcome measures, and include those for ED utilization and unplanned hospitalizations.

The Merit-Based Incentive Payment System (MIPS)

MIPS is a value-based program for individual and group outpatient physician practices. It is a program that started in 2017, and it was enacted by the MACRA Act of 2015. Together with the APMs program, MIPS comprises Medicare's **Quality Payment Program** (**QPP**). It replaces and consolidates previous value-based programs, such as the **Physician Quality Reporting System** (**PQRS**) and the **Value Modifier (VM)** program. Provider groups are required to participate in MIPS if they bill a certain amount from or have a certain amount of Medicare patients. In MIPS, providers are evaluated based on four categories:

- Quality
- Advancing care information
- Improvement activities
- Cost

The breakdown for determining a practice's final MIPS score for 2017 is the following: 60% quality, 25% advancing care information, and 15% improvement activities. Beginning in 2018, the cost will also determine the final MIPS score.

Let's take a detailed look at the four performance categories.

Quality

For the quality category, providers choose six measures from a list that includes 271 measures as of 2018. Examples of measures include *Acute Otitis Externa (ear infection): Topical Therapy* and *Varicose Vein Treatment with Saphenous Ablation: Outcome Survey*. All medical specialties are represented so that providers can choose the measures most suitable for them. The providers then collect and submit the data corresponding to the specifications of the measure.

Advancing care information

This category includes measures that are related to advancing health information technology. There are 15 measures in this category. Examples of measures include reconciling patient information, reporting clinical data to a data registry, and prescribing medication electronically.

Improvement activities

For this category, providers must demonstrate that they have taken steps to improve their practices in the areas of care coordination, patient engagement, and patient safety. Providers must demonstrate that they have completed up to four measures for 3 months.

Cost

For the final category, the cost of care will be determined from claims data, and providers who provide the most efficient care will be rewarded. The inclusion of this category into the MIPS final score will begin in 2018.

Other value-based programs

Aside from the value-based programs discussed above that are administered by the CMS, there are also additional programs that are administered by other agencies. Let's take a look at those here.

The Healthcare Effectiveness Data and Information Set (HEDIS)

The HEDIS is used to measure the quality of health insurance plans. It is administered by the **National Committee for Quality Assurance (NCQA)**. The HEDIS includes approximately 90 measures that cover virtually every medical specialty. Many of the measures share features with those already discussed previously, or with the 271 measures found in the clinical care category of MIPS.

State measures

In 2018, almost every state has some form of value-based programs and incentives. Often, these programs apply to Medicaid patients, since Medicaid is often administered at the state level. Many states also adopt federally published measures and tweak them for their own use. For example, the State of Georgia funds the Georgia Families program (`https://dch.georgia.gov/georgia-families`), which allows Georgia Medicaid patients to choose health insurance plans. It sets goals and measures effectiveness by using HEDIS measures.

Comparing dialysis facilities using Python

In the previous section, we outlined the value-based incentive programs implemented by the CMS. One of those programs was the ESRD quality incentive program, which financially rewards dialysis facilities based on the quality of care that they provide to Medicare patients with ESRD. We described 16 measures by which each ESRD case is evaluated.

In this section, we will download the data published by the CMS on dialysis center performance across the US. We will use Python commands to wrangle this data to extract the information we can use to find out which centers are performing well and which ones may benefit from an analytic solution. Proper targeting of marketing and sales efforts will increase the efficiency of analytic solutions.

Downloading the data

To download the dialysis facility comparison data, complete the following steps.

1. Navigate to the following URL: `https://data.medicare.gov/data/dialysis-facility-compare`.
2. Locate the blue button on the page that is labeled **DOWNLOAD CSV FLAT FILES (REVISED) NOW**. (To get the right year, you may have to select the **GET ARCHIVED DATA** button instead). Click the button. A `.zip` file will begin to download.
3. Extract the `.zip` file using the appropriate Windows/Mac program or Linux command.
4. Take note of the directory and path for the file named `ESRD QIP - Complete QIP Data - Payment Year 2018.csv`.

Importing the data into your Jupyter Notebook session

To import the `.csv` file into a Jupyter Notebook session, open the Jupyter Notebook program as we did in `Chapter 1`, *Introduction to Healthcare Analytics*. Open a new notebook. Then, in the first cell, type the following (substituting in your file path for that which is shown here) and hit the **Play** button:

```
import pandas as pd

df = pd.read_csv(
    'C:\\Users\\Vikas\\Desktop\\Bk\\Data\\DFCompare_Revised_FlatFiles\\' +
    'ESRD QIP - Complete QIP Data - Payment Year 2018.csv', header=0
)
```

The preceding code uses the `read_csv()` function of the `pandas` library to import the `.csv` file as a DataFrame. The `header` parameter tells the notebook that the first line contains column names.

Notice that the backslashes appear in groups of two. That is because \ is an escape character in Python. Also, notice that the filename was too long to fit in one line. In Python, statements can encompass multiple lines without special treatment as long as the break is enclosed by parentheses and certain other punctuation.

Exploring the data rows and columns

Let's explore the data. In the next cell, type the following:

```
print('Number of rows: ' + str(df.shape[0]))
print('Number of columns: ' + str(df.shape[1]))
```

The output is as follows:

```
Number of rows: 6825
Number of columns: 153
```

In the 2018 file, there should be 6,825 rows and 153 columns. Each row corresponds to a dialysis facility in the United States. Here we used the `shape` attribute of DataFrames, which returns a tuple containing the number of rows and number of columns.

We can also get a visualization of what the DataFrame looks like by using the `head()` function. The `head()` function takes a parameter, n, that tells it how many rows of the DataFrame to print. In the next cell, type the following and press **Play**:

```
print(df.head(n=5))
```

The output is as follows:

```
                     Facility Name  CMS Certification Number (CCN)  \
0        CHILDRENS HOSPITAL DIALYSIS                           12306
1                    FMC CAPITOL CITY                          12500
2                    GADSDEN DIALYSIS                          12501
3   TUSCALOOSA UNIVERSITY DIALYSIS                            12502
4                     PCD MONTGOMERY                           12505

. . .
```

You should see some of the columns for the first five rows, such as facility name, address, and measure scores. The `head()` function prints an abbreviated list of columns, selecting some from the beginning of the `.csv` file and some from the end, separated by an ellipsis.

Let's get a complete list of all `153` columns. Type the following and press *Enter*:

```
print(df.columns)
```

The output is as follows:

```
Index(['Facility Name', 'CMS Certification Number (CCN)', 'Alternate CCN
1',
        'Address 1', 'Address 2', 'City', 'State', 'Zip Code', 'Network',
        'VAT Catheter Measure Score',
        ...
        'STrR Improvement Measure Rate/Ratio',
        'STrR Improvement Period Numerator',
        'STrR Improvement Period Denominator', 'STrR Measure Score Applied',
        'National Avg STrR Measure Score', 'Total Performance Score',
        'PY2018 Payment Reduction Percentage', 'CMS Certification Date',
        'Ownership as of December 31, 2016', 'Date of Ownership Record
Update'],
        dtype='object', length=153)
```

Here, we use the `columns` attribute of a DataFrame, which gives us access to the column names of the DataFrame as a list. Unfortunately, again, `pandas` abbreviates the output so we can't see all 153 columns. To do so, we need to be more explicit and print each column using a `for` loop:

```
for column in df.columns:
    print(column)
```

The output is as follows:

```
Facility Name
CMS Certification Number (CCN)
Alternate CCN 1
Address 1
Address 2
City
State
Zip Code
Network
VAT Catheter Measure Score
...
```

Now you'll see all 153 column names. Use the scrollbar to skim through all of them. You'll notice that each of the 16 measures has several columns associated with it, and there are also additional columns like demographic data and total performance scores.

Now that we have gained a rough overview of our dataset, we can move on to more in-depth analysis.

Exploring the data geographically

For the remainder of this section, we will be using a lot of SQL-like operations in `pandas` to manipulate the data. Here is a conversion table between SQL and `pandas` for some basic operations:

Action	SQL syntax	pandas function	SQL example	pandas example
Selecting columns	SELECT	[[]]	SELECT col1, col2, FROM df;	df[['col1','col2']]
Selecting rows	WHERE	loc(),iloc()	SELECT * FROM df WHERE age=50;	df.loc[df['age']==50]
Sorting by a column	ORDER BY	sort_values()	SELECT * FROM df ORDER BY col1;	df.sort_values('col1')
Aggregating by a column	GROUP BY	groupby()	SELECT COUNT(*) FROM df GROUP BY col1;	df.groupby('col1').size()
Limiting the number of rows	LIMIT	head()	SELECT * FROM df LIMIT 5;	df.head(n=5)

With these conversions in mind, we can begin to explore the data geographically.

For starters, 6,825 dialysis facilities is a lot. Let's try narrowing that down by state. First, we count the dialysis facilities in each state:

```
"""Equivalent SQL: SELECT COUNT(*)
                   FROM df
                   GROUP BY State;
"""
df_states = df.groupby('State').size()
print(df_states)
```

The output is as follows:

```
State
AK        9
AL      170
AR       69
AS        1
AZ      120
CA      625
CO       75
CT       49
DC       23
DE       27
...
```

You should see a table containing 50 rows (one per state, each containing the associated count).

Let's now sort the rows in descending order:

```
"""Equivalent SQL: SELECT COUNT(*) AS Count
                   FROM df
                   GROUP BY State
                   ORDER BY Count ASC;
"""
df_states = df.groupby('State').size().sort_values(ascending=False)
print(df_states)
```

The output is as follows:

```
State
CA    625
TX    605
FL    433
GA    345
OH    314
IL    299
PA    294
NY    274
NC    211
MI    211
...
```

Let's further refine our query by limiting the output to 10 states:

```
"""Equivalent SQL: SELECT COUNT(*) AS Count
                   FROM df
                   GROUP BY State
                   ORDER BY Count DESC
                   LIMIT 10;
"""
df_states =
df.groupby('State').size().sort_values(ascending=False).head(n=10)
print(df_states)
```

According to the results, California is the state with the most dialysis centers, followed by Texas. If we wanted to filter dialysis facilities based on state, we could do that by selecting the appropriate rows:

```
"""Equivalent SQL: SELECT *
                   FROM df
                   WHERE State='CA';
"""
df_ca = df.loc[df['State'] == 'CA']
print(df_ca)
```

Displaying dialysis centers based on total performance

Almost every exploration of such provider-centered data will include analyzing facilities based on their quality scores. We will dive into that next.

First, let's get a count on the different scores received by the dialysis facilities:

```
print(df.groupby('Total Performance Score').size())
```

The output is as follows:

```
Total Performance Score
10              10
100             30
11               2
12               2
13               1
14               3
15               1
...
95              15
96               2
97              11
98               8
99              12
No Score       276
Length: 95, dtype: int64
```

One thing to notice is that the `Total Performance Score` column is in a string rather than integer format, and so to do numerical sorting, we must first convert the column to integer format. Second, after running the preceding code, you'll notice that 276 dialysis facilities have a value of `No Score` for the `Total Performance Score` column. These rows must be eliminated before converting to integer format to avoid throwing an error.

In the following code, we first eliminate the `No Score` rows, and then we use the `to_numeric()` function of `pandas` to convert the string column to an integer column:

```
df_filt= df.loc[df['Total Performance Score'] != 'No Score']
df_filt['Total Performance Score'] = pd.to_numeric(
    df_filt['Total Performance Score']
)
```

Now, we create a new DataFrame that selects just a few columns that we are interested in and sorts them, with the worst performing centers at the top. Such a code block would be helpful for identifying the worst performing dialysis centers, for example. We display the first five results:

```
df_tps = df_filt[[
    'Facility Name',
    'State',
    'Total Performance Score'
]].sort_values('Total Performance Score')
print(df_tps.head(n=5))
```

The output is as follows:

```
                                   Facility Name State  \
5622    462320 PRIMARY CHILDREN'S DIALYSIS CENTER    UT
698                 PEDIATRIC DIALYSIS UNIT AT UCSF    CA
6766                    VITAL LIFE DIALYSIS CENTER    FL
4635    BELMONT COURT DIALYSIS - DOYLESTOWN CAMPUS    PA
3763                      WOODMERE DIALYSIS LLC    NY

      Total Performance Score
5622                        5
698                         7
6766                        8
4635                        8
3763                        9
```

Alternatively, if we wished to analyze the mean total performance of each state's dialysis centers, we could do that by using numpy.mean() in conjunction with groupby():

```
import numpy as np

df_state_means = df_filt.groupby('State').agg({
    'Total Performance Score': np.mean
})
print(df_state_means.sort_values('Total Performance Score',
ascending=False))
```

The output is as follows:

```
        Total Performance Score
State
ID                    73.178571
WY                    71.777778
HI                    70.500000
UT                    70.421053
CO                    70.173333
```

```
WA                    70.146067
ME                    70.058824
OR                    70.046154
KS                    69.480769
AZ                    68.905983
...
```

According to the results of this query, Idaho and Wyoming have the nation's best performing dialysis centers. You could also add a column including the number of dialysis centers in each state using the following modification:

```
import numpy as np

df_state_means = df_filt.groupby('State').agg({
    'Total Performance Score': np.mean,
    'State': np.size
})
print(df_state_means.sort_values('Total Performance Score',
ascending=False))
```

The output is as follows:

```
       Total Performance Score   State
State
ID                   73.178571     28
WY                   71.777778      9
HI                   70.500000     26
UT                   70.421053     38
CO                   70.173333     75
WA                   70.146067     89
ME                   70.058824     17
OR                   70.046154     65
KS                   69.480769     52
AZ                   68.905983    117
...
```

The results indicate that when considering only states that have at least 100 dialysis centers, Arizona has the best total performance.

Alternative analyses of dialysis centers

The code introduced in this section can be adjusted to conduct all different types of analyses on dialysis centers. For example, instead of measuring mean performance by `State`, perhaps you wish to measure mean performance by dialysis center owner. This can be done by changing the column by which you group in the most recent example. Or maybe you wish to look at an individual measure instead of `Total Performance Score`, which again can be accomplished by just changing a column in the code.

Now that we have analyzed provider performance using dialysis centers in our first example, we will take a look at a more complex dataset, the inpatient hospital performance dataset.

Comparing hospitals

In the previous example, we analyzed the performance of dialysis centers using Python. Dialysis centers are just one small part of the healthcare provider pool – a pool which also includes hospitals, outpatient offices, nursing homes, inpatient rehabilitation facilities, and hospice providers, for example. As you were downloading the dialysis facility comparison data from `https://data.medicare.gov`, you might have noticed the presence of performance data for these other facilities. We are going to now examine the data for a more complex facility type: the inpatient hospital. The Hospital Compare dataset includes data for three of the eight CMS value-based programs. It is a large dataset, and we are going to demonstrate some advanced Python and `pandas` features using this data.

Downloading the data

To download the Hospital Compare dataset, complete the following steps:

1. Navigate to `https://data.medicare.gov/data/hospital-compare`.
2. Locate the blue button on the page that is labeled **DOWNLOAD CSV FLAT FILES (REVISED) NOW**. (To get the right year, you may have to select the **GET ARCHIVED DATA** button instead). Click the button. A `.zip` file will begin to download.
3. Extract the `.zip` file using the appropriate Windows/Mac program or Linux command.
4. Take note of the path containing the extracted `.csv` files.

Importing the data into your Jupyter Notebook session

Notice that the extracted Hospital Compare folder includes 71 files, the vast majority of which are .csv files. That's a lot of tables! Let's import some of the tables into a Jupyter Notebook:

```
import pandas as pd

pathname =
'C:\\Users\\Vikas\\Desktop\\Bk\\Data\\Hospital_Revised_Flatfiles\\'

files_of_interest = [
    'hvbp_tps_11_07_2017.csv',
    'hvbp_clinical_care_11_07_2017.csv',
    'hvbp_safety_11_07_2017.csv',
    'hvbp_efficiency_11_07_2017.csv',
    'hvbp_hcahps_11_07_2017.csv'
]

dfs = {
    foi: pd.read_csv(pathname + foi, header=0) for foi in files_of_interest
}
```

The preceding code loads the tables pertaining to the HVBP measure into the Python session. There are five total tables, with four of the tables corresponding to the four domains of the measure, and one table representing the overall scores.

Note that instead of explicitly creating and importing five dataframes, we created a dictionary of dataframes using a comprehension. We covered dictionaries, lists, and comprehensions in the Python chapter. This saves a lot of typing in this cell and in upcoming cells.

Exploring the tables

Next, let's explore the tables and check the numbers of rows and columns in each:

```
for k, v in dfs.items():
    print(
        k + ' - Number of rows: ' + str(v.shape[0]) +
        ', Number of columns: ' + str(v.shape[1])
    )
```

The output is as follows:

```
hvbp_tps_11_07_2017.csv  -  Number of rows: 2808, Number of columns: 16
hvbp_clinical_care_11_07_2017.csv  -  Number of rows: 2808, Number of
columns: 28
hvbp_safety_11_07_2017.csv  -  Number of rows: 2808, Number of columns: 64
hvbp_efficiency_11_07_2017.csv  -  Number of rows: 2808, Number of columns:
14
hvbp_hcahps_11_07_2017.csv  -  Number of rows: 2808, Number of columns: 73
```

For the preceding cell, we used the `items()` method of dictionaries to iterate over each key-DataFrame pair in the dictionary of DataFrames.

The tables all have the same number of rows. Since each row corresponds to a hospital, it is safe to assume that the hospitals in all of the tables are the same (we will test that assumption shortly).

Any analysis we perform is limited due to the separation of the tables. Since all the hospitals are (assumed to be) the same, we can combine all the columns into one table. We will do that using the `merge()` function of `pandas`. Using `pandas merge()` is akin to using `SQL JOIN` (you learned about `SQL JOIN` in Chapter 4, *Computing Foundations – Databases*). The merge is performed by specifying a common ID column present in both of the tables on which the rows will be matched. To see whether there is a common ID column in the five HVBP tables, we can print out the column names of each table:

```
for v in dfs.values():
    for column in v.columns:
        print(column)
    print('\n')
```

If you scroll through the results, you'll notice the presence of the `Provider Number` column in all of the tables. `Provider Number` is a unique identifier that can be used to link the tables.

Merging the HVBP tables

Let's try joining two of the tables:

```
df_master = dfs[files_of_interest[0]].merge(
    dfs[files_of_interest[1]],
    on='Provider Number',
    how='left',
```

```
        copy=False
)

print(df_master.shape)
```

The output is as follows:

```
(2808, 43)
```

Our merge appears to have worked since the number of columns in `df_master` is the sum of the columns of first two DataFrames, minus one (the `on` column is not copied). Let's look at the columns of the new DataFrame:

```
print(df_master.columns)
```

The output is as follows:

```
Index(['Provider Number', 'Hospital Name_x', 'Address_x', 'City_x',
'State_x',
       'Zip Code', 'County Name_x',
       'Unweighted Normalized Clinical Care Domain Score',
       'Weighted Normalized Clinical Care Domain Score',
       'Unweighted Patient and Caregiver Centered Experience of Care/Care
Coordination Domain Score',
       'Weighted Patient and Caregiver Centered Experience of Care/Care
Coordination Domain Score',
       'Unweighted Normalized Safety Domain Score',
       'Weighted Safety Domain Score',
       'Unweighted Normalized Efficiency and Cost Reduction Domain Score',
       'Weighted Efficiency and Cost Reduction Domain Score',
       'Total Performance Score', 'Hospital Name_y', 'Address_y', 'City_y',
       'State_y', 'ZIP Code', 'County Name_y',
       'MORT-30-AMI Achievement Threshold', 'MORT-30-AMI Benchmark',
       'MORT-30-AMI Baseline Rate', 'MORT-30-AMI Performance Rate',
       'MORT-30-AMI Achievement Points', 'MORT-30-AMI Improvement Points',
       'MORT-30-AMI Measure Score', 'MORT-30-HF Achievement Threshold',
       'MORT-30-HF Benchmark', 'MORT-30-HF Baseline Rate',
       'MORT-30-HF Performance Rate', 'MORT-30-HF Achievement Points',
       'MORT-30-HF Improvement Points', 'MORT-30-HF Measure Score',
       'MORT-30-PN Achievement Threshold', 'MORT-30-PN Benchmark',
       'MORT-30-PN Baseline Rate', 'MORT-30-PN Performance Rate',
       'MORT-30-PN Achievement Points', 'MORT-30-PN Improvement Points',
       'MORT-30-PN Measure Score'],
      dtype='object')
```

The duplicate columns (Hospital Name, Address, City, and so on) had suffixes _x and _y added to their names in the joined table, to indicate which table they are from, confirming that the merge worked.

Let's use a for loop to join the three remaining tables to df_master:

```
for df in dfs.values():
    df.columns = [col if col not in ['Provider_Number'] else 'Provider
Number'
        for col in df.columns]

for num in [2,3,4]:
    df_master = df_master.merge(
        dfs[files_of_interest[num]],
        on='Provider Number',
        how='left',
        copy=False
    )
print(df_master.shape)
```

The output is as follows:

```
(2808, 191)
```

In this cell, first we use a loop to rename all columns from Provider_Number to Provider Number, so we can join the tables cleanly.

Then we use a loop to join each remaining table to df_master. The number of columns in the resulting table equals the sum of the columns of the tables, minus four.

To confirm that the merge worked, we can print the columns of our new table:

```
for column in df_master.columns:
    print(column)
```

Scrolling through the output confirms that all of the columns from the five tables are present.

We leave it to you to perform additional analyses on the dataset, using the code examples from the *Comparing dialysis facilities* section.

Summary

In this chapter, we have taken a look at some prominent value-based programs that are shaping the US healthcare industry today. We have seen how these programs quantify provider performance through the use of measures. Additionally, we have downloaded the data for comparing dialysis facilities and hospitals and worked through some code examples in Python to see how to analyze this data.

One might argue that the analysis in this chapter could be accomplished by using a spreadsheet application such as Microsoft Excel rather than programming. In Chapter 7, *Making Predictive Models in Healthcare*, we will train predictive models on a healthcare dataset to predict discharge status in the ED. As you will see, this type of analysis almost certainly requires writing code.

References

Data.Medicare.gov (2018). Retrieved April 28, 2018 from https://data.medicare.gov.

MIPS Overview (2018). Retrieved April 28, 2018, from https://qpp.cms.gov/mips/overview.

What are the value-based programs? (2017, November 9th). *Centers for Medicare and Medicaid Services*. Retrieved April 28, 2018, from https://www.cms.gov/Medicare/Quality-Initiatives-Patient-Assessment-Instruments/Value-Based-Programs/Value-Based-Programs.html.

7
Making Predictive Models in Healthcare

This chapter is intended for all audiences and is an integral part of this book. We will demonstrate how to build predictive models for healthcare using example data and an example machine learning problem. We will preprocess the data one feature at a time. By the end of this chapter, you will understand how to prepare and fit a machine learning model to a clinical dataset.

Introduction to predictive analytics in healthcare

In Chapter 1, *Introduction to Healthcare Analytics,* we discussed the three subcomponents of analytics: descriptive analytics, predictive analytics, and prescriptive analytics. Predictive and prescriptive analytics form the heart of healthcare's mission to improve care, cost, and outcomes. That is because if we can predict that an adverse event is likely in the future, we can divert our scarce resources toward preventing the adverse event from occurring.

What are some of the adverse events we can predict (and then prevent) in healthcare?

- **Deaths**: Obviously, any death that is preventable or foreseeable should be avoided. Once a death is predicted to occur, preventative actions may include directing more nurses toward that patient, hiring more consultants for the case, or speaking to the family about options earlier rather than later.
- **Adverse clinical events**: These are events that are not synonymous with deaths, but highly increase the chances of morbidity and mortality. Morbidity refers to complications, while mortality refers to death. Examples of adverse clinical events include heart attacks, heart failure exacerbations, COPD exacerbations, pneumonia, and falls. Patients in which adverse events are likely could be candidates for more nursing care or for prophylactic therapies.

- **Readmissions**: Readmissions don't present an obvious danger to patients; however, they are costly, so preventable readmissions should, therefore, be avoided. Furthermore, readmission reduction is highly incentivized by the Centers for Medicare and Medicaid Services, as we saw in Chapter 6, *Measuring Healthcare Quality*. Preventative actions include assigning social workers and case managers to high-risk patients to assure that they are following up with outpatient providers and buying needed prescriptions.
- **High utilization**: Predicting patients who are likely to incur high amounts of medical spending again could potentially reduce costs by assigning more care members to their team and ensuring frequent outpatient check-ins and follow-ups.

Now that we've answered the "What?" question, the next question is, "How?" In other words, how do we make predictions about which care providers can act?

- **First, we need data**: The provider should send you their historical patient data. The data can be claims data, clinical transcripts, a dump of EHR records, or some combination of these. Whatever the type of data, it should eventually be able to be molded into a tabular format, in which each row represents a patient/encounter and each column represents a particular feature of that patient/encounter.
- **Using some of the data, we train a predictive model**: In Chapter 3, *Machine Learning Foundations*, we learned about what exactly we are doing when we train predictive models, and how the general modeling pipeline works.
- **Using some of the data, we test our model's performance**: Assessing the performance of our model is important for setting the expectations of the provider as to how accurate the model is.
- **We then deploy the model into a production environment and provide live predictions for patients on a routine basis**: At this stage, there should be a periodic flow of data from the provider to the analytics firm. The firm then responds with regularly scheduled predictions on those patients.

In the remainder of the chapter, we will go through the "How?" of building a predictive model for healthcare. First, we will describe our mock modeling task. Then, we will describe and obtain the publicly available dataset. After that, we will preprocess the dataset and train predictive models using different machine learning algorithms. Finally, we will assess the performance of our model. While we will not be using our models to make actual predictions on live data, we will describe the steps necessary for doing so.

Our modeling task – predicting discharge statuses for ED patients

Every year, millions of patients use emergency department facilities across the nation. The resources of these facilities have to be managed properly—if there is a large influx of patients at any given time, the staff and the available rooms should be increased accordingly. The mismatch between resources and patient influx could lead to wasted money and suboptimal care.

In this context, we introduce our example modeling task —predicting discharge statuses for patients presenting to the emergency room. The discharge status refers to whether patients are admitted to the hospital or sent home. Usually, the more serious cases are admitted to the hospital. Therefore, we are attempting to predict the outcome of the ED visit early on in the patient stay.

With such a model, the workflow of the hospital could be greatly improved, as well as resource flow. Many previous academic studies have looked at this problem (for an example, see Cameron et al., 2015).

You may be wondering why we didn't pick a different modeling task, such as readmission modeling or predicting CHF exacerbations. For one thing, the publicly available clinical data is very limited. The dataset that we chose is an ED dataset; there are no publicly available inpatient datasets available that are free to download without registering. Nevertheless, the task that we have chosen will serve our purposes in demonstrating how predictive healthcare models can be built.

Obtaining the dataset

In this section, we will provide step-by-step instructions for obtaining the data and its associated documentation.

The NHAMCS dataset at a glance

The dataset we have chosen for this book is part of the **National Hospital Ambulatory Medical Care Survey** (**NHAMCS**) public use data. It is survey data published and maintained by the US **Center for Disease Control and Prevention** (**CDC**). The home page for this data set is `https://www.cdc.gov/nchs/ahcd/ahcd_questionnaires.htm`.

- The NHAMCS data is survey-based data; it is populated by surveys sent to patients and healthcare providers that were seen in the hospital for encounters.
- The data files are in fixed-width format. In other words, they are text files in which each row is on a distinct line, and columns are each a set number of characters long. Information about the character length of each feature is available in the corresponding NHAMCS documentation.
- There are different sets of files depending on whether the data is from outpatient encounters or emergency department visits. We will be using the ED format in this chapter.
- The data comes with detailed documentation about the content of each feature.
- Each row of the data represents a distinct ED patient encounter.

See the following table for a summary of the emergency department data files from NHAMCS that we will be using throughout this book:

Filename	Data type and year	Number of rows (encounters)	Number of columns (features)	Broad feature categories
ED2013	ED Encounters; 2013	24,777	579	Visit date and information, Demographics, Tobacco, Arrival means, Payment, Vital signs, Triage, ED relationship, Reason for visit, Injury, Diagnoses, Chronic conditions, Services performed, Providers seen, Disposition, Hospital admission, Imputed data, ED information, Socioeconomic data

Downloading the NHAMCS data

The raw data files and supporting documentation are accessible from the CDC NHAMCS home page: `https://www.cdc.gov/nchs/ahcd/ahcd_questionnaires.htm` (the following screenshot). We recommend downloading all of the files into a directory dedicated to this book and its associated files. Also, remember which directories where they are downloaded to:

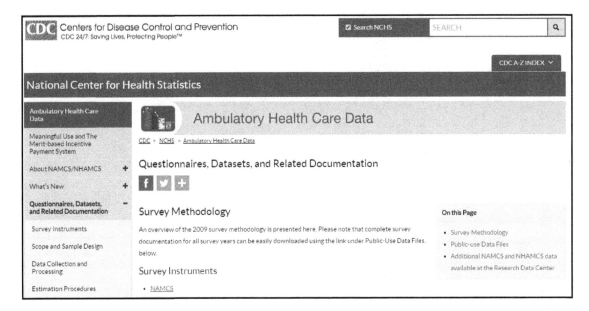

Downloading the ED2013 file

The ED2013 file contains the raw data. To download it:

1. Navigate to the CDC NHAMCS homepage: `https://www.cdc.gov/nchs/ahcd/ahcd_questionnaires.htm`.
2. Scroll to the middle of the page, to the **Public-use Data Files: Downloadable Data Files** heading.
3. Click on the link for NHAMCS. It should take you to the CDC's FTP website (`ftp://ftp.cdc.gov/pub/Health_Statistics/NCHS/Datasets/NHAMCS`). This website is pictured in the following screenshot.
4. Find the file named `ED2013.zip`. Click on it. The file will start to download.
5. Navigate to the file in your File Explorer and unzip it. In the unzipped directory, you should see a file named `ED2013` with no extension. This is the data file.

6. Move the ED2013 data file to the directory associated with the book-related files:

Index of /pub/Health_Statistics/NCHS/Datasets/NHAMCS

Name	Size	Date Modified
[parent directory]		
AS2010.zip	795 kB	1/19/17, 5:57:00 AM
ED1992.exe	1.4 MB	2/10/09, 7:00:00 PM
ed1993.exe	1.1 MB	9/27/04, 8:00:00 PM
ed1994.exe	1.0 MB	9/27/04, 8:00:00 PM
ed1995.exe	1008 kB	8/29/02, 8:00:00 PM
ed1996.exe	1.0 MB	8/29/02, 8:00:00 PM
ed1997.exe	1.3 MB	9/15/02, 8:00:00 PM
ed1998.exe	1.4 MB	9/15/02, 8:00:00 PM
ed1999.exe	1.3 MB	9/15/02, 8:00:00 PM
ed2000.exe	1.6 MB	9/15/02, 8:00:00 PM
ED2001.EXE	2.3 MB	8/28/03, 8:00:00 PM
ED2002.EXE	2.8 MB	12/9/04, 7:00:00 PM
ED2003.exe	3.1 MB	7/18/05, 8:00:00 PM
ED2004.exe	2.9 MB	8/3/06, 8:00:00 PM
ED2005.exe	3.3 MB	8/28/07, 8:00:00 PM
ED2006.exe	3.8 MB	7/10/08, 8:00:00 PM
ED2007.exe	3.5 MB	7/14/10, 8:00:00 PM
ED2008.exe	3.1 MB	4/28/11, 8:00:00 PM
ED2009.exe	3.2 MB	3/13/12, 8:00:00 PM
ED2010.exe	3.0 MB	10/15/12, 8:00:00 PM
ed2011.zip	2.5 MB	6/11/15, 8:00:00 PM
ED2012.zip	2.5 MB	4/17/16, 8:00:00 PM
ED2013.zip	2.1 MB	11/2/16, 8:00:00 PM
ED2014.zip	2.4 MB	4/10/17, 1:16:00 PM
OPD1992.exe	1.2 MB	2/10/09, 7:00:00 PM

Downloading the list of survey items – body_namcsopd.pdf

1. Navigate to the CDC NHAMCS home page: `https://www.cdc.gov/nchs/ahcd/ahcd_questionnaires.htm`.

2. Scroll to the middle of the page, to the **List of Survey Items, 1973-2012** heading.

3. Click on the link labeled **NAMCS and NHAMCS Survey Content Brochure [Revised 11/2012]**.

4. The link should take you to a PDF page at the `https://www.cdc.gov/nchs/data/ahcd/body_namcsopd.pdf` URL. This is the list of survey items.

5. Use your browser to download the file. Then use your File Explorer to move it to the desired directory.

Downloading the documentation file – doc13_ed.pdf

1. Navigate to the CDC NHAMCS home page: `https://www.cdc.gov/nchs/ahcd/ahcd_questionnaires.htm`.

2. Scroll to the middle of the page, to the **Downloadable Documentation** heading.

3. Click on the link for NHAMCS (1992-2014). It should take you to the CDC's documentation FTP website (`ftp://ftp.cdc.gov/pub/Health_Statistics/NCHS/Dataset_Documentation/NHAMCS`). This website is pictured in the following screenshot.

4. Find the file named `doc13_ed.pdf`. Click on it. A PDF should open in your browser. This PDF file contains the documentation for the ED2013 data file.

5. Use your browser to download the file. Then use your File Explorer to move it to the desired directory:

Index of /pub/Health_Statistics/NCHS/Dataset_Documentation/NHAMCS

Name	Size	Date Modified
[parent directory]		
.cache	0 B	9/3/98, 8:00:00 PM
.cache~	0 B	9/3/98, 8:00:00 PM
doc00.pdf	559 kB	9/15/02, 8:00:00 PM
doc01.pdf	752 kB	1/4/04, 7:00:00 PM
doc02.pdf	783 kB	7/28/04, 8:00:00 PM
doc03.pdf	1.4 MB	3/22/06, 7:00:00 PM
doc04.pdf	1.6 MB	8/3/06, 8:00:00 PM
doc05.pdf	875 kB	12/4/11, 7:00:00 PM
doc06.pdf	1.2 MB	12/4/11, 7:00:00 PM
doc07.pdf	1.3 MB	7/10/12, 8:00:00 PM
doc08.pdf	1.6 MB	7/10/12, 8:00:00 PM
doc09.pdf	1.5 MB	4/26/12, 8:00:00 PM
doc10_as.pdf	455 kB	1/19/17, 6:17:00 AM
doc11.pdf	2.5 MB	3/24/16, 8:00:00 PM
doc12_ed.pdf	1.1 MB	4/17/16, 8:00:00 PM
doc13_ed.pdf	1.0 MB	11/2/16, 8:00:00 PM
doc14_ed.pdf	837 kB	6/5/17, 11:59:00 AM
doc2010.pdf	1.5 MB	10/15/12, 8:00:00 PM
doc92.pdf	10.3 MB	12/13/01, 7:00:00 PM
doc93.exe	120 kB	8/18/96, 8:00:00 PM
doc94.exe	118 kB	8/18/96, 8:00:00 PM
doc95.exe	133 kB	9/22/97, 8:00:00 PM
doc96.exe	134 kB	12/30/97, 7:00:00 PM
doc97.exe	143 kB	10/27/00, 8:00:00 PM

Starting a Jupyter session

Next, we will start a Jupyter session so that we can import our data into Python and make a machine learning model. A detailed example of creating a new Jupyter Notebook was presented in Chapter 1, *Introduction to Healthcare Analytics*. Here are the steps:

1. Locate the Jupyter application on your computer and start it.
2. In the new Jupyter tab that was opened in your default browser, navigate to the directory where you wish to save the notebook.
3. Locate the **New** drop-down menu on the upper right of the console, click it, and select **Python 3**.
4. You should see a new notebook, named **Untitled**.
5. To rename your notebook, click on the name of the notebook in the upper left. A cursor should appear. Type in the desired name. We have named our notebook ED_predict.

You are now ready to import the dataset into Jupyter.

Importing the dataset

Before we load the dataset, there are some important facts about the data that must be acknowledged:

- The data is in a fixed-width format, meaning that there is no delimiter. Column widths will have to be specified manually.
- There is no header row that has column names.
- If you were to open the data file using a text editor, you would see rows of data simply containing numbers.

Because column widths are necessary for importing .fwf files, we must import those *first* into our session. We have therefore made a helper .csv file, titled ED_metadata.csv, that contains the width, name, and variable type of each column. Our data only has 579 columns, so making such a file only took a couple of hours. If you have a bigger dataset, you may have to rely on automated width detection methods and/or more team members to do the grunt work of creating a schema for your data.

Loading the metadata

With our first cell, let's import the metadata and print a small preview of it:

```
import pandas as pd
pd.set_option('mode.chained_assignment',None)

HOME_PATH = 'C:\\Users\\Vikas\\Desktop\\Bk\\health-it\\ed_predict\\data\\'

df_helper = pd.read_csv(
    HOME_PATH + 'ED_metadata.csv',
    header=0,
    dtype={'width': int, 'column_name': str, 'variable_type': str}
)

print(df_helper.head(n=5))
```

You should see the following output:

```
   width column_name   variable_type
0      2      VMONTH     CATEGORICAL
1      1       VDAYR     CATEGORICAL
2      4     ARRTIME   NONPREDICTIVE
3      4    WAITTIME      CONTINUOUS
4      4         LOV   NONPREDICTIVE
```

So the `ED_metadata.csv` file simply is a comma-separated values file containing the width, column name, and variable type as specified in the documentation. This file can be downloaded from the code repository for this book.

In the next cell, we convert the columns of the pandas DataFrame we imported into separate lists:

```
width = df_helper['width'].tolist()
col_names = df_helper['column_name'].tolist()
var_types = df_helper['variable_type'].tolist()
```

Loading the ED dataset

Next, we import the contents of the fixed-width data file into Python as a pandas DataFrame composed of string columns, using the `widths` list created in the previous cell. We then name the columns using the `col_names` list:

```
df_ed = pd.read_fwf(
    HOME_PATH + 'ED2013',
    widths=width,
    header=None,
    dtype='str'
)

df_ed.columns = col_names
```

Let's print a preview of our dataset to confirm it was imported correctly:

```
print(df_ed.head(n=5))
```

The output should look similar to the following:

```
   VMONTH VDAYR ARRTIME WAITTIME   LOV  AGE AGER AGEDAYS RESIDNCE SEX ...
\
0      01     3    0647     0033  0058  046    4     -07       01   2 ...
1      01     3    1841     0109  0150  056    4     -07       01   2 ...
2      01     3    1333     0084  0198  037    3     -07       01   2 ...
3      01     3    1401     0159  0276  007    1     -07       01   1 ...
4      01     4    1947     0114  0248  053    4     -07       01   1 ...
   RX12V3C1 RX12V3C2 RX12V3C3 RX12V3C4 SETTYPE  YEAR   CSTRATM    CPSUM
PATWT  \
0       nan      nan      nan      nan       3  2013  20113201   100020
002945
1       nan      nan      nan      nan       3  2013  20113201   100020
002945
2       nan      nan      nan      nan       3  2013  20113201   100020
002945
3       nan      nan      nan      nan       3  2013  20113201   100020
002945
4       nan      nan      nan      nan       3  2013  20113201   100020
002945
```

```
     EDWT
0    nan
1    nan
2    nan
3    nan
4    nan

[5 rows x 579 columns]
```

Looking at the column values and their meanings in the documentation confirm that the data has been imported correctly. The `nan` values correspond to blank spaces in the data file.

Finally, as another check, let's count the dimensions of the data file and confirm that there are 24,777 rows and 579 columns:

```
print(df_ed.shape)
```

The output should look similar to the following:

```
(24777, 579)
```

Now that the data has been imported correctly, let's set up our response variable.

Making the response variable

In some cases, the response variable that we are trying to predict may already be a separate well-defined column. In those cases, simply converting the response from a string to a numeric type before splitting the data into train and test sets will suffice.

In our specific modeling task, we are trying to predict which patients presenting to the ED will eventually be hospitalized. In our case, hospitalization encompasses:

- Those admitted to an inpatient ward for further evaluation and treatment
- Those transferred to a different hospital (either psychiatric or non-psychiatric) for further treatment
- Those admitted to the observation unit for further evaluation (whether they are eventually admitted or discharged after their observation unit stay)

Accordingly, we must do some data wrangling to assemble all of these various outcomes into a single response variable:

```
response_cols = ['ADMITHOS','TRANOTH','TRANPSYC','OBSHOS','OBSDIS']

df_ed.loc[:, response_cols] = df_ed.loc[:,
response_cols].apply(pd.to_numeric)

df_ed['ADMITTEMP'] = df_ed[response_cols].sum(axis=1)
df_ed['ADMITFINAL'] = 0
df_ed.loc[df_ed['ADMITTEMP'] >= 1, 'ADMITFINAL'] = 1

df_ed.drop(response_cols, axis=1, inplace=True)
df_ed.drop('ADMITTEMP', axis=1, inplace=True)
```

Let's discuss the previous code example in detail:

- The first line identifies the columns we would like to include in our final target variable by name. The target should equal 1 if the values for any of those columns is 1.
- In Line 2, we convert the columns from the string to the numeric type.
- In Lines 3-5, we create a column called ADMITTEMP that contains the row-wise sum of the five target columns. We then create our final target column, ADMITFINAL, and set it equal to 1 when ADMITTEMP is >= 1.
- In Lines 6-7, we drop the five original response columns as well as the ADMITTEMP column since we now have our final response column.

Splitting the data into train and test sets

Now that we have our response variable, the next step is to split the dataset into train and test sets. In data science, the **training set** is the data that is used to determine the model coefficients. In the training phase, the model takes into account the predictor variable values together with the response value to "discover" the rules and the weights that will guide the prediction of new data. The **testing set** is then used to measure our model performance, as we discussed in Chapter 3, *Machine Learning Foundations*. Typical splits use 70-80% for the training data and 20-30% for the testing data (unless the dataset is very large, in which case a smaller percentage can be allotted toward the testing set).

Some practitioners also have a validation set that is used to train model parameters, such as the tree size in the random forest model or the lasso parameter in regularized logistic regression.

Fortunately, the `scikit-learn` library has a handy function called `train_test_split()` that takes care of the random splitting for us, when given the test set percentage. To use this function, we must first separate the target variable from the rest of the data, we do so as follows:

```
def split_target(data, target_name):
    target = data[[target_name]]
    data.drop(target_name, axis=1, inplace=True)
    return (data, target)

X, y = split_target(df_ed, 'ADMITFINAL')
```

After running the preceding code, y holds our response variable and X holds our dataset. We feed these two variables to the `train_test_split()` function, along with `0.25` for the `test_size` and a random state for reproducibility:

```
from sklearn.model_selection import train_test_split

X_train, X_test, y_train, y_test = train_test_split(
    X, y, test_size=0.25, random_state=1234
)
```

The result is a 2 x 2 split: `X_train`, `X_test`, `y_train`, and `y_test`. We can now use `X_train` and `y_train` to train the model, and `X_test` and `y_test` to test the model performance.

An important thing to remember is that during the preprocessing phase, any transformation made to the training set must also be performed on the testing set at test time, or otherwise, the model's output for the new data will be incorrect.

As a sanity check and also to detect any target variable imbalance, let's check the number of positive and negative responses in the response variable:

```
print(y_train.groupby('ADMITFINAL').size())
```

The output is as follows:

```
ADMITFINAL
0    15996
1     2586
dtype: int64
```

Our result indicates that approximately 1 out of 7 observations in the test set have a positive response. While it is not a perfectly balanced dataset (in which case the ratio would be 1 out of 2), it is not so imbalanced that we need to do any upsampling or downsampling of the data. Let's proceed with preprocessing the predictors.

Preprocessing the predictor variables

Let's take a look at specific groups of predictor variables that commonly pop up in healthcare data.

Visit information

The first feature category in the ED2013 dataset contains information about the timing of the visit. Variables such as month, day of week, and arrival time are included here. Also included are the waiting time and length of visit variables (both in minutes).

Month

Let's analyze the VMONTH predictor in more detail. The following code prints all the values in the training set and their counts:

```
print(X_train.groupby('VMONTH').size())
```

The output is as follows:

```
VMONTH
01    1757
02    1396
03    1409
04    1719
05    2032
06    1749
07    1696
08    1034
09    1240
10    1306
11    1693
12    1551
dtype: int64
```

We can now see that the months are numbered from 01 to 12, as it says in the documentation, and that each month has representation.

One part of preprocessing the data is performing **feature engineering** – that is, combining or transforming the features in some way to come up with new features that are more predictive than the previous ones. For example, suppose we had a hypothesis that ED visitors tend to be admitted more often during the winter months. We could make a predictor called WINTER that is a combination of the VMONTH predictor such that the value is 1 only if the patient came during December, January, February, or March. We have done that in the following cell. Later on, we can test this hypothesis when we assess variable importance while making our machine learning models:

```
def is_winter(vmonth):
    if vmonth in ['12','01','02','03']:
        return 1
    else:
        return 0
X_train.loc[:,'WINTER'] = df_ed.loc[:,'VMONTH'].apply(is_winter)
X_test.loc[:,'WINTER'] = df_ed.loc[:,'VMONTH'].apply(is_winter)
```

As an informal test, let's print out the distribution of the WINTER variable and confirm that it is the sum of the preceding four winter months:

```
X_train.groupby('WINTER').size()
```

The output is as follows:

```
WINTER
0    12469
1     6113
dtype: int64
```

Sure enough, we get 6113 = 1551 + 1757 + 1396 + 1409, confirming that we engineered the feature correctly. We will see other examples of feature engineering throughout this chapter.

Day of the week

As a sanity check that the data was imported correctly, let's also explore the VDAYR variable, which indicates the day of the week that the patient visit occurred:

```
X_train.groupby('VDAYR').size()
```

The output is as follows:

```
VDAYR
1    2559
2    2972
3    2791
4    2632
5    2553
6    2569
7    2506
dtype: int64
```

As we would expect, there are seven possible values, and the observations are relatively uniformly distributed across the possible values. We could get fancy and engineer a WEEKEND feature, but engineering additional features can be very time-consuming and memory-consuming, often for minimal gain. We'll leave that exercise up to the reader.

Arrival time

The arrival time is another visit information variable included in the data. However, in its raw form, it will probably be unhelpful, since it can be an integer between 0 and 2,359. Let's make a NIGHT variable that is only positive when the patient comes in between 8 PM and 8 AM. Our reasoning behind creating this variable is the hypothesis that patients arriving at the ED outside of regular hours have more serious illnesses and will, therefore, be admitted more often to the hospital. We can use the following code to make the NIGHT variable:

```
def is_night(arrtime):
    arrtime_int = int(arrtime)
    if ((arrtime_int >= 0) & (arrtime_int < 800)):
        return 1
    elif ((arrtime_int >= 2000) & (arrtime_int < 2400)):
        return 1
    else:
        return 0
X_train.loc[:,'NIGHT'] = df_ed.loc[:,'ARRTIME'].apply(is_night)
X_test.loc[:,'NIGHT'] = df_ed.loc[:,'ARRTIME'].apply(is_night)

X_train.drop('ARRTIME', axis=1, inplace=True)
X_test.drop('ARRTIME', axis=1, inplace=True)
```

In the preceding example, we first code a function that returns 1 if the patient has arrived between 8 PM and 8 AM, and returns 0 otherwise. We then use the apply() function of pandas to "apply" this function to the ARRTIME column and make the NIGHT column. We then drop the original ARRTIME column since it is not useful in its raw form.

Wait time

The wait time spent in the ED is yet another visit information variable that could reasonably be correlated with the target variable. Hypothetically, patients with more serious illnesses could appear to be more symptomatic to the triage nurse and therefore assigned more critical triage scores, causing them to have smaller waiting times than people with less serious illnesses.

In the documentation, it states that the WAITTIME variable may take values of −9 and −7 when blank and not applicable, respectively. Whenever a continuous variable has a placeholder value like this, we *must* do some sort of imputation to remove the placeholder values. Otherwise, the model will think that the patient had a wait time of −7 minutes, and the whole model will be adjusted adversely.

In this case, mean imputation is the appropriate action. **Mean imputation** replaces those negative values with the mean of the rest of the dataset, so that during modeling time those observations will have no effect in determining the coefficient for this variable.

To perform mean imputation, we first convert the columns to the numeric type:

```
X_train.loc[:,'WAITTIME'] = X_train.loc[:,'WAITTIME'].apply(pd.to_numeric)
X_test.loc[:,'WAITTIME'] = X_test.loc[:,'WAITTIME'].apply(pd.to_numeric)
```

Next, we write a function, called mean_impute_values(), that removes values of −7 and −9 from the column and replaces them with the mean of the column. We make the function generalizable so that it may be used later on in our preprocessing for other columns:

```
def mean_impute_values(data,col):
    temp_mean = data.loc[(data[col] != -7) & (data[col] != -9), col].mean()
    data.loc[(data[col] == -7) | (data[col] == -9), col] = temp_mean
    return data

X_train = mean_impute_values(X_train,'WAITTIME')
X_test = mean_impute_values(X_test,'WAITTIME')
```

We then call the function on the data, and we are finished. Following that, we will confirm that this function has been applied correctly, but first, let's go over a few more variables.

Other visit information

The final visit information variable in this dataset is the length of the visit variable (LOV). However, the length of visit is determined only after the entire ED visit, and by that time, the decision whether to admit or discharge will have already been made. It is important to drop variables that won't be available during the time of the prediction, and for that reason, we must drop LOV. We do so as shown in the following code:

```
X_train.drop('LOV', axis=1, inplace=True)
X_test.drop('LOV', axis=1, inplace=True)
```

Now that we've finished tackling the visit information, let's move on to demographic variables.

Demographic variables

In healthcare, demographic variables are usually associated with outcomes. Age, sex, and race are major demographic variables in healthcare. In this dataset, ethnicity and residence type have also been included. Let's sort out these variables as follows.

Age

As people get older, one can expect them to be sicker and to be admitted to the hospital more frequently. This hypothesis will be tested once we see the variable importance results of our model.

There are three variables that reflect the age in the dataset. AGE is an integer value that gives the age in years. AGEDAYS is an integer value that gives the age in days if the patient is less than 1 year old. AGER is the age variable, except that it has been converted to a categorical variable. Let's convert the AGE variable to a numeric type, leave the AGER variable as is, and remove the AGEDAYS variable since it will be not applicable in the vast majority of cases:

```
X_train.loc[:,'AGE'] = X_train.loc[:,'AGE'].apply(pd.to_numeric)
X_test.loc[:,'AGE'] = X_test.loc[:,'AGE'].apply(pd.to_numeric)

X_train.drop('AGEDAYS', axis=1, inplace=True)
X_test.drop('AGEDAYS', axis=1, inplace=True)
```

Sex

In healthcare, women have often been found to have longer life expectancies and be healthier overall than men, so let's include the SEX variable in our model. It is already categorical, so we can leave it as is.

Ethnicity and race

Ethnicity (Hispanic/Latino versus non-Hispanic/Latino) and race are also included in the data. Often, races that are prone to poor socioeconomic status have worse outcomes in healthcare. Let's leave the unimputed ethnicity and race variables (ETHUN and RACEUN) as is. We can remove the redundant RACER variable as well as the imputed versions of ethnicity and race (ETHIM and RACERETH):

```
X_train.drop(['ETHIM','RACER','RACERETH'], axis=1, inplace=True)
X_test.drop(['ETHIM','RACER','RACERETH'], axis=1, inplace=True)
```

Other demographic information

The patient residence is included in the data. Since it is categorical, there is no need to alter it.

Let's see what we have so far and print the first five rows using the head() function:

```
X_train.head(n=5)
```

Scrolling horizontally through the output, you should confirm that all of our transformations and variable drops have been done correctly.

Triage variables

Triage variables are important for emergency department modeling tasks. Triage encompasses assigning a risk score to a patient based on their initial presentation and vital signs. It is usually completed by a nurse specialized to perform triage and encompasses both subjective and objective information. Triage scores usually range from 1 (critical) to 5 (non-urgent). The IMMEDR variable (item number 34 in the documentation) is the triage score in this dataset. We will certainly include it.

Other variables we can categorize as triage variables include whether or not the patient arrived via EMS (ARREMS; usually correlated with worse outcomes) and whether or not the patient has been seen and discharged within the last 72 hours (SEEN72). We will also include these variables in our model.

Financial variables

The method of payment of the patient is commonly included in healthcare datasets and usually, certain payment types are associated with better or worse outcomes. Patients with no expected source of payment (NOPAY), or with Medicaid (PAYMCAID) or Medicare (PAYMCARE), typically are less healthy than patients with private insurance (PAYPRIV) or who are paying on their own (PAYSELF). Let's include all of the financial variables except for the PAYTYPER variable, which is just a nonbinary expansion of the other payment variables:

```
X_train.drop('PAYTYPER', axis=1, inplace=True)
X_test.drop('PAYTYPER', axis=1, inplace=True)
```

Vital signs

Vital signs are an important source of information for patients in healthcare modeling, for many reasons:

- They are easy to collect.
- They are typically available at the beginning of the clinical encounter.
- They are objective.
- They are numerical indicators of patient health.

The vital signs included in this dataset are temperature, pulse, respiratory rate, blood pressure (systolic and diastolic), oxygen saturation percentage, and whether they are on oxygen. Height and weight are commonly also categorized as vital signs, but they are not included in our data. Let's take a look at each vital sign in turn.

Temperature

Temperature is usually measured using a thermometer early during the patient encounter and can be recorded in degrees Celsius or Fahrenheit. A temperature of 98.6° F (37.1° C) is usually considered a normal body temperature. Temperatures markedly above this range can be termed as **fever** or **hyperthermia** and usually reflect infection, inflammation, or environmental overexposure to the sun. Temperatures below normal by a certain amount are termed **hypothermia** and usually reflect environmental exposure to cold. The more the temperature deviates from normal, usually the more serious the illness is.

In our dataset, the TEMPF temperature has been multiplied by 10 and stored as an integer. Also, some values are blank (indicated by -9) and we must impute those, since temperature is a continuous variable. Following that, we first convert the temperature to a numeric type, use our previously written mean_impute_values() function to impute the missing values in TEMPF, and then use a lambda function to divide all temperatures by 10:

```
X_train.loc[:,'TEMPF'] = X_train.loc[:,'TEMPF'].apply(pd.to_numeric)
X_test.loc[:,'TEMPF'] = X_test.loc[:,'TEMPF'].apply(pd.to_numeric)

X_train = mean_impute_values(X_train,'TEMPF')
X_test = mean_impute_values(X_test,'TEMPF')

X_train.loc[:,'TEMPF'] = X_train.loc[:,'TEMPF'].apply(lambda x:
float(x)/10)
X_test.loc[:,'TEMPF'] = X_test.loc[:,'TEMPF'].apply(lambda x: float(x)/10)
```

Let's print out 30 values of just this column to confirm that our processing was performed correctly:

```
X_train['TEMPF'].head(n=30)
```

The output is as follows:

```
15938      98.200000
5905       98.100000
4636       98.200000
9452       98.200000
7558       99.300000
17878      99.000000
21071      97.800000
20990      98.600000
4537       98.200000
7025       99.300000
2134       97.500000
5212       97.400000
9213       97.900000
```

```
2306        97.000000
6106        98.600000
2727        98.282103
4098        99.100000
5233        98.800000
5107       100.000000
18327       98.900000
19242       98.282103
3868        97.900000
12903       98.600000
12763       98.700000
8858        99.400000
8955        97.900000
16360       98.282103
6857        97.100000
6842        97.700000
22073       97.900000
Name: TEMPF, dtype: float64
```

We can see that the temperatures are now of the float type and that they are not multiplied by 10. Also, we see that the mean value, 98.282103, has been substituted where values were previously blank. Let's move on to the next variable.

Pulse

Pulse measures the frequency of the heartbeat in the patient. The normal range is 60-100. Having a pulse faster than 100 is termed **tachycardia** and usually indicates some underlying cardiac dysfunction, volume depletion, or infection (sepsis). A pulse lower than 60 is termed **bradycardia**.

We must use mean imputation to impute the missing values. First, we convert the pulse to a numeric type:

```
X_train.loc[:,'PULSE'] = X_train.loc[:,'PULSE'].apply(pd.to_numeric)
X_test.loc[:,'PULSE'] = X_test.loc[:,'PULSE'].apply(pd.to_numeric)
```

Then, we write a mean_impute_vitals() function that is similar to our mean_impute_values() function, except that the placeholder values have been changed from -7 and -9 to -998 and -9:

```
def mean_impute_vitals(data,col):
    temp_mean = data.loc[(data[col] != 998) & (data[col] != -9),
col].mean()
    data.loc[(data[col] == 998) | (data[col] == -9), col] = temp_mean
    return data
```

```
X_train = mean_impute_vitals(X_train,'PULSE')
X_test = mean_impute_vitals(X_test,'PULSE')
```

Respiratory rate

The respiratory rate indicates the rate at which the person takes breaths. 18-20 is considered normal. Tachypnea (abnormally elevated respiratory rate) is seen commonly in clinical practice and indicates an oxygen shortage in the body, usually due to either a cardiac or pulmonary cause. Bradypnea is an abnormally low respiratory rate.

In the following code, we convert the RESPR variable to a numeric type and then perform a mean imputation of the missing values:

```
X_train.loc[:,'RESPR'] = X_train.loc[:,'RESPR'].apply(pd.to_numeric)
X_test.loc[:,'RESPR'] = X_test.loc[:,'RESPR'].apply(pd.to_numeric)

X_train = mean_impute_values(X_train,'RESPR')
X_test = mean_impute_values(X_test,'RESPR')
```

Blood pressure

The blood pressure measures the amount of force per unit area that the blood exerts on the blood vessel walls. Blood pressure consists of two numbers – the **systolic blood pressure** (blood pressure during the systolic phase of the heartbeat) and the **diastolic blood pressure** (blood pressure during the diastolic phase). Normal blood pressure is usually somewhere between 110 to 120 mmHg for the systolic blood pressure and 70 to 80 mmHg for the diastolic blood pressure. Elevated blood pressure is called **hypertension**. The most common cause of elevated blood pressure is essential hypertension, which is primarily genetic (but multifactorial). Low blood pressure is called **hypotension**. Both hypertension and hypotension have complex etiologies that are often difficult to identify.

In our dataset, systolic and diastolic blood pressure are in separate columns (BPSYS and BPDIAS, respectively). First, we process the systolic blood pressure by converting it to a numeric type and mean imputing the missing values as we have done already for other columns:

```
X_train.loc[:,'BPSYS'] = X_train.loc[:,'BPSYS'].apply(pd.to_numeric)
X_test.loc[:,'BPSYS'] = X_test.loc[:,'BPSYS'].apply(pd.to_numeric)

X_train = mean_impute_values(X_train,'BPSYS')
X_test = mean_impute_values(X_test,'BPSYS')
```

Diastolic blood pressure is a bit more complex. The value `998` means that the pressure was `PALP`, meaning that it was too low to be detected by a sphygmamometer but high enough to feel by touch (palpation). After we convert it to a numeric type, we will substitute a numeric value of `40` for the `PALP` values:

```
X_train.loc[:,'BPDIAS'] = X_train.loc[:,'BPDIAS'].apply(pd.to_numeric)
X_test.loc[:,'BPDIAS'] = X_test.loc[:,'BPDIAS'].apply(pd.to_numeric)
```

We write a new function called `mean_impute_bp_diast()` that does the conversion of `PALP` values to `40` and the missing values to the mean:

```
def mean_impute_bp_diast(data,col):
    temp_mean = data.loc[(data[col] != 998) & (data[col] != -9),
col].mean()
    data.loc[data[col] == 998, col] = 40
    data.loc[data[col] == -9, col] = temp_mean
    return data

X_train = mean_impute_values(X_train,'BPDIAS')
X_test = mean_impute_values(X_test,'BPDIAS')
```

Oxygen saturation

Oxygen saturation measures the oxygen level in the blood. It is reported as a percentage, with higher values being more healthy. We convert it to a numeric type and perform mean imputation as follows:

```
X_train.loc[:,'POPCT'] = X_train.loc[:,'POPCT'].apply(pd.to_numeric)
X_test.loc[:,'POPCT'] = X_test.loc[:,'POPCT'].apply(pd.to_numeric)

X_train = mean_impute_values(X_train,'POPCT')
X_test = mean_impute_values(X_test,'POPCT')
```

Let's examine the vital sign transformations we've done so far by selecting those columns and using the `head()` function:

```
X_train[['TEMPF','PULSE','RESPR','BPSYS','BPDIAS','POPCT']].head(n=20)
```

The output is as follows:

	TEMPF	PULSE	RESPR	BPSYS	BPDIAS	
15938	98.200000	101.000000	22.0	159.000000	72.000000	98.000000
5905	98.100000	70.000000	18.0	167.000000	79.000000	96.000000
4636	98.200000	85.000000	20.0	113.000000	70.000000	98.000000
9452	98.200000	84.000000	20.0	146.000000	72.000000	98.000000
7558	99.300000	116.000000	18.0	131.000000	82.000000	96.000000
17878	99.000000	73.000000	16.0	144.000000	91.000000	99.000000
21071	97.800000	88.000000	18.0	121.000000	61.000000	98.000000
20990	98.600000	67.000000	16.0	112.000000	65.000000	95.000000
4537	98.200000	85.000000	20.0	113.000000	72.000000	99.000000
7025	99.300000	172.000000	40.0	124.000000	80.000000	100.000000
2134	97.500000	91.056517	18.0	146.000000	75.000000	94.000000
5212	97.400000	135.000000	18.0	125.000000	71.000000	99.000000
9213	97.900000	85.000000	18.0	153.000000	96.000000	99.000000
2306	97.000000	67.000000	20.0	136.000000	75.000000	99.000000
6106	98.600000	90.000000	18.0	109.000000	70.000000	98.000000
2727	98.282103	83.000000	17.0	123.000000	48.000000	92.000000
4098	99.100000	147.000000	20.0	133.483987	78.127013	100.000000
5233	98.800000	81.000000	16.0	114.000000	78.000000	97.311242
5107	100.000000	95.000000	24.0	133.000000	75.000000	94.000000
18327	98.900000	84.000000	16.0	130.000000	85.000000	98.000000

Examining the preceding table, it looks like we are in good shape. We can see the imputed mean values for each column (values having extra precision). Let's move onto the last vital sign we have in our data, the pain level.

Pain level

Pain is a common indication that something is wrong with the human body, and pain level is usually asked in every medical interview, whether it is the initial history and physical or the daily SOAP note. Pain levels are usually reported on a scale from 0 (non-existent) to 10 (unbearable). Let's first convert the `PAINSCALE` column to the numeric type:

```
X_train.loc[:,'PAINSCALE'] =
X_train.loc[:,'PAINSCALE'].apply(pd.to_numeric)
X_test.loc[:,'PAINSCALE'] = X_test.loc[:,'PAINSCALE'].apply(pd.to_numeric)
```

Now, we have to write a separate function for mean-imputing pain values, since it uses -8 as a placeholder value instead of -7:

```
def mean_impute_pain(data,col):
    temp_mean = data.loc[(data[col] != -8) & (data[col] != -9), col].mean()
    data.loc[(data[col] == -8) | (data[col] == -9), col] = temp_mean
    return data

X_train = mean_impute_pain(X_train,'PAINSCALE')
X_test = mean_impute_pain(X_test,'PAINSCALE')
```

Together, vital signs provide an important picture of the health of the patient. In the end, we will see how important a role these variables play when we do the variable importance.

Now, we can move on to the next variable category.

Reason-for-visit codes

The reason-for-visit variables encode the reason for the patient visit, which can be seen as the chief complaint of the visit (we talked about chief complaints in `Chapter 2`, *Healthcare Foundations*). In this dataset, these reasons are coded using a code set called *A Reason for Visit Classification for Ambulatory Care* (refer to *Page 16* and *Appendix II* of the 2011 documentation for further information; a screenshot of the first page of the *Appendix* is provided at the end of the chapter). While the exact code may not be determined early during the patient encounter, we include it here because:

- It reflects information available early during the patient encounter.

- We would like to demonstrate how to process a coded variable (all the other coded variables occur too late in the patient encounter to be of use for this modeling task):

2011 NHAMCS MICRO-DATA FILE DOCUMENTATION	PAGE 167

APPENDIX II
REASON FOR VISIT CLASSIFICATION

A. SUMMARY OF CODES

MODULE	CODE NUMBER
SYMPTOM MODULE	
General Symptoms	1001-1099
Symptoms Referable to Psychological and Mental Disorders	1100-1199
Symptoms Referable to the Nervous System (Excluding Sense Organs)	1200-1259
Symptoms Referable to the Cardiovascular and Lymphatic Systems	1260-1299
Symptoms Referable to the Eyes and Ears	1300-1399
Symptoms Referable to the Respiratory System	1400-1499
Symptoms Referable to the Digestive System	1500-1639
Symptoms Referable to the Genitourinary System	1640-1829
Symptoms Referable to the Skin, Nails, and Hair	1830-1899
Symptoms Referable to the Musculoskeletal System	1900-1999
DISEASE MODULE	
Infective and Parasitic Diseases	2001-2099
Neoplasms	2100-2199
Endocrine, Nutritional, Metabolic, and Immunity Diseases	2200-2249
Diseases of the Blood and Blood-forming Organs	2250-2299
Mental Disorders	2300-2349

Coded variables require special attention for the following reasons:

- Often there are multiple entries designated in the table for more than one code, and the reason-for-visit codes are no exception. Notice that this dataset contains three RFV columns (RFV1, RFV2, and RFV3). A code for asthma, for example, may appear in any of these columns. Therefore, it is not enough to do one-hot encoding for these columns. We must detect the presence of each code in *any* of the three columns, and we must write a special function to do that.
- Codes are categorical, but the numbers themselves usually carry no meaning. For easier interpretation, we must name the columns accordingly, using suitable descriptions. To do this, we have put together a special .csv file that contains the typed description for each code (available for download at the book's GitHub repository).

- One output format possibility is a column for each code, where a 1 indicates the presence of that code and a 0 indicates its absence (as done in Futoma et al., 2015). Any desired combinations/transformations can then be performed. We have used that format here.

Without further ado, let's start transforming our reason-for-visit variables. First, we import the RFV code descriptions:

```
rfv_codes_path = HOME_PATH + 'RFV_CODES.csv'

rfv_codes = pd.read_csv(rfv_codes_path,header=0,dtype='str')
```

Now we will do our RFV code processing.

First, to name the columns properly, we import the sub() function from the re module (re stands for regular expression).

Then we write a function that scans any given RFV columns for the presence of an indicated code, and returns the dataset with a new column, with a 1 if the code is present and a 0 if the code is absent.

Next, we use a for loop to iterate through every code in the .csv file, effectively adding a binary column for every possible code. We do this for both the training and testing sets.

Finally, we drop the original RFV columns, since we no longer need them. The full code is as follows:

```
from re import sub

def add_rfv_column(data,code,desc,rfv_columns):
    column_name = 'rfv_' + sub(" ", "_", desc)
    data[column_name] = (data[rfv_columns] ==
rfv_code).any(axis=1).astype('int')
    return data

rfv_columns = ['RFV1','RFV2','RFV3']
for (rfv_code,rfv_desc) in zip(
    rfv_codes['Code'].tolist(),rfv_codes['Description'].tolist()
):
    X_train = add_rfv_column(
        X_train,
        rfv_code,
        rfv_desc,
        rfv_columns
    )
    X_test = add_rfv_column(
```

```
        X_test,
        rfv_code,
        rfv_desc,
        rfv_columns
    )
# Remove original RFV columns
X_train.drop(rfv_columns, axis=1, inplace=True)
X_test.drop(rfv_columns, axis=1, inplace=True)
```

Let's take a look at our transformed dataset with the `head()` function:

```
X_train.head(n=5)
```

Notice that there are now 1,264 columns. While the full DataFrame has been truncated, if you scroll horizontally, you should see some of the new `rfv_` columns appended to the end of the DataFrame.

Injury codes

Injury codes are also included in the data. While the reason-for-visit codes apply to all visits, injury codes only apply if the patient has undergone either physical injury, poisoning, or adverse effects of medical treatment (including suicide attempts). Because the exact reason for injury may not be known until a full workup has been performed, and that workup usually occurs after a decision to admit has already been made. Therefore, we will remove the injury code variables, since they potentially contain future information that will not be available at prediction time. However, if you wish to use such codes for your modeling task, remember that coded data can be processed in a manner similar to that shown earlier. Refer to the documentation for additional details on injury variables:

```
inj_cols = [
    'INJURY','INJR1','INJR2','INJPOISAD','INJPOISADR1',
    'INJPOISADR2','INTENT','INJDETR','INJDETR1','INJDETR2',
    'CAUSE1','CAUSE2','CAUSE3','CAUSE1R','CAUSE2R','CAUSE3R'
]

X_train.drop(inj_cols, axis=1, inplace=True)
X_test.drop(inj_cols, axis=1, inplace=True)
```

Diagnostic codes

The dataset also contains ICD-9-DM codes to classify diagnoses associated with each visit. Notice that there are three diagnostic code columns. This is consistent with what we said about coded variables in the *Reason-for-Visit codes* section. Because ICD-9 codes are usually assigned to visits after the workup has been performed and the cause of the symptoms determined, we will have to omit them from this modeling task:

```
diag_cols= [
    'DIAG1','DIAG2','DIAG3',
    'PRDIAG1','PRDIAG2','PRDIAG3',
    'DIAG1R','DIAG2R','DIAG3R'
]

X_train.drop(diag_cols, axis=1, inplace=True)
X_test.drop(diag_cols, axis=1, inplace=True)
```

Medical history

As we discussed in `Chapter 2`, *Healthcare Foundations*, individuals that have chronic conditions are usually less healthy and have poorer health outcomes than those who do not have chronic health conditions. The dataset includes information on the presence of 11 common chronic conditions for each visit. These conditions are cancer, cerebrovascular disease, chronic obstructive pulmonary disease, a condition requiring dialysis, congestive heart failure, dementia, diabetes, history of myocardial infarction, history of pulmonary embolism or deep vein thrombosis, and HIV/AIDS. Because past medical history is often available electronically for previously seen patients and is usually established early during patient triage, we have decided to include these variables here. Because they are already binary, no processing of these variables is needed.

There is also a continuous variable, called `TOTCHRON`, that tallies the total number of chronic disease for each patient, which we mean-impute as follows:

```
X_train.loc[:,'TOTCHRON'] = X_train.loc[:,'TOTCHRON'].apply(pd.to_numeric)
X_test.loc[:,'TOTCHRON'] = X_test.loc[:,'TOTCHRON'].apply(pd.to_numeric)

X_train = mean_impute_values(X_train,'TOTCHRON')
X_test = mean_impute_values(X_test,'TOTCHRON')
```

Tests

Medical tests, while important, occur post-prediction time and must be omitted for this use case. They may be used for other modeling tasks, such as readmission prediction or mortality:

```
testing_cols = [
    'ABG','BAC','BLOODCX','BNP','BUNCREAT',
    'CARDENZ','CBC','DDIMER','ELECTROL','GLUCOSE',
    'LACTATE','LFT','PTTINR','OTHERBLD','CARDMON',
    'EKG','HIVTEST','FLUTEST','PREGTEST','TOXSCREN',
    'URINE','WOUNDCX','URINECX','OTHRTEST','ANYIMAGE',
    'XRAY','IVCONTRAST','CATSCAN','CTAB','CTCHEST',
    'CTHEAD','CTOTHER','CTUNK','MRI','ULTRASND',
    'OTHIMAGE','TOTDIAG','DIAGSCRN'
]

X_train.drop(testing_cols, axis=1, inplace=True)
X_test.drop(testing_cols, axis=1, inplace=True)
```

Procedures

We omit procedures because, similar to the tests, they often occur post-prediction time:

```
proc_cols = [
    'PROC','BPAP','BLADCATH','CASTSPLINT','CENTLINE',
    'CPR','ENDOINT','INCDRAIN','IVFLUIDS','LUMBAR',
    'NEBUTHER','PELVIC','SKINADH','SUTURE','OTHPROC',
    'TOTPROC'
]

X_train.drop(proc_cols, axis=1, inplace=True)
X_test.drop(proc_cols, axis=1, inplace=True)
```

Medication codes

The data includes ample information on medications given in the ED and/or prescribed at discharge. In fact, information on up to 12 medications is allotted in various columns. Obviously, medication administration occurs after the decision to admit the patient has been made, so we cannot use these columns for this use case.

Nevertheless, we encourage you to peruse the documentation and read about the coding systems used for medications if you wish to use such information in your own predictive modeling:

```
med_cols = [
    'MED1','MED2','MED3','MED4','MED5',
    'MED6','MED7','MED8','MED9','MED10',
    'MED11','MED12','GPMED1','GPMED2','GPMED3',
    'GPMED4','GPMED5','GPMED6','GPMED7','GPMED8',
    'GPMED9','GPMED10','GPMED11','GPMED12','NUMGIV',
    'NUMDIS','NUMMED',
]

X_train.drop(med_cols, axis=1, inplace=True)
X_test.drop(med_cols, axis=1, inplace=True)
```

Provider information

Provider columns indicate which type(s) of medical providers participated in the medical encounter. We have omitted these variables:

```
prov_cols = [
    'NOPROVID','ATTPHYS','RESINT','CONSULT','RNLPN',
    'NURSEPR','PHYSASST','EMT','MHPROV','OTHPROV'
]

X_train.drop(prov_cols, axis=1, inplace=True)
X_test.drop(prov_cols, axis=1, inplace=True)
```

Disposition information

Because disposition variables are directly related to the outcome, we cannot leave them in the data. We omit them here (recall that we previously removed several of the disposition variables right after we created our final target column):

```
disp_cols = [
    'NODISP','NOFU','RETRNED','RETREFFU','LEFTBTRI',
    'LEFTAMA','DOA','DIEDED','TRANNH','OTHDISP',
    'ADMIT','ADMTPHYS','BOARDED','LOS','HDDIAG1',
    'HDDIAG2','HDDIAG3','HDDIAG1R','HDDIAG2R','HDDIAG3R',
    'HDSTAT','ADISP','OBSSTAY','STAY24'
]
```

```
X_train.drop(disp_cols, axis=1, inplace=True)
X_test.drop(disp_cols, axis=1, inplace=True)
```

Imputed columns

These columns indicate those that contain imputed data. For the most part, we have
included the unimputed counterparts in our data and therefore do not need the imputed
columns, so we remove them:

```
imp_cols = [
    'AGEFL','BDATEFL','SEXFL','ETHNICFL','RACERFL'
]

X_train.drop(imp_cols, axis=1, inplace=True)
X_test.drop(imp_cols, axis=1, inplace=True)
```

Identifying variables

When combined, the identifying variables provide a unique key for each encounter. While
this may come in handy in many situations, fortunately, `pandas` DataFrames already
uniquely assign an integer to each row, so we can remove the ID variables:

```
id_cols = [
    'HOSPCODE','PATCODE'
]

X_train.drop(id_cols, axis=1, inplace=True)
X_test.drop(id_cols, axis=1, inplace=True)
```

Electronic medical record status columns

The dataset includes dozens of columns that indicate the technological level of the facility at
which the patient was seen. We discussed this in the *EHR technology and meaningful
use* section in `Chapter 2`, *Healthcare Foundations*. We omit these columns since they are
valued on a per-hospital basis rather than a per-encounter basis:

```
emr_cols = [
    'EBILLANYE','EMRED','HHSMUE','EHRINSE','EDEMOGE',
    'EDEMOGER','EPROLSTE','EPROLSTER','EVITALE','EVITALER',
    'ESMOKEE','ESMOKEER','EPNOTESE','EPNOTESER','EMEDALGE',
    'EMEDALGER','ECPOEE','ECPOEER','ESCRIPE','ESCRIPER',
    'EWARNE','EWARNER','EREMINDE','EREMINDER','ECTOEE',
```

```
        'ECTOEER','EORDERE','EORDERER','ERESULTE','ERESULTER',
        'EGRAPHE','EGRAPHER','EIMGRESE','EIMGRESER','EPTEDUE',
        'EPTEDUER','ECQME','ECQMER','EGENLISTE','EGENLISTER',
        'EIMMREGE','EIMMREGER','ESUME','ESUMER','EMSGE',
        'EMSGER','EHLTHINFOE','EHLTHINFOER','EPTRECE','EPTRECER',
        'EMEDIDE','EMEDIDER','ESHAREE','ESHAREEHRE','ESHAREWEBE',
        'ESHAREOTHE','ESHAREUNKE','ESHAREREFE','LABRESE1','LABRESE2',
        'LABRESE3','LABRESE4','LABRESUNKE','LABRESREFE','IMAGREPE1',
        'IMAGREPE2','IMAGREPE3','IMAGREPE4','IMAGREPUNKE','IMAGREPREFE',
        'PTPROBE1','PTPROBE2','PTPROBE3','PTPROBE4','PTPROBUNKE',
        'PTPROBREFE','MEDLISTE1','MEDLISTE2','MEDLISTE3','MEDLISTE4',
        'MEDLISTUNKE','MEDLISTREFE','ALGLISTE1','ALGLISTE2','ALGLISTE3',
        'ALGLISTE4','ALGLISTUNKE','ALGLISTREFE','EDPRIM','EDINFO',
        'MUINC','MUYEAR'
]

X_train.drop(emr_cols, axis=1, inplace=True)
X_test.drop(emr_cols, axis=1, inplace=True)
```

Detailed medication information

More detailed drug information is available in these columns. These columns include information on drug categories, which is coded. We must omit these columns because they represent future information. However, this information could be immensely useful in other machine learning problems:

```
drug_id_cols = [
    'DRUGID1','DRUGID2','DRUGID3','DRUGID4','DRUGID5',
    'DRUGID6','DRUGID7','DRUGID8','DRUGID9','DRUGID10',
    'DRUGID11','DRUGID12'
]

drug_lev1_cols = [
    'RX1V1C1','RX1V1C2','RX1V1C3','RX1V1C4',
    'RX2V1C1','RX2V1C2','RX2V1C3','RX2V1C4',
    'RX3V1C1','RX3V1C2','RX3V1C3','RX3V1C4',
    'RX4V1C1','RX4V1C2','RX4V1C3','RX4V1C4',
    'RX5V1C1','RX5V1C2','RX5V1C3','RX5V1C4',
    'RX6V1C1','RX6V1C2','RX6V1C3','RX6V1C4',
    'RX7V1C1','RX7V1C2','RX7V1C3','RX7V1C4',
    'RX8V1C1','RX8V1C2','RX8V1C3','RX8V1C4',
    'RX9V1C1','RX9V1C2','RX9V1C3','RX9V1C4',
    'RX10V1C1','RX10V1C2','RX10V1C3','RX10V1C4',
    'RX11V1C1','RX11V1C2','RX11V1C3','RX11V1C4',
    'RX12V1C1','RX12V1C2','RX12V1C3','RX12V1C4'
]
```

```
drug_lev2_cols = [
    'RX1V2C1','RX1V2C2','RX1V2C3','RX1V2C4',
    'RX2V2C1','RX2V2C2','RX2V2C3','RX2V2C4',
    'RX3V2C1','RX3V2C2','RX3V2C3','RX3V2C4',
    'RX4V2C1','RX4V2C2','RX4V2C3','RX4V2C4',
    'RX5V2C1','RX5V2C2','RX5V2C3','RX5V2C4',
    'RX6V2C1','RX6V2C2','RX6V2C3','RX6V2C4',
    'RX7V2C1','RX7V2C2','RX7V2C3','RX7V2C4',
    'RX8V2C1','RX8V2C2','RX8V2C3','RX8V2C4',
    'RX9V2C1','RX9V2C2','RX9V2C3','RX9V2C4',
    'RX10V2C1','RX10V2C2','RX10V2C3','RX10V2C4',
    'RX11V2C1','RX11V2C2','RX11V2C3','RX11V2C4',
    'RX12V2C1','RX12V2C2','RX12V2C3','RX12V2C4'
]

drug_lev3_cols = [
    'RX1V3C1','RX1V3C2','RX1V3C3','RX1V3C4',
    'RX2V3C1','RX2V3C2','RX2V3C3','RX2V3C4',
    'RX3V3C1','RX3V3C2','RX3V3C3','RX3V3C4',
    'RX4V3C1','RX4V3C2','RX4V3C3','RX4V3C4',
    'RX5V3C1','RX5V3C2','RX5V3C3','RX5V3C4',
    'RX6V3C1','RX6V3C2','RX6V3C3','RX6V3C4',
    'RX7V3C1','RX7V3C2','RX7V3C3','RX7V3C4',
    'RX8V3C1','RX8V3C2','RX8V3C3','RX8V3C4',
    'RX9V3C1','RX9V3C2','RX9V3C3','RX9V3C4',
    'RX10V3C1','RX10V3C2','RX10V3C3','RX10V3C4',
    'RX11V3C1','RX11V3C2','RX11V3C3','RX11V3C4',
    'RX12V3C1','RX12V3C2','RX12V3C3','RX12V3C4'
]

addl_drug_cols = [
    'PRESCR1','CONTSUB1','COMSTAT1','RX1CAT1','RX1CAT2',
    'RX1CAT3','RX1CAT4','PRESCR2','CONTSUB2','COMSTAT2',
    'RX2CAT1','RX2CAT2','RX2CAT3','RX2CAT4','PRESCR3','CONTSUB3',
    'COMSTAT3','RX3CAT1','RX3CAT2','RX3CAT3','RX3CAT4','PRESCR4',
    'CONTSUB4','COMSTAT4','RX4CAT1','RX4CAT2','RX4CAT3',
    'RX4CAT4','PRESCR5','CONTSUB5','COMSTAT5','RX5CAT1',
    'RX5CAT2','RX5CAT3','RX5CAT4','PRESCR6','CONTSUB6',
    'COMSTAT6','RX6CAT1','RX6CAT2','RX6CAT3','RX6CAT4','PRESCR7',
    'CONTSUB7','COMSTAT7','RX7CAT1','RX7CAT2','RX7CAT3',
    'RX7CAT4','PRESCR8','CONTSUB8','COMSTAT8','RX8CAT1',
    'RX8CAT2','RX8CAT3','RX8CAT4','PRESCR9','CONTSUB9',
    'COMSTAT9','RX9CAT1','RX9CAT2','RX9CAT3','RX9CAT4',
    'PRESCR10','CONTSUB10','COMSTAT10','RX10CAT1','RX10CAT2',
    'RX10CAT3','RX10CAT4','PRESCR11','CONTSUB11','COMSTAT11',
    'RX11CAT1','RX11CAT2','RX11CAT3','RX11CAT4','PRESCR12',
    'CONTSUB12','COMSTAT12','RX12CAT1','RX12CAT2','RX12CAT3',
    'RX12CAT4'
]
```

```
    ]

    X_train.drop(drug_id_cols, axis=1, inplace=True)
    X_train.drop(drug_lev1_cols, axis=1, inplace=True)
    X_train.drop(drug_lev2_cols, axis=1, inplace=True)
    X_train.drop(drug_lev3_cols, axis=1, inplace=True)
    X_train.drop(addl_drug_cols, axis=1, inplace=True)

    X_test.drop(drug_id_cols, axis=1, inplace=True)
    X_test.drop(drug_lev1_cols, axis=1, inplace=True)
    X_test.drop(drug_lev2_cols, axis=1, inplace=True)
    X_test.drop(drug_lev3_cols, axis=1, inplace=True)
    X_test.drop(addl_drug_cols, axis=1, inplace=True)
```

Miscellaneous information

Finally, there are several columns at the end that are irrelevant for our purposes, so we remove them:

```
    design_cols = ['CSTRATM','CPSUM','PATWT','EDWT']

    X_train.drop(design_cols, axis=1, inplace=True)
    X_test.drop(design_cols, axis=1, inplace=True)
```

Final preprocessing steps

Now that we have gone through all of the variable groups, we are almost ready to build our predictive models. But first, we must expand all of our categorical variables into binary variables (also known as one-hot encoding or a 1-of-K representation) and convert our data into a format suitable for input into the `scikit-learn` methods. Let's do that next.

One-hot encoding

Many classifiers of the scikit-learn library require categorical variables to be one-hot encoded. **One-hot encoding**, or a **1-of-K representation**, is when a categorical variable that has more than two possible values is recorded as multiple variables each having two possible values.

For example, let's say that we have five patients in our dataset and we wish to one-hot encode a column that encodes the primary visit diagnosis. Before one-hot encoding, the column looks like this:

patient_id	primary_dx
1	copd
2	hypertension
3	copd
4	chf
5	asthma

After one-hot encoding, this column would be split into *K* columns, where *K* is the number of possible values, and each column takes a value of 0 or 1 depending on whether the observation takes the value corresponding to that column:

patient_id	primary_dx_copd	primary_dx_hypertension	primary_dx_chf	primary_dx_asthma
1	1	0	0	0
2	0	1	0	0
3	1	0	0	0
4	0	0	1	0
5	0	0	0	1

Note that we have converted the strings of the previous column into an integer representation. This makes sense since machine learning algorithms are trained on numbers, not words! This is why one-hot encoding is necessary.

scikit-learn has a OneHotEncoder class in its preprocessing module. However, pandas has a get_dummies() function that accomplishes one-hot encoding in a single line. Let's use the pandas function. Before we do that, we must identify the columns that are categorical in our dataset to be passed to the function. We do this by using the metadata to identify the categorical columns and seeing which of those columns intersect with the columns that remain in our data:

```
categ_cols = df_helper.loc[
    df_helper['variable_type'] == 'CATEGORICAL', 'column_name'
]

one_hot_cols = list(set(categ_cols) & set(X_train.columns))

X_train = pd.get_dummies(X_train, columns=one_hot_cols)
```

We must also one-hot encode the test data:

```
X_test = pd.get_dummies(X_test, columns=one_hot_cols)
```

As a final note, we should mention that there is the possibility that the testing set will contain categorical values that haven't been seen in the training data. This may cause an error when assessing the performance of the model using the testing set. To prevent this, you may have to write some extra code that sets any missing columns in the testing set to zero. Fortunately, we do not have to worry about that with our dataset.

Numeric conversion

Let's now convert all of the columns into numeric format:

```
X_train.loc[:,X_train.columns] =
X_train.loc[:,X_train.columns].apply(pd.to_numeric)
X_test.loc[:,X_test.columns] =
X_test.loc[:,X_test.columns].apply(pd.to_numeric)
```

NumPy array conversion

The final step is taking the NumPy array of the pandas DataFrame that will be passed directly into the machine learning algorithm. First, we save the final column names, which will assist us when we assess variable importance later on:

```
X_train_cols = X_train.columns
X_test_cols = X_test.columns
```

Now, we use the `values` attribute of the `pandas` DataFrames to access the underlying NumPy array for each DataFrame:

```
X_train = X_train.values
X_test = X_test.values
```

Now, we are ready for to build the models.

Building the models

In this section, we'll build three types of classifiers and assess their performance: a logistic regression classifier, a random forest, and a neural network.

Logistic regression

We discussed the intuition behind and basics of logistic regression models in Chapter 3, *Machine Learning Foundations*. To build a model on our training set, we use the following code:

```
from sklearn.linear_model import LogisticRegression

clfs = [LogisticRegression()]

for clf in clfs:
    clf.fit(X_train, y_train.ravel())
    print(type(clf))
    print('Training accuracy: ' + str(clf.score(X_train, y_train)))
    print('Validation accuracy: ' + str(clf.score(X_test, y_test)))
    coefs = {
        'column': [X_train_cols[i] for i in range(len(X_train_cols))],
        'coef': [clf.coef_[0,i] for i in range(len(X_train_cols))]
    }
    df_coefs = pd.DataFrame(coefs)
    print(df_coefs.sort_values('coef', axis=0, ascending=False))
```

Prior to the `for` loop, we import the `LogisticRegression` class and set `clf` equal to a `LogisticRegression` instance. The training and testing occur in the `for` loop. First, we use the `fit()` method to fit the model (for example, to determine the optimal coefficients) using the training data. Next, we use the `score()` method to assess the model performance on both the training data and the testing data.

In the second half of the `for` loop, we print out the coefficient values of each feature. In general, features with coefficients that are farther from zero are the most positively/negatively correlated with the outcome. However, we did not scale the data prior to training, so it is possible that more important predictors that are not scaled appropriately will have lower coefficients.

The output of the code should look like the following:

```
<class 'sklearn.linear_model.logistic.LogisticRegression'>
Training accuracy: 0.888978581423
Validation accuracy: 0.884261501211
        coef                                         column
346  2.825056              rfv_Symptoms_of_onset_of_labor
696  1.618454              rfv_Adverse_effect_of_drug_abuse
95   1.467790                rfv_Delusions_or_hallucinations
108  1.435026  rfv_Other_symptoms_or_problems_relating_to_psy...
688  1.287535                            rfv_Suicide_attempt
895  1.265043                                       IMMEDR_01
```

```
520  1.264023  rfv_General_psychiatric_or_psychological_exami...
278  1.213235                                     rfv_Jaundice
712  1.139245     rfv_For_other_and_unspecified_test_results
469  1.084806                         rfv_Other_heart_disease
. . .
```

First, let's discuss the performance of the training and testing sets. They are close together, which indicates the model did not overfit to the training set. The accuracy is approximately 88%, which is on par with performance in research studies (Cameron et al., 2015) for predicting emergency department status.

Looking at the coefficients, we can confirm that they make intuitive sense. The feature with the highest coefficient is related to the onset of labor in pregnancy; we all know that labor results in a hospital admission. Many of the features pertaining to severe psychiatric disease, which almost always result in an admission due to the risk the patient poses to themselves or to others. The IMMEDR_1 feature also has a high coefficient; remember that this feature corresponds to a value of 1 on the triage scale, which is the most critical value:

```
. . .
898  -0.839861                               IMMEDR_04
823  -0.848631                               BEDDATA_03
625  -0.873828                    rfv_Hand_and_fingers
371  -0.960739                          rfv_Skin_rash
188  -0.963524                        rfv_Earache_pain_
217  -0.968058                            rfv_Soreness
899  -1.019763                               IMMEDR_05
604  -1.075670             rfv_Suture__insertion_removal
235  -1.140021                          rfv_Toothache
30   -1.692650                                LEFTATRI
```

In contrast, scrolling to the bottom reveals some of the features that are negatively correlated with an admission. Having a toothache and needing sutures to be removed show up here, and they are not likely to result in admissions since they are not urgent complaints.

We've trained our first model. Let's see whether some of the more complex models will improve.

Random forest

A convenient feature of `scikit-learn` is that many of the classifiers have identical methods so that models can be built interchangeably. We see that in the following code, when we use the `fit()` and `score()` methods of the `RandomForestClassifier` class to train the model and assess its performance, respectively:

```
from sklearn.ensemble import RandomForestClassifier

clfs_rf = [RandomForestClassifier(n_estimators=100)]

for clf in clfs_rf:
    clf.fit(X_train, y_train.ravel())
    print(type(clf))
    print('Training accuracy: ' + str(clf.score(X_train, y_train)))
    print('Validation accuracy: ' + str(clf.score(X_test, y_test)))
    imps = {
        'column': [X_train_cols[i] for i in range(len(X_train_cols))],
        'imp': [clf.feature_importances_[i] for i in
range(len(X_train_cols))]
    }
    df_imps = pd.DataFrame(imps)
    print(df_imps.sort_values('imp', axis=0, ascending=False))
```

The output should look similar to the following:

```
<class 'sklearn.ensemble.forest.RandomForestClassifier'>
Training accuracy: 1.0
Validation accuracy: 0.885391444713
                                  column       imp
1                                    AGE  0.039517
13                                 PULSE  0.028348
15                                 BPSYS  0.026833
12                                 TEMPF  0.025898
16                                 BPDIAS 0.025844
0                               WAITTIME  0.025111
14                                 RESPR  0.021329
17                                 POPCT  0.020407
29                              TOTCHRON  0.018417
896                            IMMEDR_02  0.016714
...
```

This time the validation accuracy was similar to that of the logistic regression model, approximately 88%. However, the accuracy on the training data was 100%, indicating that we overfit the model to the training data. We'll discuss potential ways of improving our models at the end of this chapter.

Looking at the feature importance, again the results make sense. This time the vital signs seem to be the most important predictors, along with the age predictor. Scrolling to the bottom reveals those features that had no impact on predictability. Note that in contrast to regression coefficients, with the variable importance of random forest, the frequency with which the variable was positive plays a role in the importance; this may explain why IMMEDR_02 is ranked as more important than IMMEDR_01.

Neural network

Finally, we arrive at the neural network model. Note that our training set only has approximately 18,000 observations; the most successful neural network models (for example, "deep learning" models) typically use millions or even billions of observations. Nevertheless, let's see how our neural network model fares. For neural networks, it is recommended that the data is scaled appropriately (for example, having a **standard distribution** with a mean equal to 0 and a standard deviation equal to 1). We use the StandardScaler class to accomplish this:

```
from sklearn.preprocessing import StandardScaler
from sklearn.neural_network import MLPClassifier

# Scale data
scaler = StandardScaler()
scaler.fit(X_train)
X_train_Tx = scaler.transform(X_train)
X_test_Tx = scaler.transform(X_test)

# Fit models that require scaling (e.g. neural networks)
hl_sizes = [150,100,80,60,40,20]
nn_clfs = [MLPClassifier(hidden_layer_sizes=(size,), random_state=2345,
verbose=True) for size in hl_sizes]

for num, nn_clf in enumerate(nn_clfs):
    print(str(hl_sizes[num]) + '-unit network:')
    nn_clf.fit(X_train_Tx, y_train.ravel())
    print('Training accuracy: ' + str(nn_clf.score(X_train_Tx, y_train)))
    print('Validation accuracy: ' + str(nn_clf.score(X_test_Tx, y_test)))
```

Once you run the preceding cell, you will see iterations being completed, and once the iterations fail to result in improvements to the model, the training will stop and the accuracies will be printed. In our run, the validation accuracy of the model having 150 cells in its hidden layer was 87%, higher than the other hidden layer sizes.

Using the models to make predictions

We have finished preprocessing the data, and making and scoring the model. The AUC is similar to that reported in previous academic studies that predict ED outcomes (see Cameron et al., 2015 for an example).

The next step would be to save and deploy the model and use it to make live predictions. Fortunately, all of the classifiers in the scikit-learn library include several functions for making predictions:

- For most classifiers, the `predict()` function takes a matrix, X, that contains unlabeled data as input and simply returns the class predictions with no further information.
- The `predict_proba()` function takes a matrix, X, that contains unlabeled data as input and returns the probabilities with which the observations belong to each class. These should add up to 1 for each observation.
- The `predict_log_proba()` function is similar to the `predict_proba()` function except that it returns the log probabilities with which the observations belong to each class.

Keep the following important fact in mind: *When making predictions, the unlabeled data must be preprocessed identically to the manner in which the training data was preprocessed.* This includes:

- Column additions and deletions
- Column transformations
- Imputation of missing values
- Scaling and centering
- One-hot encoding

Just one column that is not preprocessed properly can have an extremely negative impact on the model predictions.

Improving our models

Although in this chapter we have built a rudimentary model that matches the performance of academic research studies, there is certainly room for improvement. The following are some ideas for how the model can be improved, and we leave it to the reader to implement these suggestions and any other tricks or techniques the reader might know to improve performance. How high will your performance go?

First and foremost, the current training data has a large number of columns. Some sort of feature selection is almost always performed, particularly for logistic regression and random forest models. For logistic regression, common methods of performing feature selection include:

- Using a certain number of predictors that have the highest coefficients
- Using a certain number of predictors that have the lowest p-values
- Using lasso regularization and removing predictors whose coefficients become zero
- Using a greedy algorithm such as forward- or backward-stepwise logistic regression that removes/adds predictors systematically according to rules
- Using a brute-force algorithm, such as best subset logistic regression, that tests every predictor permutation/combination for a given number of predictors

For random forests, using the variable importance and selecting a certain number of predictors with the highest importance is very common, as is performing grid searches.

Neural networks have their own unique improvement techniques.

- For one thing, more data is always good, particularly with neural networks.
- The specific optimization algorithm used can factor into the performance.
- In this example, our neural networks only had one hidden layer. In the industry, models with multiple hidden layers are becoming increasingly common (although they may take a long time to train).
- The specific nonlinear activation function used may also impact the model's performance.

Summary

In this chapter, we have built a predictive model for predicting outcomes in the emergency department. While there are many machine learning problems in healthcare, this exercise has demonstrated the issues typically faced as one preprocesses healthcare data, trains and scores models, and makes predictions with unlabeled data. This chapter marks the end of the coding portion of this book.

Now that we have seen the construction of a predictive model firsthand, the next logical question to ask is how predictive models have fared when compared with traditional statistical risk scores in predicting clinical outcomes. We explore that question in the next chapter.

References and further reading

Cameron A, Rodgers K, Ireland A, et al. (2015). A simple tool to predict admission at the time of triage. *Emerg Med J* 2015;32:174-179.

Futoma J, Morris J, Lucas J (2015). A comparison of models for predicting early hospital readmissions. Journal of Biomedical Informatics 56: 229-238.

Healthcare Predictive Models – A Review

8

This chapter is intended for all audiences and marries the traditional risk score model commonly used in healthcare with the theory and features underlying machine learning models similar to those developed in Chapter 7, *Making Predictive Models in Healthcare*. If you come from a data science background, this chapter will be a good introduction to some of the widely used clinical risk scores and will indicate which features should be included in your models, whether general or disease-specific. If you come from a healthcare background, this chapter will be a review of some of the clinical risk scores and will explain how machine learning algorithms can enhance traditional risk assessment.

Predictive healthcare analytics – state of the art

As we touched upon in Chapter 3, *Machine Learning Foundations*, healthcare is no stranger to complex risk factor assessments. For almost every major disease, one can find several risk-scoring models that are used widely by physicians to assess the risk of having a disease or suffering morbidity/mortality from that disease. When we use the term "risk score," we are largely referring to criterion tables, in which risk factors are allotted point values, and the points for all of the risk factors are summed to give an overall risk based on the total. These scoring systems are used widely in medicine; interestingly, many of them are based on research involving logistic regression models (similar to the one developed in Chapter 7, *Making Predictive Models in Healthcare*). The crucial question of the last several decades is whether machine learning can improve our ability to predict whether an individual has or will have a disease, how much care that disease will require, and whether the patient will die from the disease in a certain time period.

That question is addressed in this chapter. We organize this chapter by having sections on several leading causes of morbidity and mortality in developed countries for which risk scores have been developed. The covered entities include overall cardiovascular risk, congestive heart failure, cancer, and all-cause readmission. The first three entities are leading causes of mortality, and the fourth entity is a common way to measure quality in healthcare. We then explore the subsequent machine learning literature to see whether machine learning has improved the traditional risk assessment used for that disease. By the end of this chapter, you should have a thorough understanding of how machine learning can be used to improve disease prediction.

Overall cardiovascular risk

We start with overall cardiovascular risk assessment since it is one of the most important areas in personal health and the exploration of cardiovascular risk factors has such a long and storied history.

Cardiovascular risk refers to the risk of developing a subset of the cardiac disease known as cardiovascular disease. **Cardiovascular disease** (CVD) refers to dysfunction of the circulatory system caused by a narrowing and/or clogging of the arteries that supply blood to tissues, a process known as atherosclerosis. It encompasses a broad set of cardiac diseases, which include the following:

- **Coronary artery disease** (CAD): This occurs when the blood vessels that supply blood to the heart become narrowed due to atherosclerosis. CAD is deadly because it can lead to sudden occlusion of the coronary arteries, which is known as a myocardial infarction (or a heart attack).
- **Congestive heart failure** (CHF): This is the failure of the heart to pump blood to the rest of the body. It is caused by the long-term effects of CAD on the heart. It has an onset that is more gradual than myocardial infarction, however, its course is often characterized by sudden exacerbations and hospitalizations before ultimately leading to death.
- **Peripheral vascular disease** (PVD): This is when arteries that supply blood to the arms or legs become narrowed and occluded, which can lead to problematic symptoms such as pain (known as **claudication**) and may result in amputations.
- **Cerebrovascular disease**, or atherosclerosis of the vessels supplying the brain: This puts individuals at higher risk for ischemic and hemorrhagic stroke. Stroke is when the blood supply to the brain is cut off, which can lead to death and also can lead to devastating sequelae.

Now that you know what CVD is, you should also know its devastating effects on humans. Globally, it is the leading cause of morbidity and mortality (Weng et al., 2017). CHF alone is related to 3-5% of hospital admissions and is the leading cause of hospital admissions for healthcare professionals and accounts for up to 2% of total healthcare expenditures in developed countries (Tripoliti et al., 2016).

Although CVD had been a prominent cause of disability and death in the United States since the beginning of the twentieth century, in the 1940s, people still had no idea what caused it. In fact, during that time, little was understood about the risk and prevention of CVDs (and disease in general). At the time, it was believed that CVD was the destiny of whomever it affected, independent of lifestyle decisions.

The Framingham Risk Score

In 1948, the National Heart Institute embarked on an ambitious project in conjunction with Boston University, called the Framingham Heart Study. Its goal: to find which factors cause CVD. In 1948, 5,209 men and women were recruited from the town of Framingham, Massachusetts that had not yet been affected visibly by CVD (Framingham Heart Study, 2018a). Every 2 years, these individuals underwent a detailed medical history, physical examination, and laboratory testing. Over the years, new generations of patients were recruited and subjects have continued to return every 2 years for assessment, until today.

It was through this long-term, prospective study that the risk factors for CVD were first identified. The link between smoking and CVD was first reported in 1960 (Framingham Heart Study, 2018b). After that, cholesterol, high blood pressure, and diabetes were eventually linked to CVD as well. Starting in the 1990s, risk scores for developing specific types of CVD (for example, myocardial infarction, PVD, CHF) began being published. In 2008, the general Framingham Risk Score was published. The Framingham Risk Score assigns individuals a risk score for experiencing CVD events within a 10-year period based on five major CVD risk factors: age, high blood pressure, cholesterol levels, smoking status, and diabetes. The following is a summary of the general cardiovascular risk-scoring criteria for women (D'Agostino et al., 2008).

Men have similar criteria with slightly different point values:

Points	Age (y)	HDL cholesterol	Total cholesterol	SBP not treated	SBP treated	Smoker	Diabetic
-3				<120			
-2		60+					
-1		50-59			<120		
0	30-34	45-49	<160	120-129		No	No
1		35-44	160-190	130-139			
2	35-39	<35		140-149	120-129		
3			200-239		130-139	Yes	
4	40-44		240-279	150-159			Yes
5	45-49		280+	160+	140-149		
6					150-159		
7	50-54				160+		
8	55-59						
9	60-64						
10	65-69						
11	70-74						
12	75+						

Today, these same five risk factors (four of them being preventable) are continuously expounded by our doctors when we visit their offices.

To calculate the total score, the values for each of the six risk factors (age, HDL level, total cholesterol, SBP not treated, SBP treated, smoker, diabetic) are added. The following table shows how point values correspond to 10-year risk scores (D'Agostino et al., 2008):

Points	Risk (%)	Points	Risk (%)	Points	Risk (%)
<-2	<1	6	3.3	14	11.7
-1	1.0	7	3.9	15	13.7
0	1.2	8	4.5	16	15.9
1	1.5	9	5.3	17	18.5
2	1.7	10	6.3	18	21.5
3	2.0	11	7.3	19	24.8
4	2.4	12	8.6	20	28.5
5	2.8	13	10.0	21 +	> 30

You may be wondering, "What is the method behind the madness?" To develop these scores, the study's authors used the Cox proportional hazards regression, which is similar to logistic regression, except that instead of determining how variables are associated with a binary outcome, it determines how variables are related to the quantity of time before an event occurs. They even calculated the C-statistic of their risk score (analogous to the area under the curve, discussed in `Chapter 3`, *Machine Learning Foundations*) which was 0.76 to 0.79. This is a very good score that can be obtained just from a patient history, physical examination, and some simple blood tests.

Cardiovascular risk and machine learning

As you know, scientific progress is never complacent. When a result is obtained, it is only a matter of time before people begin wondering how to improve upon it. The same is the case with cardiovascular risk assessment. Key questions that were asked include the following:

- What are some other risk factors that are as (or even more) important than the five risk factors in the Framingham Risk Score?
- Can the newer machine learning algorithms outperform statistical models, such as regression, to yield higher discriminability and performance?

One study, by the University of Nottingham in England, addressed those questions (Weng et al., 2017). It was a prospective study that monitored the electronic medical records of 378,256 patients from the year 2005 to 2015. For each patient, they used data on the 8 risk factors included in the Framingham Risk Score, as well as 22 additional variables that were thought to be correlated with cardiovascular risk from previous literature and consultation with physicians. The 22 additional variables encompassed information such as socioeconomic status; history of other illnesses including kidney disease, arthritis, and atrial fibrillation; newer lab tests such as C-reactive protein and gamma-glutamyl transferase; and ethnicity. They trained four types of machine learning algorithms on the patient data – logistic regression, random forest, neural networks, and gradient-boosting machines. All four of the algorithms improved performance over the baseline risk prediction algorithm; in fact, the neural network algorithm predicted 355 more correct cases of cardiovascular events than the established algorithm. As they looked at the variables of top importance, while many resembled the Framingham criteria, many were new. Ethnicity appeared in the top three variables in all of the algorithms. Socioeconomic status (Townsend Deprivation Index) appeared in the top ten for all four algorithms. Chronic kidney disease was also found to be linked to cardiovascular risk. For cardiovascular risk, it is clear that machine learning has enriched our knowledge of predicting cardiac events.

Congestive heart failure

Of all the cardiac events mentioned in the *Overall cardiovascular risk* section, CHF deserves a special section of its own. That is for three main reasons:

- CHF is the most common cause of hospital admission in developed countries
- Its cost of management is very high, accounting for up to 2% of total healthcare expenditures
- Its cost of diagnosis is also very high, requiring expensive echocardiograms to be performed, read, and interpreted by specialized personnel and physicians (Tripoliti et al., 2016)

Diagnosing CHF

While CHF can be deemed probable in patients with particular symptoms, risk factors, electrocardiogram findings, and laboratory results, a definitive diagnosis can only be made through echocardiography or a cardiac MRI. Echocardiography requires skilled personnel to administer the test, and then a specialist physician (usually a cardiologist or radiologist) must read the study and visually assess how well the heart is pumping. This is usually done by estimating the **ejection fraction** (**EF**), which is the fraction of blood the left ventricle ejects during its contraction. An EF of 65% is considered normal, 40% indicates heart failure, and 10-15% is seen in advanced stages of CHF. The following diagram was taken from an echocardiogram, which shows the four chambers of the heart. You can imagine that it may be unreliable to quantify heart function using the fuzzy images produced by sound waves:

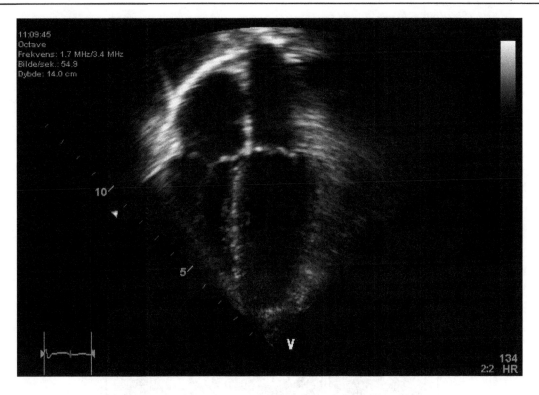

A cardiac MRI, while more expensive, is more accurate in measuring EF and is considered the gold standard for CHF diagnosis; however, it requires a cardiologist to spend up to 20 minutes reading an individual scan. In the following diagram, we see:

- *A*) An illustration of the heart with the imaging plane used for cardiac MRI also shown.
- *B*) A 3-D angiogram of the heart (an angiogram is a study in which dye is injected into the bloodstream while images are taken to better visualize the blood vessels).

- C), D), and E) images of normal, damaged, and ischemic left ventricles, respectively, obtained from cardiac MRIs:

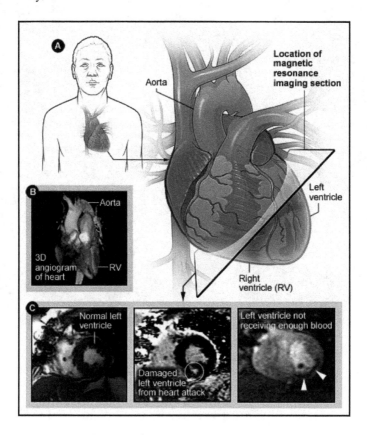

Given the nontrivial nature of CHF diagnosis, again we ask the same questions we asked previously: Can new risk factors be discovered and better performance be achieved with respect to CHF diagnosis by using machine learning algorithms?

CHF detection with machine learning

One approach to improve CHF detection with machine learning is to sidestep the use of expensive and time-consuming imaging studies. A recent study from Keimyung University in South Korea used rough sets, decision trees, and logistic regression algorithms, and compared their performance to a physician's diagnosis of heart disease, which was used as the gold standard (Son et al., 2012).

Rough sets are similar to best subset logistic regression (for example, subsets of variables are tested for their informativeness, and the most informative subsets are chosen for the final decision rules). The algorithms were trained on demographic characteristics and lab findings only. The models achieved over 97% sensitivity and 97% specificity in differentiating CHF from non-CHF-related shortness of breath. That's astonishingly close to the human performance, with much less data, time, and resources used.

A second approach we should mention is the use of automated algorithms to read the echocardiography and cardiac MRI scans used to diagnose CHF. This problem was the subject of the 2015 Data Science Bowl, sponsored by the data science competition website Kaggle and Booz Allen Hamilton, the consulting company. For more on this competition, you can visit the Kaggle competition website: `https://www.kaggle.com/c/second-annual-data-science-bowl`. It goes to show the interest that machine learning in healthcare has garnered.

Other applications of machine learning in CHF

While the detection and diagnosis of disease in humans is always a problem, there are other applications of ML in CHF management. These applications are well-documented in a review paper by the University of Ioannina in Greece (Tripoliti et al., 2017). In addition to CHF detection, discussed problems in that paper relevant to CHF management include severity estimation, CHF subtype classification, exacerbation and hospital readmission prediction, and mortality.

Cancer

In `Chapter 2`, *Healthcare Foundations*, we cited several reasons why fighting cancer via ML is an important endeavor, its significant global morbidity, mortality, and emotional consequences notwithstanding. In this section, let's take a closer look at some important concepts and background about cancer, potential machine learning applications for fighting cancer, important features for cancer risk and survivability modeling, and some of the work that has already been done in the area of breast cancer as an example.

What is cancer?

Cancer can be described as the growth and proliferation of abnormal cells. These cells differ from normal cells in their aggressive reproductive capabilities and their ability to starve normal cells from important resources such as blood and nutrients. Cancer is usually either benign, meaning that it is self-contained to a local area of the body, or malignant, meaning that it has the ability to spread to other bodily tissues. Malignant cancers almost always result in death if untreated, and many even when treated. The progression toward death depends on a number of factors, including the type of cancer, clinical stage of the cancer when detected, pathologic grade of the tumor, and clinical risk factors. Benign cancers aren't as problematic as malignant cancers, although they may cause symptoms and can still result in death (for example, a benign acoustic neuroma that causes high pressure in the brain). Treatment involves some combination of chemotherapy, radiotherapy, biological agents, and/or surgical resection of the tumor and possibly the surrounding tissue and organs.

As you know, cancer is usually classified by the bodily area in which it first appears. The four most deadly types of cancer in the US are lung cancer, breast cancer, prostate cancer, and colon cancer.

ML applications for cancer

Two comprehensive review papers thoroughly document and summarize the ML research that has been performed for cancer in the last three decades. The first review paper is by the University of Alberta in Canada and provides a thorough review of the studies undertaken prior to it writing in 2006 (*Cruz and Wishart*, 2006). The second paper is a more recent one and comes from the University of Ioannina in Greece (Kourou et al., 2015). Both papers have broken down the types of subproblems in the area of cancer ML quite well and match well with some of the subproblems that were discussed in `Chapter 2`, *Healthcare Foundations*. These problems include:

- **Early detection/screening of cancer**: Can machine learning models be trained to identify individuals with a high risk of developing cancer before symptoms appear?
- **Diagnosis of cancer**: How can machine learning aid oncologists/radiologists in making definitive diagnoses of cancer and classifying the cancer stage and grade?

- **Cancer recurrence**: In an individual who has been treated successfully with initial cancer, how likely is that cancer to recur?
- **Life expectancy and survivability**: In which patients will cancer likely cause mortality? Which patients are likely to be alive in 5 years? In 10 years?
- **Tumor drug sensitivity**: Which tumors are likely to respond to specific treatments for cancer (for example, chemotherapy, radiotherapy, biological agents, or surgery).

Important features of cancer

A number of variables are particularly important for machine learning with cancer use cases. Let's take a look at those now.

Routine clinical data

Clinical data that is routinely available in electronic medical records of all patients is particularly valuable, since it is inexpensive and can be easily included in retroactive modeling studies. Such clinical data is summarized in the following table. It should be noted that there are many exceptions to these rules; for example, while elderly age is an important risk factor for most cancers, bone cancers and some leukemias tend to occur most commonly in children (National Cancer Institute, 2015). The National Cancer Institute is an excellent resource for a more detailed breakdown of clinical risk factors for cancer (www.cancer.gov):

Risk factor	Increases cancer risk	Decreases cancer risk
Elderly age	×	
Positive family history	×	
High-fat diet	×	
High-fiber diet		×
Diets high in fruits and vegetables		×
Obesity	×	
Tobacco use	×	
Alcohol use	×	
Sun exposure	×	

Cancer-specific clinical data

After the primary site of the tumor has been identified, almost every tumor can be further classified into subtypes, both clinically and pathologically. The clinical stage of the tumor classifies the extent of the neoplasm. The TNM staging system is the most common; under this system, staging is determined from three factors:

- The size of the tumor (T)
- The involvement of nearby lymph nodes (N)
- The metastasis of the tumor to other bodily sites (M)

Usually, survival rates are given depending on the clinical stage, which in turn is determined by the TNM staging criteria, which differs for each tumor.

The pathologic grade of the tumor concerns the cellular characteristics of its cells. Things that pathologists look for when setting a tumor grade include the similarity of tumor cell appearance to normal cell appearance (differentiation) and the existence of normal cell organelles (National Cancer Institute, 2015).

Imaging data

Radiographic findings from x-rays, CT scans, and MRIs can also be used in models that are related to cancer severity and prognosis. Later in this section, we will look at a breast cancer study that trained a neural network on mammogram features, such as the presence and shape of breast tumor microcalcifications and surrounding skin characteristics (Ayer et al., 2010).

Genomic data

Although gene results are not always easy to obtain in prospective studies, nor are they available in retrospective studies, they are important predictors when available. Specific features include the presence of single nucleotide polymorphisms (SNPs; point mutations) in the patient's DNA and the presence of certain genes (such as BRCA1 in hereditary breast cancer) (Morin et al. Harrison's, 2005).

Proteomic data

The presence of specific proteins associated with the tumor also influences risk. Examples of significant proteins include tumor-associated biomarkers (for example, CA 19-9 in pancreatic cancer) and hormones (for example, HER-2/neu in breast cancer) (Longo et al., 2005).

An example – breast cancer prediction

Let's take a look at how machine learning has enhanced the screening and diagnosis of breast cancer, one of the most common cancers worldwide.

Traditional screening of breast cancer

Screening of breast cancer is a complex problem. Risk scores generally perform poorly; a systematic review of the literature for the performance of the Gail model for predicting breast cancer risk found AUCs that were typically between 0.55 and 0.65 (a random classifier would have an AUC of 0.5) (Wang et al., 2018).

The next least invasive test for breast cancer screening is a clinical breast exam or self-breast exam. The sensitivity and specificity for breast exams vary widely according to age, breast density, and research setting; one study found that sensitivity can be as low as 57%, although the same study found the specificity to be 88% (Baines et al., 1989). Because a good screening test has a high sensitivity, there is a consensus that physical breast examination alone is not adequate for breast cancer screening.

Imaging is the next least invasive screening test for breast cancer. Imaging modalities used for breast cancer screening include mammography, MRI, and ultrasound. In 2016, the **US Preventive Services Task Force** (**USPSTF**) recommended biennial mammograms (see the following diagram showing a mammogram of the breast with a whitish area diagnosed as colloid carcinoma; National Cancer Institute, 1990) for women aged 50 and older, due to the high sensitivity (77% to 95%) and high specificity (94% to 97%) of mammograms in this age group combined with their low potential for causing patient harm (US Preventive Services Task Force, 2016).

Biopsies are the most invasive options for breast cancer detection, and in fact, are used for definitive diagnosis when screening tests are positive.

Breast cancer screening and machine learning

The machine learning literature in breast cancer research is vast (Cruz and Wishart, 2006; Kourou et al., 2015). Here we summarize one study that highlights the potential for machine learning to aid in breast cancer diagnosis, when used in conjunction with mammography and EMRs. The study is from the University of Wisconsin, Madison and consisted of 48,744 mammograms (Ayer et al., 2010).

For each mammogram, information about 36 categorical variables was collected, including clinical data (age, past medical history, family history) and mammographic findings, such as tumor mass characteristics, surrounding skin and nipple characteristics, lymph node examination, and calcification characteristics. An artificial neural network consisting of 1,000 hidden layers was trained and the generated labels were compared to the true label of benign versus malignant. Eight radiologists also reviewed varying numbers of mammograms and classified the scan as benign versus malignant. The total AUC of the neural network was 0.965, while that of the radiologists was 0.939. This study, combined with other studies we will read about in the final chapter, demonstrate how ML can be used as an effective tool in the fight against cancer:

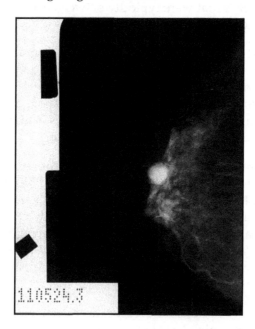

Readmission prediction

Predicting the likelihood of all-cause patient readmissions is outside the scope of a typical clinician's knowledge base, since it is not tied to a specific organ system or disease. However, it is becoming a problem of increasing importance in the healthcare world, since preventable hospital readmissions are a major cause of elevated healthcare expenditures in the United States and other countries. We discussed the incentive and rationale for predicting hospital readmissions and the US government's **Hospital Readmission Reduction Program (HRRP)** in Chapter 6, *Measuring Healthcare Quality*. Let's now review how machine learning algorithms can be used to augment simpler readmission risk scores.

LACE and HOSPITAL scores

The most well-known readmission risk score is the LACE score, which was developed in 2010 by Canadian researchers (van Walraven et al., 2010). "LACE" stands for the four predictors used to calculate the score, and the full score calculation ranges from 0-19 and is shown in the following table. The Charlson comorbidity index is a score that assigns scores to patients based on the presence of certain illnesses in their past medical history, including myocardial infarction, cancer, CHF, and HIV infection:

Component	Attribute	Value	Points
L	Length of stay (days)	<1	0
		1	1
		2	2
		3	3
		4-6	4
		7-13	5
		>13	7
A	Acuity (emergence of admission)	Yes	3
C	Comorbidity (Charlson comorbidity index)	0	0
		1	1
		2	2
		3	3
		>3	5
E	ED visits during last 6 months	0	0
		1	1
		2	2
		3	3
		<3	4

To derive this index, the study authors entered over a dozen variables thought to be related to readmission risk for 2,393 patients into a multivariable logistic regression model, and were left with these four variables as the significant predictors in the model. They then developed the scoring system and externally validated it using 1,000,000 records from a Canadian patient database. Their own reported C-statistic for predicting early death or urgent readmission within 30 days was 0.684.

Another example of a hospital readmission risk score is the more recently developed HOSPITAL score (Donze et al., 2013; Donze et al., 2016). Again "HOSPITAL" stands for the seven predictors used in the score as listed in the following table:

Component	Attribute	Value	Points
H	Hemoglobin < 12 g/dL at discharge	Yes	1
O	Oncology service discharge	Yes	2
S	Sodium < 135 mmol/L at discharge	Yes	1
P	Procedure during hospital stay	Yes	1
IT	Index admission type: urgent	Yes	1
A	Admission count during the previous year	0-1	0
		2-5	2
		>5	5
L	Length of stay > 5 days	Yes	2

The HOSPITAL score ranges from 0-13 points. The score was derived using the seven factors independently related to hospital readmission, also using a multivariable logistic regression model (Donze et al., 2013). The score was externally validated using 117,065 discharges from four countries and the authors reported a C-statistic of 0.72 (Donze et al., 2016).

Readmission modeling

Let's look at two recent studies that have applied machine learning to the readmission risk identification problem.

The first study comes by Duke University (Futoma et al., 2014). In this study, 3.3 million hospital admissions from New Zealand were studied. For each admission, demographic information, background information, **diagnosis-related group** (DRG) codes, and **International Classification of Diseases** (ICD) diagnosis and procedure codes were used. The matrix was then fed into six different machine learning algorithms:

- Logistic regression
- Logistic regression with the multistep variable selection
- Penalized logistic regression
- Random forest
- Support vector machine
- Deep learning

Of the first five methods, the random forest had the best performance, achieving an AUC of 0.684. The deep learning models were used to predict readmissions on five patient cohorts: pneumonia, **chronic obstructive pulmonary disease** (COPD), CHF, MI, and total hip/knee arthroplasty. The highest performance was achieved for pneumonia, with an AUC of 0.734. It should be noted that no direct comparison to LACE or HOSPITAL risk scores was performed.

The second study comes from the Advocate Health Care hospital system (Tong et al., 2016). The study consisted of 162,466 index (for example, initial) hospital admissions. For each index admission, 19 data elements were collected including the four LACE score components and 15 other EMR variables, such as past medical history, previous clinical encounters, employment status, and lab results. They trained three different machine learning models on this data:

- Logistic regression with the stepwise forward-backward variable selection
- Logistic regression with lasso regularization
- Boosting

They found that when they used 80,000 index admissions for the training/validation sets, the LACE model had an AUC of ~0.65, while the three machine learning models all had AUCs of ~0.73. The results suggest the significance of additional variables outside of the four variables used for the LACE score, and they further reinforce the use of machine learning for healthcare.

Other conditions and events

There are many other conditions for which machine learning algorithms have been used to improve risk assessment and prediction over traditional risk scores. COPD, pneumonia, sepsis, stroke, and dementia are just a few examples.

Summary

In this chapter, we have reviewed different types of healthcare models and the features they use to achieve efficacy. We have omitted some emerging trends in healthcare from our discussion, however; these include the use of newer technologies such as social media, the Internet of Things, and deep learning algorithms to push the healthcare prediction envelope even further. We'll examine these trends in the next chapter.

References and further reading

Ayer T, Alagoz O, Chhatwal J, Shavlik JW, Kahn Jr. CE, Burnside ES (2010). Breast Cancer Risk Estimation with Artificial Neural Networks Revisited: Discrimination and Calibration. *Cancer* 116 (14): 3310-3321.

Baines CJ (1989). Breast self-examination. *Cancer* 64(12 Suppl): 2661-2663.

Cruz JA, Wishart DS (2006). Applications of Machine Learning in Cancer Prediction and Prognosis. *Cancer Informatics* 2: 59-77.

D'Agostino RB, Vasan RS, Pencina MJ, Wolf PA, Cobain M, Massaro JM, Kannel WB (2008). *General Cardiovascular Risk Profile for Use in Primary Care: The Framingham Heart Study.* *Circulation* 117 (6): 743-753.

Donze J, Aujesky D, Williams D, Schnipper JL (2013). Potentially avoidable 30-day hospital readmissions in medical patients: derivation and validation of a prediction model. *JAMA Intern Med* 173(8): 632-638.

Donze JD, Williams MV, Robinson EJ et al. (2016). International Validity of the "HOSPITAL" Score to Predict 30-day Potentially Avoidable Readmissions in Medical Patients. *JAMA Intern Med* 176(4): 496-502.

Framingham Heart Study (2018a). *History of the Framingham Heart Study.* https://www.framinghamheartstudy.org/fhs-about/history/. Accessed June 16, 2018.

Framingham Heart Study (2018b). *Research Milestones.* https://www.framinghamheartstudy.org/fhs-about/research-milestones/. Accessed June 16, 2018.

Futoma J, Morris J, Lucas J (2015). A comparison of models for predicting early hospital readmissions. *Journal of Biomedical Informatics* 56: 229-238.

Kourou K, Exarchos TP, Exarchos KP, Karamouzis MV, Fotiadis DI (2015). Machine learning applications in cancer prognosis and prediction. *Computational and Structural Biotechnology Journal* 13: 8-17.

Lenes K (2005). *File: Echocardiogram 4chambers.jpg.* https://commons.wikimedia.org/wiki/File:Echocardiogram_4chambers.jpg. Accessed June 23, 2018.

Longo DL (2005). "*Approach to the Patient with Cancer.*" In Kasper DL, Braunwald E, Fauci AS, Hauser SL, Longo DL, Jameson JL. eds. *Harrison's Principles of Internal Medicine*, 16e. New York, NY: McGraw-Hill.

Morin PJ, Trent JM, Collins FS, Vogelstein B (2005). "Cancer Genetics." In Kasper DL, Braunwald E, Fauci AS, Hauser SL, Longo DL, Jameson JL. eds. *Harrison's Principles of Internal Medicine*, 16e. New York, NY: McGraw-Hill.

National Cancer Institute (1990). Mammogram Showing Cancer. Unknown Photographer, American College of Radiology. https://commons.wikimedia.org/wiki/File:Mammogram_showing_cancer.jpg. Accessed June 23, 2018.

National Cancer Institute (2015a). *Breast Cancer Screening (PDQ®)-Health Professional Version.* https://www.cancer.gov/types/breast/hp/breast-screening-pdq#section/all. Accessed June 23, 2018.

National Cancer Institute (2015b). *Risk Factors for Cancer.* https://www.cancer.gov/about-cancer/causes-prevention/risk. Accessed June 23, 2018.

National Heart Lung and Blood Institute (2013). File:Cardiac_Mri.jpg. https://commons.wikimedia.org/wiki/File:Cardiac_mri.jpg. Accessed June 23, 2018.

Son C, Kim Y, Kim H, Park H, Kim M (2012). Decision-making model for early diagnosis of congestive heart failure using rough set and decision tree approaches. *Journal of Biomedical Informatics* 45: 999-1008.

Tong L, Erdmann C, Daldalian M, Li J, Esposito T (2016). Comparison of predictive modeling approaches for 30-day all-cause non-elective readmission risk. *BMC Medical Research Methodology* 2016(16): 26.

Tripoliti EE, Papadopoulos TG, Karanasiou GS, Naka KK, Fotiadis DI (2017). Heart Failure: Diagnosis, Severity Estimation and Prediction of Adverse Events Through Machine Learning Techniques. *Computational and Structural Biotechnology Journal* 15: 26-47.

US Preventive Services Task Force (2016). *Final Recommendation Statement: Breast Cancer: Screening.* https://www.uspreventiveservicestaskforce.org/Page/Document/RecommendationStatementFinal/breast-cancer-screening1. Accessed June 23, 2018.

van Walraven C, Dhalla IA, Bell C, Etchells E, Stiell IG, Zarnke K, Austin PC, Forster AJ (2010). Derivation and validation of an index to predict early death or unplanned readmission after discharge from hospital to the community. *Canadian Medical Association Journal* 182(6): 551-557.

Wang X, Huang Y, Li L, Dai H, Song F, Chen K (2018). Assessment of performance of the Gail model for predicting breast cancer risk: a systematic review and meta-analysis with trial sequential analysis. *Breast Cancer Research* 20: 18.

Weng SF, Reps J, Kai J, Garibaldi JM, Qureshi N (2017). *Can machine-learning improve cardiovascular risk prediction using routine clinical data? PLOS One* 12(4): e0174944. https://doi.org/10.1371/journal.pone.0174944

The Future – Healthcare and Emerging Technologies

9

So far in this book, we've examined the exciting history of healthcare analytics and some of the ways it currently impacts our healthcare system. In this chapter, we provide a sense of the latest developments in the field and what will likely be coming to healthcare analytics in the not-so-distant future. We'll delve into healthcare and the internet, specifically the **Internet of Things** (**IoT**) and social media applications, to see how they are playing roles in improving health. Next, we'll take a look at some of the new algorithms (collectively referred to as "deep learning") that are achieving state-of-the-art performance in medical prediction tasks. Finally, although this book has presented the state of healthcare analytics in a hopeful and optimistic fashion, there are still some considerable obstacles and barriers that must be overcome for healthcare analytics to disruptively impact our healthcare system for the better. We'll discuss those at the end of the book.

Healthcare analytics and the internet

Physically, the **internet** is a specific computer network that connects millions of computing devices worldwide. Practically, it is an infrastructure that provides services to applications such as email, social networks, data storage, and communication (Kurose and Ross, 2013). The internet rose to prominence in the 1990s and affected virtually every industry in the global economy; healthcare is no exception. As we discussed in Chapter 2, *Healthcare Foundations*, clinical data is increasingly being stored electronically on computers, and third parties who perform analytics with this data often receive the data via the internet and use the cloud to store this data. Furthermore, the results of the analytics are often communicated back to the healthcare organization via an internet technology known as an **application programming interface** (**API**) by which the healthcare organization sends a request for specific information to a server and receives that information.

Aside from the typical data exchange cycle discussed throughout this book, which obviously relies heavily on the internet, there are some fringe methods through which the internet is affecting healthcare. Let's take a look at two of those methods here:

- Internet of Things
- Social media

Healthcare and the Internet of Things

Although, traditionally, we think of the internet as a network for computers, in recent years, additional types of devices have joined the fray. The IoT is a network of physical devices embedded with sensors, software, and internet connectivity, enabling these devices to exchange data (Dimitrov, 2016). To date, much work has been done with the IoT in the healthcare space, and the implications of the IoT for healthcare are considerable. One emerging function of the IoT is to be able to remotely monitor patient health (Ma et al., 2017). A prototypical example is provided by a group of researchers at UCLA who developed a weight, activity, and blood pressure patient-monitoring system for CHF called **WANDA** (Suh et al., 2011). Increased weight due to fluid retention, decreased activity, and uncontrolled blood pressure are critical markers of CHF decompensation; WANDA uses weight scales and blood pressure monitors to communicate measurements about the patient to the patient's phone via Bluetooth. The phone then sends this data to a backend database in the cloud, along with activity and symptom information about the patient collected from a phone-based app. The data can then be used to perform logistic regression (similar to that we discussed in `Chapter 2`, *Healthcare Foundations* and `Chapter 7`, *Making Predictive Models in Healthcare*) to alert a physician in case the patient is at risk of CHF decompensation. All of this is done privately and securely. This is a prime example of how one of the deadliest and most morbid chronic diseases can be fought using the IoT.

Although the IoT-healthcare partnership has promise, major obstacles and barriers include effective interdevice communication (device companies often use their own proprietary languages), maintenance of patient privacy and security, and ease of use for the patient (Dimitrov, 2016). Certainly, the IoT space will be one to watch as we look toward the future.

Healthcare analytics and social media

A different type of internet application for improving health is the use of social media applications, such as Facebook and Twitter, to monitor and forecast disease epidemics. An **epidemic** is a sudden and widespread occurrence of a particular disease in a community.

Social media is well adapted for tracking epidemics because they create senses of anonymity and freedom to express personal feelings and information (Charles-Smith et al., 2015). The analysis of language used on social media sites has shed light on various disease outbreaks including alcohol and drug abuse, congestive heart failure, and infectious diseases (Brathwaite et al., 2016). Here we take a look at how social media is being used to combat two prominent epidemics: influenza and suicide.

Influenza surveillance and forecasting

One recent study by Johns Hopkins University in Maryland sought to determine whether user "tweets" or messages on Twitter can be used to forecast or predict the rate of influenza in the following weeks (Paul et al., 2014). They used a basic linear autoregressive model, which is similar to logistic regression except that the features are the influenza rates of the previous weeks and the coefficients are determined by least squares regression. They compared models that used only the CDC's published weekly rates with models that also used a Twitter influenza surveillance system that analyzes tweets to determine whether they are about influenza infections. Their study found that incorporating Twitter data helps reduce errors in the predicted influenza rate by 15 - 30% up to 10 weeks into the future. Similarly, a review study analyzing the use of social media for monitoring disease found that joint information from social media sites and national health statistics predicted outbreaks before standard outbreak surveillance systems (Charles-Smith et al., 2015).

Predicting suicidality with machine learning

Suicide is the 10th leading cause of death in the United States, and its incidence is rising, placing unprecedented emotional and financial burdens on its victims' families (Brathwaite et al., 2016). In the afore-cited study, by Brigham Young University, researchers recruited 135 participants through Amazon's Mechanical Turk (www.mturk.com) and asked them to complete three clinically validated questionnaires for assessing suicide risk. In addition, the researchers analyzed the tweets of each participant using a language analysis tool that extracts features from the text. The features largely measure the frequency of certain word categories including "family," "anger," and "sadness." They used Python and the scikit-learn library to then build models that classified each of these "training set" participants as suicidal or not suicidal. To test their model on previously unseen data, they used leave-one-out cross-validation, a procedure in which only one participant was used as test data, and this was repeated 135 times. Their decision tree model obtained an accuracy of 91.9% and had a sensitivity of 53% and a specificity of 97%. Certainly, this is encouraging for identifying suicidal patients before they commit suicidal acts, although it remains to be seen how privacy would be preserved in such a suicide-monitoring system.

Healthcare and deep learning

No book on healthcare analytics would be complete without a discussion of deep learning. In recent years, unparalleled results have been achieved in the areas of speech recognition, face recognition, language understanding, and object identification using deep learning algorithms (Goodfellow et al., 2016). Almost in tandem have been the breakthroughs in healthcare; from cancer detection on pathology slides and radiology scans to predicting mortality and readmissions, time and time again, results are being seen that rival (and in some cases surpass) committees of expert physicians.

We have already discussed some aspects of deep learning briefly. In Chapter 1, *Introduction to Healthcare Analytics*, we discussed a historical paper that is seen by many to have been a seminal event for deep learning as a field, in Chapter 3, *Machine Learning Foundations*, we discussed deep neural networks as a medical decision-making framework, and in Chapter 8, *Healthcare Predictive Models – A Review*, we discussed some studies that used deep learning algorithms to achieve their results. Let's now briefly discuss what deep learning is and what distinguishes it from traditional machine learning and neural networks. We will then discuss some promising studies that use the following subtypes of deep learning algorithms in reaching their conclusions:

- Deep feed-forward networks
- **Convolutional neural networks (CNN)**
- **Recurrent neural networks (RNN)**

I have decided to keep discussion of the theory of deep learning out of this book since a brief, simplistic chapter on deep learning theory would not do the field justice. There are, however, some excellent courses on Coursera (www.coursera.org) that explain what deep learning is mathematically in a very easy-to-follow manner.

What is deep learning, briefly?

Deep learning has been defined as an approach to artificial intelligence in which high-level understanding is obtained through the expression and combination of simpler, low-level representations (Goodfellow et al., 2016).

Today, the use of the term *deep learning* to describe a machine learning method or algorithm usually implies the following:

- The algorithm is loosely modeled after the human neuron, using artificial neurons. In other words, the building block of a deep neural network is an artificial neuron that takes a **sum of weighted input** (similar to a regression model) and then applies a **nonlinear transformation** to that sum.
- Unlike regression, a deep neural network usually has many layers of neurons, with an **input layer** at the beginning of the model, an **output layer** at the end of the model, and at least one **hidden layer** in between the input and output layers. The output of one layer is then fed into the next layer until the output layer is reached.
- To train the weights of the model to predict the output correctly, since there are so many, we must use many, many examples (billions in some cases). A high number of training examples is implied in deep learning. The deeper and more complex the network, the more training examples we need.
- Deep learning uses the **backpropagation** algorithm to train the weights properly, and the backpropagation algorithm relies on calculus and linear algebra.

Deep learning in healthcare

There have been many studies that have applied this new class of algorithms to healthcare problems. Let's now take a tour.

Deep feed-forward networks

In `Chapter 8`, *Healthcare Predictive Models – A Review*, we discussed a study by Duke University that predicted hospital readmissions using a variety of algorithms (Futoma et al., 2015). In the second part of the study, they used a deep feed-forward network (similar to the one schematically depicted previously) that had three hidden layers, each consisting of 200-750 neurons depending on the specific condition. As their nonlinear activation function, they used the `sigmoid` function for almost all of the layers except for the output layer, where they used the `softmax` function (a common practice in deep learning). They made a model for each of the five CMS incentivized conditions (pneumonia, congestive heart failure, chronic obstructive pulmonary disease, myocardial infarction, and total hip/knee arthroplasty) and pretrained each network with all of the observations pertaining to each disease (recall that there were approximately 3,000,000 observations in total).

They used a number of other tricks to achieve maximal performance, including ridge regression penalization, dropout, and early stopping (see Goodfellow et al., 2016, for an explanation of these techniques). They achieved better results than the best non-deep learning algorithm for all of the five conditions (although the improvement was significant for only three of the five diseases). Their reported AUC is better than the previously reported AUC for the LACE and HOSPITAL readmission scores. Therefore, this is an example that demonstrates the promise of deep learning for solving complex prediction problems in healthcare, although it also highlights the difficulty and complexity with which such models are trained.

Convolutional neural networks for images

In the previous section, it was stated that neural networks employ weighted sums followed by nonlinear transformations to determine what values are used in the next layer. While this is generally true for feed-forward networks, this does not have to be true for all networks; different mathematical functions can be used apart from weighted sums to determine the next layer's input. In a different type of neural network, called a CNN, a convolution operation is used to determine the next layer's input. Typically, convolution operations are immediately followed by **pooling** operations (such as **max pooling**, in which the largest value is chosen from a discrete area to pass on to the next layer).

Networks that employ these types of operations are well-suited to data that is regularly sampled, such as images or time series data. Therefore, convolutional neural networks are popular in healthcare for processing data taken from pathology slides, radiology scans, and other images, and for detecting various diseases from them.

Pathology is a branch of medicine concerned with the evaluation of cross-sectional microscopic slides taken from human tissue samples. Examination of the slides is often done to classify tissue as cancerous or non cancerous. A pathologist sometimes has to examine very large images to look for any signs of cancerous tissue, which is very time-consuming and susceptible to errors. A recent study by Google, Inc. sought to determine whether a convolutional neural network could do a better job than pathologists at detecting breast cancer in lymph node tissue (Liu et al., 2017). For the study, slides as large as 100,000 x 100,000 pixels were used. The model was able to achieve an AUC between 0.965 and 0.986, while the pathologists achieved an AUC of 0.966. More significantly, the model produced its classification virtually instantaneously, while the human pathologist took 30 hours! This is an example of how artificial intelligence can be combined with human breadth and depth of knowledge to enhance cancer detection from pathology images. Similar types of studies can be performed on radiology scans as well.

Recurrent neural networks for sequences

Another type of specialized deep neural network is called a **recurrent neural network**, which is particularly suited to sequential data. A variant of recurrent neural networks is referred to as **long short-term memory networks** (**LSTMs** for short) (Hochreiter and Schmidhuber, 1997). LSTM networks contain **LSTM cells**, which are cells that receive an input vector and produce an output vector. The LSTM cell is intricate and consists of various "gates" that regulate the output of the cell known as **input gates**, **output gates**, and **forget gates**. The gates, in turn, are partially controlled by the input at the previous time step. LSTMs have been the networks behind many of the successful results achieved in handwriting recognition, speech recognition, language translation, and image captioning (Goodfellow et al., 2016).

A recent study, again by Google, Inc., used deep learning architectures, including an LSTM architecture, to predict in-hospital mortality, unplanned readmission, prolonged length of stay, and final discharge diagnoses (Rajkomar et al., 2018). They achieved state-of-the-art results.

Obstacles, ethical issues, and limitations

Given our touting of recent analytic and machine learning results throughout this book, why haven't doctors been replaced by computers yet? The truth is that there are many **obstacles** that stand in the way of implementing analytics in healthcare. **Ethical issues** introduced by this technology are also fiercely debated and must be considered. Finally, while obstacles imply a possibility of being overcome, there are also **limitations** to this technology, or aspects that likely will not be solved anytime soon. Let's discuss all three of these things in this section.

Obstacles

What are some of the current obstacles that must be overcome in order to achieve widespread use of analytics for improving healthcare?

- Healthcare has traditionally been slow to adopt emerging technologies, and this is a challenge that must be overcome. Healthcare has been described as a conservative field, one that is slow to embrace change. For example, there was some initial resistance to the idea of using electronic blood pressure cuffs in hospitals. Also facing skepticism and resistance was the advancement of electronic medical records, because of concerns that it takes away from the patient-physician interaction and increases the time required to write notes. Analytics and machine learning is certainly no exception; it is simply another new, unfamiliar technology, and while industries such as automotive and manufacturing embraced it with little issue, healthcare will likely be a different story.

- Perhaps an important underlying reason why doctors resist analytics and machine learning is the fear that computers are trying to "take over" or "replace" physicians. Certainly, we are a long way off from having that conversation, in terms of money, technology, and time. The machine learning studies we have discussed in this book are trained in very specific tasks, and of course, they rely on human intuition and judgment when being trained and interpreted. More likely, successful health analytics and machine learning will be achieved by utilizing a team approach, in which human strengths (such as generalizability and breadth of knowledge) are combined with computing strengths (speed and computational precision) to yield the best possible result. Still, the concern that physicians have about being replaced by computers is a real possibility, however distant, and we must find ways for physicians and artificial intelligence to work together rather than against one another.

- Another reason for skepticism toward analytics is the "hope versus hype" debate. Buzzphrases such as "big data" and "deep learning" sometimes carry negative connotations because of the hype surrounding them. Some people think that belief in these fields is overinflated. Specifically, skeptics of analytics and machine learning argue that most big data applications, while they "sound cool," rarely save lives or money. Certainly, these concerns are valid; contributing positively to society is something that all machine learning studies should strive for, rather than simply demonstrating that something can be done.

Ethical issues

Ethics has always been a part of considering new technologies, including computer science, and must not be ignored here. What are some of the ethical issues introduced by healthcare analytics?

- First and foremost, in my opinion, is the inability to place a value or a number on human feelings and painlessness. Many machine learning models are trained using a cost function. What should the cost function be? Should it be based on decreasing costs, increasing quality and outcomes, or decreasing pain and heartbreak? Who determines the ratio with which these seemingly opposing goals should be pursued?
- Another ethical issue introduced by artificial intelligence is the question of responsibility. If a machine learning model makes an errant prediction, who is to be held responsible? Should it be the physician who oversaw the patient? Or should it be the team of data scientists that made the model?
- A third issue lies in the realm of patient privacy. We discussed HIPAA laws in `Chapter 2`, *Healthcare Foundations*. Is it right to use patient data to train models? Should it require consent or not? Which data points should be allowed to be used?
- Finally, there is the problem of bias. There is a concern that predicting outcomes on patients may depend on things such as race, gender, and age. This may lead to patient discrimination.

Limitations

Limitations are those aspects of healthcare analytics that may never be overcome. What are some limitations of healthcare analytics?

- Robots and computers are not human, and they currently cannot replace a human's ability to offer comfort and empathy in the face of pain, illness, or death.
- Technologies such as neural networks, while they may offer accurate predictions, suffer from the black box problem—they cannot explain their reasoning or logic to the patient. Therefore, a patient may not trust a neural network completely the way a patient trusts a good physician.

- While the field of machine learning is constantly changing, time series and natural language processing are particularly important in the field of healthcare, and these areas are weaknesses of machine learning algorithms as opposed to structured clinical data. It may be some time before an algorithm can be written that reads text, makes generalizations, and asks relevant questions like humans do.

Conclusion of this book

In this book, we focused on healthcare analytics with the triple aim of healthcare: reducing cost, improving outcomes, and increasing care quality. Now that you have read the book, you can hopefully see more clearly how healthcare analytics can accomplish that. It can reduce healthcare costs by diagnosing problems correctly (with the help of inexpensive machine learning algorithms) and preventing unnecessary tests. It can improve healthcare outcomes by diagnosing problems sooner rather than later, allowing for corrective action to take place. Finally, it can increase quality by determining which hospitals are providing proper and timely care, and rewarding those hospitals for doing so.

With the aim of improving healthcare throughout the world, this book has introduced to you several friends that will help you to achieve that task:

- The Python language, including the base language and external libraries such as pandas and scikit-learn
- The SQL language
- Machine learning algorithms
- Healthcare domain knowledge
- Some math

Thank you for reading about what has become a central goal and mission in my life. Now let's improve healthcare, one model at a time.

References and further reading

Brathwaite SR, Giraud-Carrier C, West J, Barnes MD, Hanson CL (2016). Validating Machine Learning Algorithms for Twitter Data Against Established Measures of Suicidality. *JMIR Ment Health* 3(2): e21.

Charles-Smith LE, Reynolds TL, Cameron MA, Conway M, Lau EHY, Olsen JM, Pavlin JA, Shigematsu M, Streichert LC, Suda KJ, Corley CD (2015). Using Social Media for Actionable Disease Surveillance and Outbreak Management: A Systematic Literature Review. *PLoS ONE* 10(10): e0139701.

Dimitrov DV (2016). Medical Internet of Things and Big Data in Healthcare. *Healthcare Inform Res* 22(3): 156-163.

Futoma J, Morris J, Lucas J (2015). A comparison of models for predicting early hospital readmissions. *J Biomedical Informatics* 56: 229-238.

Goodfellow I, Bengio Y, Courville A (2016). Deep Learning. Boston, MA: MIT Press.

Liu Y, Gaepalli K, Norouzi M, Dahl GE, Kohlberger T, Boyko A, Venugopalan S, Timofeev A, Nelson PQ, Corrado GS, Hipp JD, Peng L, Stumpe MC (2017). Detecting Cancer Metastases on Gigapixel Pathology Images. `arXiv:1703.02442` [cs.CV]

Ma J, Nguyen H, Mirza F, Neuland O (2017). Two Way Architecture Between IoT Sensors and Cloud Computing for Remote Health Care Monitoring Applications. In Proceedings of the 25th European Conference on Information systems (ECIS), Guimaraes, Portugal, June 5-10, 2017 (pp. 2834-2841). Research-in-Progress Papers.

Paul MJ, Dredze M, Broniatowski D (2014). Twitter Improves Influenza Forecasting. *PLoS Curr* October 28; 6. PubMed PMID: 25642377.

Rajkomar A, Oren E, Chen K, Dai AM, Hajaj N, Hardt M, et al. (2018). Scalable and accurate deep learning with electronic health records. *npj Digital Medicine* 1:18; doi:10.1038/s41746-018-0029-1.

Suh M, Chen C, Woodbridge J, Tu MK, Kim JI, Nahapetian A, Evangelista LS, Sarrafzadeh M (2011). A Remote Patient Monitoring System for Congestive Heart Failure. *J Med Syst* 35(5): 1165-1179.

Other Books You May Enjoy

If you enjoyed this book, you may be interested in these other books by Packt:

Learning Social Media Analytics with R

Raghav Bali, Dipanjan Sarkar, Tushar Sharma

ISBN: 978-1-78712-752-4

- Learn how to tap into data from diverse social media platforms using the R ecosystem
- Use social media data to formulate and solve real-world problems
- Analyze user social networks and communities using concepts from graph theory and network analysis
- Learn to detect opinion and sentiment, extract themes, topics, and trends from unstructured noisy text data from diverse social media channels
- Understand the art of representing actionable insights with effective visualizations
- Analyze data from major social media channels such as Twitter, Facebook, Flickr, Foursquare, Github, StackExchange, and so on
- Learn to leverage popular R packages such as ggplot2, topicmodels, caret, e1071, tm, wordcloud, twittR, Rfacebook, dplyr, reshape2, and many more

Predictive Analytics with Tensorflow
Md. Rezaul Karim

ISBN: 978-1-78839-892-3

- Get a solid and theoretical understanding of linear algebra, statistics, and probability for predictive modeling
- Develop predictive models using classification, regression, and clustering algorithms
- Develop predictive models for NLP
- Learn how to use reinforcement learning for predictive analytics
- Factorization Machines for advanced recommendation systems
- Get a hands-on understanding of deep learning architectures for advanced predictive analytics
- Learn how to use deep Neural Networks for predictive analytics
- See how to use recurrent Neural Networks for predictive analytics
- Convolutional Neural Networks for emotion recognition, image classification, and sentiment analysis

Leave a review - let other readers know what you think

Please share your thoughts on this book with others by leaving a review on the site that you bought it from. If you purchased the book from Amazon, please leave us an honest review on this book's Amazon page. This is vital so that other potential readers can see and use your unbiased opinion to make purchasing decisions, we can understand what our customers think about our products, and our authors can see your feedback on the title that they have worked with Packt to create. It will only take a few minutes of your time, but is valuable to other potential customers, our authors, and Packt. Thank you!

Index

text editor
  installing 26
training set 172
tree-like reasoning
  about 52
  categorical reasoning with algorithms and trees
    52, 54
  corresponding machine learning algorithms 55

U

unstructured data 46
US Medicare value-based programs
  about 135
  End-Stage Renal Disease (ESRD) quality
    incentive program 141
  Home Health Value-Based Program (HHVBP)
    143
  Hospital Readmission Reduction (HRR) program
    138
  Hospital Value-Based Purchasing (HVBP)
    program 135
  Hospital-Acquired Conditions (HAC) program
    138
  Merit-Based Incentive Payment System (MIPS)
    143
  Skilled Nursing Facility Value-Based Program
    (SNFVBP) 142

V

Value Modifier (VM) program 143
value-based care 30

value-based programs
  about 144
  Healthcare Effectiveness Data and Information
    Set (HEDIS) 145
  state measures 145
values 111
variable types
  about 66, 107
  numeric types 109
  strings 107, 109
visit information, predictor variables
  arrival time 176
  day of week 175, 176
  month 174, 175
  visit information 178
  wait time 177
vital signs, predictor variables
  blood pressure 183
  oxygen saturation 184
  pain level 186
  pulse 182
  respiratory rate 183
  temperature 181

W

WANDA 228
World Health Organization (WHO) 40

Z

zero imputation 129

Printed in the USA
CPSIA information can be obtained
at www.ICGtesting.com
JSHW050827101223
53419JS00010B/80